Shakespeare

Shakespeare & Love

The Inside Story of the Crime that
Stunned the Book World

Mike Kelly

Ashgrove Publishing
London

Dedication

To Raymond

Contents

Prologue: Wherefore Art Thou Folio? – 7
1 – Much Ado About Nicking – 11
2 – The First Folio: A Comedy Of Errors – 15
3 – Our Man In Havana – 25
4 – Heidy Hi – 31
5 – Mr Scott Goes To Washington – 41
6 – An Inspector Calls – 49
7 – Bling Lear – 55
8 – All the World's A Stage – 63
9 – The Tempest – 73
10 – Cranky Noodle Dandy – 81
11 – Snackbeth – 87
12 – Bombay Bad Boys – 93
13 – Crime And Punishment – 103
14 – Measure For Measure – 111
15 – Guns And Poses – 125
16 – The Tome Raiders – 135
17 – The Third Man – 141
18 – The Play What I Wrote – 151
19 – Honourable Men – 167
20 – Call The Copse – 179
21 – The Trial Of Raymond S – 183
22 – The Unusual Suspect – 199
23 – A Shakespeare Tragedy In A Sentence – 211
24 – Keep Calm And Carry On Appealing – 231
Epilogue: Exit Raymond, Stage Left – 241

Prologue:

Wherefore Art Thou Folio?

Lying in the shadow of Durham Cathedral and Durham Castle, Palace Green is easy on the eye, particularly for lovers of history. Even for those unmoved by archaic symbols of grand days of yore, there is a pleasing tranquility to the surroundings.

It's a nice place to sit and watch the world amble past, to contemplate the architecture dating from the 15th century and gaze at the steady stream of academics, students and genteel sightseers meandering around the Green. Its history is palpable.

Home of, reputedly, England's third university behind Oxford and Cambridge, students first walked through its doors in 1837. The Palace Green library dates back to nearly 170 years before that – 1669 – when it was established by the then Bishop of Durham, John Cosin, as an endowed public library for local clergy and people of scholarly interests.

Its printed stock contains over 5,000 titles including nine incunabula – printed books dating from before 1501 – around 1,380 titles printed in England from 1500 to 1700 and 600 foreign 16th-century titles. Notable treasures include a *Book of Common Prayer* from 1619, annotated with Cosin's proposals for its 1662 revision, an example of that 1662 *Book of Common Prayer* and when our story begins, its jewel in the crown, a Shakespeare First Folio.

Widely regarded as the most important secular book in the English language – some would argue in any language – it is the first collected edition of Shakespeare's plays. In December 1998, the book took pride of place in one of two glass-topped display cabinets in Cosin's Library as a focal point of an exhibition of English literature through the ages, which had been running since August. VIPs, academics and the plain curious wandered in to peer at the calfskin-bound book, two of its 907 pages opened for them to catch a glimpse of one of the 36 plays it contained.

At the time, First Folios in excellent condition had an estimated value of £1 million. And the Durham edition was in pristine condition as it had been there, more or less, since Bishop Cosin acquired it soon after its publication in 1623. It had been protected from centuries of wear and tear other copies had endured as they moved frequently between owners, some not as careful as others.

Yet, security during the daytime amounted to library staff keeping a non-intrusive eye on the visitors. At night, vigilance was a little more rigorous with security staff employed to watch over the cabinets which, at the end of each day, were covered with light-protective cloths.

By December 1998, the exhibition was all but at an end and had been due to close on a Friday. However, a large business-delegation was then in Durham and it was decided to keep the exhibits open for them until the following Tuesday. This was to prove a fateful decision. For it wasn't just lovers of literature who were drawn to the glass-topped cabinets offering a tantalizing glimpse of literary treasures.

On the Thursday after the closure of the exhibition, library staff pulled back the light-protective cloths to clear things for the Christmas break, revealing a terrible sight. Two of the display cabinets had been forced open and the contents removed. There were no alarms on the cabinets and whoever had carried out the theft had merely replaced the light-protective cloth to cover their tracks.

The First Folio itself is a very large book, around fourteen inches high, nine inches wide and more than three inches thick. It is not something that can be slipped into your pocket or even concealed within a jacket, no matter how voluminous, without being noticed. A bag would have been needed to carry it and the other items stolen.

These were an early handwritten translation of the New Testament dating back to the late 14th or early 15th century, a 15th-century manuscript that included two handwritten stanzas of a Chaucer

Prologue: Wherefore Art Thou Folio?

poem to the Blessed Virgin; two works by the 10th century poet Aelfric, printed in 1566 and 1709; an edition of *Beowulf*; and a 1612 book of maps and poetry – a total haul worth up to £15 million.

Staff had not conducted searches of bags and no visitors had been reported to have acted suspiciously. Yet, someone, or perhaps more than one, had strolled into the research room, jemmied the cabinets open, slipped the stolen items into an inconspicuous bag and had strolled out again, back through the library, out the front door onto Palace Green and had simply vanished while unsuspecting visitors absorbed the historic splendour of the surroundings.

Staff at Durham University and in the world of letters at large were aghast at the dreadful news. Speaking shortly after the discovery, Beth Rainey, who had looked after the collection for the past 30 years, said: 'I am devastated. The Shakespeare folio is an extremely significant book for the North-East and for the country. It is irreplaceable.'

Speculation began in earnest as to who could have been responsible. Miss Rainey said: 'It may be that someone wanted a very great book, or else that whoever has stolen it doesn't really know what they've got. We will obviously have to have a major review of our security. There is always a tension between security and use. We have a duty of curation, but at the same time books are for use. People do not normally walk around with a jemmy.' Apart from, of course, thieves who know valuable items when they see them.

The University's spokesman at the time, Keith Seacroft, said: 'These books are landmarks in the history of English literature, and we were obviously very shaken and upset to discover they had been taken. They were in a working area of the library, so we believe the thieves must have taken advantage of a few minutes when the room was not otherwise occupied.'

Detective Inspector Andy Summerbell of Durham Police said his officers were pursuing a number of lines of inquiry. 'While it is possible that the crime was committed by local thieves it is very likely they would have identified a buyer for such a specialist haul.'

When antiquarian booksellers and collectors were alerted to the

Prologue: Wherefore Art Thou Folio?

theft, a group of anonymous benefactors offered a £5,000 reward for information leading either to the conviction of the thieves or the safe recovery of the books.

There were a series of stories about the fate of the Folio, some more fanciful than others. One in the Newcastle *Evening Chronicle* reported a theory it had been stolen to raise cash for drug deals. The byline on it was Charlie Westberg, who later became a Durham police spokesman and was to help deal with inquiries about the extraordinary events surrounding the Folio which were to unfold a decade later.

What everybody was agreed on was that it would be impossible to sell on the legitimate market. As a result of an exhaustively researched census carried out on all of the known copies left in the world, totalling around 230, each Folio was easily identifiable by its specific size as well as tell-tale typographical errors, missing pages, idiosyncratic notations, tears and blemishes – all of which formed a kind of unique literary DNA. To come to auction, it would first have to be authenticated by an establishment which would have expert knowledge of this DNA, for example, the Folger Shakespeare Library in Washington DC in the USA.

As Raymond Rickett Scott, who lived just 12 miles away from Durham at the time of the First Folio theft was later to put it, 'It would be like stealing the Mona Lisa and trying to sell it to the Louvre.'

And Scott, a self-styled (or as he liked to say, *soi-disant*) playboy and dilettante who lived at home with his elderly mother, Hannah, and had a string of convictions for book thefts to his name, was in an expert position to know.

For in 2008, ten years after the First Folio disappeared from Durham University, that was exactly what he tried to do.

Chapter One

Much Ado About Nicking

On July 10th 2008, Raymond Scott was pruning roses in the garden of the modest home he shared with his mother, Hannah, in Washington, Tyne and Wear. Then aged fifty-one, he could have passed for someone in his mid-forties, with a full head of dark brown hair, flecked with just a hint of grey, and brown eyes most of the time hidden behind one of a number of pairs of designer sunglasses. Slim built, 5' 10", he walked with the self-conscious gait of a thespian treading the boards, as if eager to find a chance to quote at length, in his idiosyncratic nasal tones, from his beloved Shakespeare. Even in everyday conversation he would sound as if he were on a stage. In his bedroom he was surrounded by books, a love for which he had cultivated over the years.

He struck a curious, but liked, figure among locals. Neighbours would sometimes see him emerge in his silk dressing-gown to clean his succession of high-powered sports cars parked outside his house only to be observed later taking the bus to the shops with his mother. His latest was a silver Ferrari 456M with a top speed of 200mph which had replaced, in turn, a Lamborghini Countach and a yellow Ferrari Dino.

On this day Scott had been distracted. He had been in contact with an expert in America about a book he said he acquired while in Cuba and which he hoped would make his fortune and lead to the life he had always dreamed of with the woman he loved.

But the conversation with the expert had taken an unexpected, and concerning, turn. Scott was determined to ring him at 4 p.m. to sort the matter out. He checked his watch, it was 3 p.m. Then, Hannah walked into the garden with two men following close behind her. She said they were detectives from the Durham police force who wanted a word with him. They went into the house and they said he was being arrested for the theft of books from Durham University 10 years ago.

Scott, perplexed, said, 'No, no, not me.' He was wearing a T-shirt and shorts and they told him to get changed into something more appropriate.

Scott went quietly, there were no handcuffs. The matter was handled tactfully in front of his mother. As he was escorted out of the front door, Scott told her to look in the Yellow Pages to find him a firm of solicitors and tell them he was going to Durham police station.

Despite the agreeable nature of the arresting officers, Scott would later recall the events with his own literary allusions. 'It was like something out of Kafka, you are accused of an offence but don't know what it is. Like Arthur Koestler's *Darkness at Noon*. I had to pinch myself I wasn't having a dream and it was real.'

But unlike Koestler's main character, Rubashov, who was charged with treason against the Soviet state, Scott was not facing execution. 'This is fair England,' he consoled himself. 'It's not like being in Paraguay, North Korea or Chile under Pinochet, otherwise I would have been apprehensive. I didn't think it was a political crime. I wasn't planning to assassinate Tony Blair when he went to the Trimdon Social Club.'

Still, even though he claimed to be somewhat nonplussed as to what the nature of his crime was, he found the officers making the arrest impressively high flying. 'They made it quite clear they were part of the major crime team, they were the elite of the detective force. They are called in when a major crime has been committed and in the majority of cases they investigate murders.'

As Scott was taken to Durham police station, other officers began emptying the house of his extensive private collection of books. It was quite an eclectic mix, totalling some 1300 volumes. Neighbours looked on as three vans left filled to the brim with belongings from the house.

The most valuable book was *Mrs Dalloway* by Virginia Woolf

that Scott believed was worth about £300. Other titles included *The Illustrated Library Shakespeare* limited edition by Robert Frederick, and a facsimile edition of *A Dictionary of the English Language,* in two volumes, by Samuel Johnson. 'A great hero of mine,' as Scott described him, 'a true Renaissance man.'

As well as the scores of historical texts, there were modern-day books like John Le Carré's *Smiley's People,* Lou Reed's *Emotion in Action* and *The Cuban Flavour Cookbook.* Also finding their way into police custody were *Playboy 50 Years, Erotic Lingerie* and *The Book of Sensual Massage.*

Bizarrely, officers even confiscated an Argos catalogue. Other property taken by the police included designer clothes and accessories, financial documents and his passport. They also seized the silver Ferrari leaving behind the other, more modest family car, a Kia Picanto.

Speaking of his arrival at Durham police station Scott said: 'I managed three jokes in the preliminaries. The first was to assure them I did not have any Irish grandparents – harking back to the days of fitting up Irish terrorists. The cops at the front desk were laughing – regulation laughs, not belly laughs. The arresting officers were very stony faced. They started to pat me down. For my second joke I said I am sure there are some gentlemen who like this sort of thing but it does nothing for me. They put a pair of rubber gloves on and I said I can assure you I have no rare books or manuscripts secreted up my anal passage.'

He said this just elicited a gruff 'I'm glad to hear that'.'

On being given a menu he told the officers: 'I'll have the lobster thermidor or the pheasant. They said they weren't in season and I'd have to have the microwaved lasagne.'

He was questioned at length that Thursday night and he provided a written statement in which he denied being responsible for the theft of the Shakespeare First Folio and other items taken in 1998 from Durham University.

University authorities had long given up any hope of their retrieval until Scott turned up 10 years later at the prestigious Folger

Shakespeare Library in Washington DC presenting a First Folio to experts there for authentication. The Folger's raising of the alert had led to Scott's arrest.

It seemed an act of pure folly, presenting the foremost authorities on Shakespeare First Folios with what was thought to be the copy stolen from Durham University. It showed him to be stupid or naive, desperate or crazy, a dupe or a thief. But which?

I first met Scott in January 2009, some six months after his initial arrest. Investigations into the matter were proceeding frustratingly slowly at that time for him, as officers more used to dealing with good old-fashioned murders, assaults and robberies got their heads around the rarefied, byzantine world of antique book theft.

It was a complex case, part Lovejoy, part Agatha Christie, part Brian Rix farce, with a healthy dose of Shakespearian comedy and, at the end, tragedy, thrown in for good measure.

Over the months I drank more wine and watched Scott drink more champagne than I care to remember as he related his tale. Showgirls, Fidel Castro bodyguards, expensive limousines and pot noodles – all had their particular place in it.

It was a story that traversed the globe from Washington DC to Monte Carlo to Paris to humble Wigeon Close in Washington, Tyne and Wear. But it all started in 17th-century England when the friends of a man now acknowledged as England's greatest ever playwright took on the troublesome task of saving his work for posterity.

Chapter Two

The First Folio: A Comedy Of Errors

Mr William Shakespeare's Comedies, Histories & Tragedies, commonly known as the First Folio, is a behemoth of a book, roughly the equivalent in size to a phonebook.

It contains 36 of Shakespeare's plays, printed on 907 pages of, even for the standards of the early 17th century, so-so quality paper mainly made out of boiled and dissolved linens including discarded handkerchiefs and undergarments. It is littered with typographical errors – around 1700 were discovered when a Second Folio was being prepared nine years later. Some areas of text are barely legible as the inking process had been so erratic. Also, lines have either been squeezed together to fit on a page – with verse sometimes turned to prose – or spread out to reach the bottom of a page. To add a further twist, the whole complicated process was overseen by a head printer who was blind and his motley assortment of junior underlings included at least one apparent illiterate. The leather-covered inking tools used had to be soaked in urine overnight to keep them supple, and left occasional stains over the book's pages.

In short, the end result is not a thing of beauty.

However, they are the first collected works of a literary genius and this, coupled with fire, plague, obsession and the acquisitiveness of a small band of wealthy men over the centuries, has turned it the First Folio into one of the most valuable books in the history of print, rivalled only by the Gutenberg Bible.

Yet it is a miracle of sorts it was ever printed in the first place. It began as the idea of ageing actors, John Heminges and Henry Condell, to collect Shakespeare's plays together in one book shortly after his death in 1616. They were two of the three surviving members of the company of actors to which Shakespeare belonged through most of his career. The other was the ailing Richard Burbage who died in 1619. Heminges and Condell were the last people with a truly intimate knowledge of Shakespeare's plays, and this was to prove invaluable in the arduous task.

Their first problem was that not one manuscript written by Shakespeare had survived. Some had perished in the 1613 Globe Theatre fire when, rather unwisely in a building made of wood with a thatched roof, cannons were fired during a performance of the play *All Is True*, now known as *Henry VIII*. The thatched roof caught alight and it took a few moments for the packed crowd to realize the unscheduled pyrotechnics weren't part of the act before they fled.

Half of the plays contained within the Folio had not been published at all. So Heminges and Condell had to lay their hands on any remnants of his work. There were a number of possible sources.

Elizabethan playwrights would often first produce drafts of plays for the actors, often referred to as 'foul papers'. From these, a transcript or 'fair copy' would be prepared by the author or a scribe. Detailed stage directions and other information needed for performance would be added to create a 'prompt book'.

Rivalry between playhouses was intense, so as soon as a play was written, it was produced. Rival theatre companies would send their members to attend performances to make notes and produce alternative versions of the plays. These unauthorized and inferior text copies were called Quarto Texts.

Heminges and Condell scoured London for as many rough drafts, 'prompt books', fair and foul copies and illicit quarto editions they could find for the base material for the Folio. And, of course, they could rely on their own, fading memories of performing the plays.

It was only then that they walked through the doors of printer and publisher William Jaggard, who was an unlikely choice. He was described by Paul Collins in *The Book of William, How Shakespeare's First Folio Conquered The World*, as 'the one man in the world that we know Shakespeare disliked'.

The First Folio: A Comedy of Errors

Jaggard had published *The Passionate Pilgrime* by a certain W. Shakespeare. Little of this very slim volume contained anything actually written by Shakespeare, and that he neither knew of nor was asked permission for its publication under his name had not bothered Jaggard one bit. Jaggard was typical of the contemporary publishing trade, a cutthroat business where such acts of piracy were commonplace thanks to the absence of general copyright laws.

Jaggard had launched his business in 1595 and not long afterwards came into possession of two unpublished sonnets by Shakespeare. They had been written for a patron around 1593 when Shalespeare's career was on hold after London theatres were temporarily closed following an outbreak of bubonic plague. (The bubonic plague held many terrors for Shakespeare as he'd lost his sisters, Joan and Margaret, and his brother, Edmund, to it. His only son, Hamnet, is also believed to have died as a result of it in 1596). Now known as Sonnets 138 and 144, they were never meant for publication and had never been registered or sold to any printer.

Sonnet 138 begins:

> When my love swears that she is made of truth,
> I do believe her though I know she lies.

The opening line is a pun on 'maid of truth', meaning 'virgin'. It was pretty racy stuff for the 16th century and Jaggard knew he had hit pay dirt. The sonnets were short so he interspersed them with lyrics lifted from a recently pirated version of Shakespeare's *Love's Labour's Lost*, as well as a clutch of unattributed poems from other writers with a vaguely similar style. Thus, the *The Passionate Pilgrime* was published.

Shakespeare was not best pleased and let it be known he had been much offended with how Jaggard had 'presumed to make so bold' with his name.

So why Heminges and Condell chose this printer is open to debate as by the time they approached Jaggard with their proposition, he was blind. It says much about the quality of printers in London at the time that being blind didn't necessarily put you out of business. Perhaps his rates might have been a bit more reasonable than potential competitors and maybe his contacts in the netherworld of Elizabethan publishing were essential to the project.

The ownership of plays was often transferred to the companies that published them. They protected themselves by registering ownership with the Worshipful Company of Stationers and Newspaper Makers – the Stationer's Company for short. Over the years, quarto-sized editions of individual Shakespeare plays had been printed by a variety of sources. Many were old pirating cronies of Jaggard, so he knew where to hunt them out. They set about either paying for their use in the Folio or, for those with rights to the most desirable plays like *Henry V*, *Hamlet*, *Love's Labour's Lost*, *Romeo and Juliet*, *Much Ado About Nothing* and *Henry IV part two*, they hit on the plan of including these owners in a 'Shakespeare syndicate'.

Some plays had become 'derelict' and were not owned by anybody – A *Midsummer Night's Dream* for one – and were planned for inclusion. There were people who point-blank refused to allow inclusion of the plays they owned, which ruled out *Pericles* and *Cardenio*. There was no trace of *Love's Labour's Wonne*, and Heminges and Condell discounted a number of plays attributed to Shakespeare that they knew to be bogus.

It was decided that the volume would be in Folio format. This large size was a highly unusual choice for an author then viewed just as a populist playwright – the Folio size was typically for serious works, such as bibles. However, a precedent had been set in 1616 when a collection of Ben Jonson's works were published in the same format.

The Folio was typeset and bound in 'sixes' – where three sheets of paper, taken together, are folded down the middle like a modern tabloid newspaper to form a booklet-like quire or gathering of six leaves, twelve pages.

Once printed, the 'sixes' were assembled and bound together to make the book. The sheets were printed in two page forms, meaning that pages 1 and 12 of the first quire were printed simultaneously on one side of one sheet of paper (the outer side), then pages 2 and

The First Folio: A Comedy of Errors

11 were printed on the other side of the same sheet (the inner side). The same was done on pages 3 and 10, and 4 and 9 on the second sheet, and pages 5 and 8, and 6 and 7 on the third. Then the first quire could be assembled with its pages in the correct order. Each of the 75-or-so quires was printed using the same method.

The text being printed had to be 'cast off' – the compositors had to plan beforehand how much text would fit onto each page. As they were working at times with messy and corrected manuscripts, their calculations would have been frequently off by varying amounts, resulting in the need to expand or compress the text. This is why some lines of verse in Shakespeare's First Folio were typeset as two lines, or verse printed as prose, or, worse still, lines or passages omitted altogether.

When the book first went to print, the play *Troilus and Cressida* was omitted as they weren't sure of their right to use it. However, when they discovered they could, the presses were stopped and it was inserted without page numbers and the title omitted from the contents page. To achieve this, some text from *Romeo and Juliet* had to be left out – including the famous balcony scene. Another oddity is that *Troilus and Cressida* can also be found in the tragedy section of the Folio while, in earlier quarto editions, it was called *The History of Troilus and Cressida*. However, needs must. Finally, in the third printrun of the Folio, the full text of *Romeo and Juliet* was included.

The original two printruns – or issues – were not pulped and some are still in existence today, their rarity making them very valuable commodities.

The uncertainty over the eventual inclusion of *Troilus and Cressida* was to play a part nearly 400 hundred years later in proving that the Folio that Scott took to the Folger Shakespeare Library was the stolen Durham edition. One of the identifying marks of the Durham copy is that the title of *Troilus and Cressida* is written in freehand on the contents page.

Opposite the title page is, some would say, the infamous portrait of Shakespeare from an engraving by Martin Droeshout. Until recently it was thought Droeshout the Younger was the artist. However, now it is believed – and accepted by the *Oxford Dictionary of National Biography*, for one – that it was the work of his uncle, Droeshout the Elder, who was in his fifties at the time of the First Folio's publication.

What Droeshout used as a basis for the engraving is not known – perhaps a portrait of Shakespeare which has never been found or a description or rough sketch by Heminges and Condell. What is known is the reaction of the vast majority of Shakespeare scholars to it – absolute horror.

The problem for the critics is the image is not that of some romantic literary hero made flesh by Joseph Fiennes in the film *Shakespeare in Love*. What we are faced with is a simpering vicar or non-descript accountant, not a member of a rumbustious acting company who wrote the greatest ever plays in the English language. He has a curiously large, bulb-shaped head with ill-cut, reedy hair, blank and slightly askew eyes, all balanced precariously on top of a shovel-shaped ruff below which is the body of a child.

The words 'monstrous' and 'ludicrous' sum up the consensus among these critics. Yet, on the opposite page his fellow playwright and fan, Ben Jonson, who of course knew what Shakespeare looked like in the flesh, praised it thus: 'O, could he but have drawne his wit/As well in brasse, as he hath hit/His face; the Print would then surpasse/All, that was ever writ in brasse.'

In other words, if Shakespeare was as handsome as his words, it would have been the most beautiful picture ever. Or – great plays, shame about the face.

In all, it took about two years for the book to be completed. It was first advertised in the catalogue of the Frankfurt Book Fair as being due out in mid–1622, but in the end the title page bore the date 1623, and the final copies weren't completed until the following year. The printers on the book are identified as Isaac Jaggard and Edward Blount.

They were sold at 15s (unbound) and £1 (bound in calfskin). There is some conjecture as to how many First Folios were printed, ranging from 500 to 1,000. Nearer 1,000 would appear the best estimate given that there are 230 known surviving copies today. Over the century after its publication its value actually fell, as the better-produced and more handsome-looking Second, Third and Fourth Folios were published in 1632, 1663 and 1685 respectively.

The Third Folio contained seven further plays including *Pericles, Prince of Tyre* and others now known not to be by Shakespeare such as *Locrine*, *The London Prodigal* and *The Puritan*. It is very rare, as many unsold copies were destroyed in the Great Fire of London in 1666. While not unaffected by the conflagration, the First Folio escaped similar wholesale destruction as ownership of it had moved out to the countryside and abroad.

In 1687, a First Folio sold for eight shillings, less than half its cover price. There its value in the eyes of book buyers remained and it was only in the 1700s that its original £1 price was surpassed. In 1756, a copy fetched £3 3s, and by the 1790s the average price had risen to about £35.

The acceleration of its value continued into the 19th century thanks in no small part to one of England's most celebrated bibliophiles, the Reverend Thomas Dibdin. In 1824, he conducted a census in which he located 30 First Folios in the London area, grading them as to their condition. Not only were they collectible; each copy now had an indisputable provenance.

By the mid 19th century they were changing hands for over £300. Then in the 20th century, prices began to soar. It was a sign of things to come when in 1906 the Bodleian Library in Oxford paid £3,000 to buy back a First Folio it had originally received in 1623 by arrangement with the Stationer's Company. It had been sold it into private hands around 1663 to trade up to a Third Folio, a decision the Bodleian came to rue.

This copy ended up in the hands of the Turbutt family and when the son, an Oxford undergraduate, made known the intention to sell, an audacious bid of £3,000 was made on behalf of a wealthy American industrialist – twice the then asking price of a First Folio. The Bodleian was given until March 31st 1906 to match the price, which it eventually managed to do through a public appeal.

It was one of the few reverses in the war of acquisition launched by the industrialist, which was to transform the value of the First Folio forever. His name was Henry Clay Folger.

Born in 1857, Folger was a tenth-generation descendant of the Nantucket settler Peter Folger, whose daughter, Abiah, was the mother of Benjamin Franklin.

Henry Folger's fascination with Shakespeare began in 1879, when, as a senior at Amherst College in Massachusetts, he was inspired by a lecture by Ralph Waldo Emerson. He read other works by Emerson, including a speech written in 1864 on the 300th anniversary of Shakespeare's birth, which kindled in the young Folger a lifelong devotion to the playwright.

In 1889, Folger purchased his first rare book, a copy of the Fourth Folio for $107.50, and this was the beginning of a lifelong quest. His work was helped by the worldwide census of First Folios by Sir Sidney Lee in 1902, which identified 158 extant copies. At that time there were 100 in the UK and 39 in the US. Today, thanks largely to Folger, there are 145 copies in the US and 44 in Britain.

After outbidding everyone at auction when a First Folio came up for sale, Folger, using Lee's census, tracked down the owners and made them generous offers. By the time of his death in 1930, Folger had bought 79 copies, all now housed in the Folger Shakespeare Library, which opened in 1932.

Up and up the value went. In 1960, a copy fetched £26,473 and soon after this a new name appeared on the scene – Mitsuo Kodama. A past president of Meisei University outside Tokyo, he was inspired after a meeting with a British Library rare-book specialist to collect Shakespeare and he set about it with the same single-minded determination as Folger had done a half-century before.

By the time of his death in the mid 1980s, he had snapped up 57 of the various folios and quartos including 12 First Folios, all now kept in the Kodama Memorial Library at Meisei University. This perhaps partly explains why the purchase price leapt from £76,923 in 1978 to £690,000 in 1989.

The First Folio: A Comedy of Errors

In the new Millennium, the value went to over seven figures. A copy sold at Christie's in New York in October 2001 for $6.16m (then £3.73m). Oriel College, Oxford, raised a rumoured £3.5 million from the sale of its First Folio to Sir Paul Getty in 2003.

In July 2006, one of the approximately 40 complete copies extant of the First Folio owned by Dr Williams's Library in London, sold for £2.5 million at Sotheby's auction house.

Another census is now being conducted with obsessive thoroughness by Anthony James West. He began his work in 1990 and, when complete, it will amount to five volumes under the title, *The Shakespeare First Folio: The History of the Book*. The first volume charts the price which people have been prepared to pay for it, the second traces the ownership of each copy over the centuries. He has criss-crossed the globe in his quest, admitting to Paul Collins in the 'Book of William', that he had spent 'a fucking fortune' doing so. So not only does the book obsess buyers, it obsesses those tracing buyers.

West puts the amount of extant First Folios at 230 and expects to track down at least another dozen or so un-catalogued copies. They can turn up in the most unlikely of places. One was found in the public library in Skipton, North Yorkshire, where it had been mislabelled and forgotten.

In 2004, Anne Humphries of Bramhall, Stockport, was left one in the will of Frances Cottle of Tottenham, London, a relative she didn't know she had. It had taken a genealogist two years to find her.

However, in all his years West had never come across an extant copy in Cuba. Yet a man who would later say he was not able to tell a Jackie Collins from a First Folio was to claim he had done just that, thanks to a former bodyguard of Fidel Castro and a beautiful showgirl.

Chapter Three

Our Man in Havana

Scott said he first went to Havana when he was in his mid-30s because of a discussion about his drink problem with his 'personal physician'.

'He was actually my GP but it sounds better if you say "personal physician". Even in those days I was drinking too much and my personal physician, a young-ish doctor with novel ideas, said, "So Raymond, you always want to have a glass to your mouth?" He said as a physician he couldn't advocate cigarettes, but had I ever thought of putting a nine-inch Cuban in my mouth? A phrase open to serious mis-interpretation.

'He explained he was partial to a cigar and used the aroma to flavour his mouth before exhaling. Like Bill Clinton – also a fan of cigars as Monica Lewinsky testified – he didn't inhale. It would act as a placebo.'

As ever when something fired his imagination, Scott set about it with single-mindedness. 'I went to a shop in Grey Street, Newcastle, which is not there anymore, that sold Cuban cigars. I was astonished at the price but bought a box of 25 anyway. It's an acquired taste but they were pretty good and I began to wonder what the real thing tasted like.' Up to that point in his life he had never been to Cuba. Paris, Monte Carlo and St Moritz were his favoured destinations.

'But then I tried a place in Mayfair in London that supplies cigars to the nouveau riche and the aristocracy. I bought a Cohiba Esplendido.' The Cohiba began as a cigar smoked by a bodyguard of Fidel Castro's named Bienvenido 'Chico' Perez which had been especially rolled for him by his friend, Eduardo Rivera, who worked at La Corona cigar factory in Havana. Castro took a fancy to them and approached Rivera about rolling cigars for him personally and set him up with five other rollers in a former diplomatic mansion in a suburb of Havana known as *El Laguito* - Spanish for 'the little lake'.

Later, the factory became the first to be staffed entirely by women *torcedoras*, or cigar rollers. Security was tightly regulated, with only designated officials and workers allowed entry into the most critical work areas of the factory. The cigars were reserved for Castro and other high-ranking Cuban officials, and were often presented to foreign dignitaries as gifts. Additionally, with rumours and fears of a CIA assassination attempt running rampant, it made sense for Castro to smoke only cigars that were manufactured under extremely secure and secret conditions.

The CIA had, allegedly, contemplated using exploding cigars as a means of assassinating Castro. Castro himself was said to be particularly fond of the long, thin cigars rolled for him, especially the sizes that would become the Lancero and Corona Especial.

Castro decided to release his personal cigars as a premium cigar brand for public consumption when the 1982 World Cup was held in Spain.

Scott said: 'It was the best thing that I'd ever tasted. If you want a comparison, suppose you've been used to drinking Lambrini – that dreadful thing teenagers buy at off-licences – then you taste Krug, Dom Pérignon, Cristal, or a white burgundy, *un grand vin de Bordeaux*, a Château Lafite Rothschild.'

Having tasted a Cuban cigar bought in England, he was determined to head to the country itself and try some freshly made there. 'I knew the best of the best were Havana cigars and I started on an odyssey of trying to find the Holy Grail of cigars.'

On his first trip to Cuba he bought the same Cohiba Esplendido. 'I couldn't believe it was the same cigar. It was so fresh. I paid £25 for a single one in England yet in Cuba I paid something like £2. It was so much better, I can't articulate it.'

He said he began visiting Cuba regularly. 'I was drinking just as much and in addition to that I was smoking a box of 25 cigars a week. My physician's advice had opened a new vista of enjoyment for me, but hadn't cured my drink habit.

'If I find something pleasurable it's very, very difficult for me to stop and draw the line. They say total pleasure is one degree less than excess. The aroma of a fine cigar is an aphrodisiac and now I'm never happy unless I have a nine-inch Cuban in my mouth.'

And there were other attractions. He particularly liked Monte Carlo, a playground for the super rich, but despite his aspirations, the benevolence of his mother Hannah – Lady Bountiful as he called her – and his own money gathering activities which would later prove to be of great interest to the police, he couldn't compete.

'Unless you have a yacht the size of the Ark Royal you're a nobody in Monte Carlo. I've walked around the harbour area and I've seen Roman Abramovich's yacht. It's the only place in the world you have to remember the number plate of your Ferrari, Lamborghini or Bugatti because there are so many. You go to Cuba with a few thousand pounds to spread around and everyone assumes you have a big yacht in Monte Carlo.'

From 1915 to 1930, tourism had been one of Cuba's major sources of hard currency, behind only the sugar and the tobacco industries. Havana, where a kind of laissez-faire attitude in all things leisurely was the norm, was the Caribbean's most popular destination, particularly with US citizens, keen to escape the restrictions of Prohibition.

Following a severe drop in the influx of tourists to the island resulting from the Great Depression, the end of Prohibition in the United States and the outbreak of World War II, Havana began to welcome visitors in significant numbers again in the 1950s. It was also during this period that US organized crime secured control of much of the leisure and tourism industries in the country. The island became the mob's most secure link in the drug-trafficking chain to the United States and Cuba gained a reputation for sensuality and *la dolce vita*, earning it the name 'the Latin Las Vegas'. Meyer Lansky, a great friend of the dictator and Cuban President Fulgencio Batista, built the Hotel Riviera, Santo Trafficante came to own shares in the Sevilla and a casino was opened at the Hotel Plaza.

It was tourism's association with the world of gambling and prostitution which made Fidel Castro's government, established in 1959 after the revolution, view the entire sector as a social evil to be eradicated. Many bars and gambling venues were closed down and a government body, the National Institute of the Tourism Industry, took over many facilities traditionally available to the wealthy and made them accessible to the general public.

With the deterioration of Cuba–US relations and the imposition of a trade embargo on the island in 1961, tourism dropped drastically and did not return to anything close to its pre-revolution levels until 1989. The revolutionary government in general – and Fidel Castro in particular – initially opposed any considerable development of tourism, linking it to the debauchery and criminal activities of the past.

However, in the late 1970s, Castro changed his stance and, in 1982, the Cuban government passed a foreign investment code which opened a number of sectors, tourism included, to foreign capital. Through the creation of firms open to such foreign investment, such as Cubanacan, established in 1987, Cuba began to attract capital for hotel development, managing to almost triple the number of tourists to 326,000 by the end of the 1980s.

As a result of the collapse of the Soviet Union and its Eastern European allies in 1989 and the early 1990s, Cuba was plunged into a severe economic crisis and saw itself in desperate need of foreign currency. The answer, again, was to be found in tourism, and the Cuban government spent considerable sums to attract visitors. Following heavy investment, by 1995, the industry had become Cuba's main source of foreign income.

One of the areas developed as a result of this change of stance was Varadero, a resort town in the province of Mantanzas 140km east of Havana. And it was here Scott stayed on his first visit to Cuba in 1998. He checked into the plush Hotel Nacional de Cuba, the site of a number of Mafia leader meetings during Batista's time in power. In the evenings Scott would visit the adjacent Parisien Cabaret, a venue which was to play a major part in events to come a decade later.

'It's a really touristy place where westerners go to get married. Beach holidays are not my thing. I prefer cities. Very, very exciting cities.'

On his next trip he stayed at the Meliá Cohiba, a Five Star hotel in the centre of Havana where the most expensive suite costs $500 a night.

'I stayed in the best suite, suite 1804,' said Scott. 'The great attraction is it's used by all the aircrews like the Air Italia hostesses.'

There followed a number of visits and it was in October 2007 that Scott was to meet the woman who was to change his life.

Chapter Four

Heidy Hi

On a balmy night in October 2007, Scott ventured out to one of his usual haunts, the Cabaret Parisien. Like the Moulin Rouge but with no nudity, for an admission fee of about £30 visitors are treated to a night of exotic dancing by a cavalcade of ornately dressed entertainers. It was a popular place for well-to-do visitors to Cuba and Scott fit right in. He was wearing his favourite pair of handmade crocodile-skin shoes bought for £800 from a shop in London's Jermyn Street, silver trousers, and a midnight-blue Valentino silk shirt that normally costs £295 but that Scott bought for just £39.95 from TK Maxx in Byker, Newcastle.

His outfit was completed by his trademark Tiffany sunglasses, two bulky gold- and diamond-encrusted Versace rings and a Rolex watch which had belonged to his late father.

'I looked very prosperous. People against me would call it camouflage as far as the clothes are concerned. What you wear is something very personal. You are what you wear and what you drive.'

Scott was as much enamoured with the shady history of the hotel as the delights it held in the present. 'All the mafia bosses like Santos Trafficante, who was said to be involved in the assassination of JFK, Meyer Lansky and Lucky Luciano used to stay in the Hotel Nacional. Frank Sinatra used to be the bag man, bringing money in and out of Cuba for the Mafia.'

Scott, on his own, paid for a stage-side seat and tucked into £50 plates of lobster washed down by a bottle of relatively modest Moët costing £100, and watched the evening's entertainment unfold.

It was not long before his eye was caught by the central dancer, a shapely, statuesque brunette with olive skin, chocolate-brown eyes and luscious red lips. He was enraptured.

'They say communism is on its last legs and when I saw hers I thought "Viva Fidel, Viva Castro. Communism is on its last legs and these are the legs". I suppose it was love at first sight.'

The show, which started at 10 p.m., went on for two hours.

'We made eye contact and she was probably aware of me looking at her. There were lots of pretty girls but I was only looking at her. She was sort of smiling. I was sitting in the best seat by myself, a sad sort of tosser I suppose.'

Scott never moved from his seat. During the interval he gestured for the Master of Ceremonies to come to his table. 'I said could you introduce me to her. I said I was staying at the Meliá Cohiba and would like to meet her afterwards.' Scott gave him the equivalent of a £50 tip in Cuban Convertible Pesos – about three times the average monthly Cuban salary – to effect the introduction.

He soon returned to Scott's table. 'He said the show's going to finish at midnight. She'll meet you outside.'

The rest of the evening passed in a blur as he waited for the show to end. At last, the curtain came down and he met her, in time-honoured tradition, at the stage door.

Scott recalled: 'She was wearing just a T-shirt and jeans. She looked stunning. She could wear a bin bag with two holes in it and still look beautiful. The elaborate Cinderella costumes the girls wear are owned by the Government. They take them off and leave them by the back entrance after the show and go back to their homes in their Cinderella rags.

'I introduced myself as Raymond Scott. I'm a billionaire with a yacht in Monte Carlo. No, no,' he laughed.

'She spoke English and told me her name was Heidy. I spoke a little Spanish. Her English was much better than my Spanish. We talked a bit about the show and I suggested we go back to the bar at my hotel. She said she couldn't go to a tourist's hotel as it was against the law, but she knew a bar around the corner. I said OK.'

Heidy Garcia Rios was twenty-one and lived in Santos Suarez, a Havana suburb, rundown like many others. With houses of cracked plaster, faded paint and worn-down sidewalks, it contrasted starkly with the glitz of the Cabaret Parisien. Heidy shared a two-bedroom home with her mother, grandmother and two aunts.

'Once upon a time, before the revolution,' Scott said, 'Santos Suarez was a middle-class area of accountants, doctors and civil servants. Her house was sadly dilapidated. I've been there and it's quaint and has a certain charm but I wouldn't like to live there.

'What would have happened if it wasn't for me, Prince Charming, talking to her that night? She would have got on the bus together with the other dancers, male and female, and been dropped off to walk back to her dilapidated home on unpaved and ill-lit streets.

'She told me most of the guys, really good-looking guys, are gay with no interest in the girls, which was good news to me in regard to opposition. We went to the Cuban bar around the corner. I went native and didn't ask for champagne and instead had a Mojito, a rum cocktail. I stood out, obviously, because of the way I was dressed, but there was no antagonism.

'We talked for about an hour. Her mother and father had separated shortly after her birth so in a Sigmund Freud way perhaps she looked on me as a father figure. I am older than her father by six years. I don't try to look younger than I am. I am quite open about my date of birth – the 12th of February 1957.

'I'm not really interested in longevity, I don't want to live as long as my father who was seventy-six when he passed away. Although, it would be great to live until I was a hundred and get shot in the back by a jealous husband as I was making love to his twenty-something year-old wife, but you've got to be realistic about these things when you drink heavily.'

'I just had one Mojito. They're strong stuff and the barman wasn't short on the measures. Heidy doesn't drink alcohol – opposites attract – and was drinking mango juice despite my best efforts to ply her with alcohol. No, no,' Scott laughed.

'I decided it was best to take it softly, softly. Obviously I was sexually attracted to her. I'm a heterosexual male. I wanted her. I just said I'd really like to see you again tomorrow afternoon and take you shopping.'

He put her in a taxi home and returned to his hotel suite. 'I didn't sleep. I was on cloud nine. I was in love again. Shakespeare tried to put it into words – "Shall I compare thee to a summer's day? Thou art more lovely and more temperate". The world's a wonderful place when you're in love. You can walk down the street and lampposts have a certain charm, even the pieces of dog shit look good.'

The following afternoon Heidy met Scott outside his hotel and he took her to Miramar, an upmarket suburb of Havana where many ambassadorial residences and the Russian Embassy are located, as well as several stylish shops. To pay for goods in these shops, customers have to use Cuban Convertible Pesos, one of two currencies in the country, the other being the Cuban Peso.

The Convertible Peso had been in limited use from 1994 to 2004 when it was treated as the equivalent of the US Dollar and both were used for tourism and to purchase luxury items. The ordinary peso was used for basic goods and non-luxury items. In 2004, the Cuban Government had removed the US Dollar from circulation in retaliation against further US sanctions.

'In Cuba they have a joke that the ordinary peso is only good for the toilet. If you have Convertible Pesos you can go to the tourist shops and those where the diplomats and their wives go to buy the things the vast majority of Cubans could not even dream about.' He had a wallet full of Convertible Pesos and spent, he recalls, the equivalent of about £200 on dresses and shoes for Heidy.

'Things she could wear in the tourist restaurants like El Floridita, an old haunt of Ernest Hemingway. All these wonderful places where people pay as much for a starter as Cubans earn in an entire week. The service is impeccable, all run by the Government of course, to make sure the people who service you are good. Obviously, you give them a generous tip, which is why they are sought-after jobs. Being a waiter at El Floridita, or any of the hotels in Havana, is far better than being a university professor or even a brain surgeon in a state-owned hospital because the tourists come along and give you a tip which is the equivalent of a week's or a month's salary.'

On this trip, Scott had been in Cuba for a week of his fortnight's holiday. The day with Heidy went well and she swapped time off with another dancer to spend the rest of the week with Scott.

'We enjoyed the high life. Every day we went out shopping because here you have a young woman of twenty-one who had been exposed to the glamorous side of life from TV and the Cabaret. The clothes I bought for her, the jewellery, were meant to be worn by beautiful girls like her. The prices were very, very reasonable. There was no Versace, Armani or Karl Lagerfeld, that sort of thing. What there was, was just quality merchandise without those fancy labels which would have cost thousands of pounds in the West End of London or in Paris.'

Scott was a little coy when discussing when he and Heidy began sleeping together. 'We did manage to have sexual relations I think on about the third night as a result of me, basically, approaching the guy who was in charge of security at the hotel and bribing him to turn a blind eye when Heidy got in the lift. She didn't get in the lift beside me, but in front of me. She wasn't dressed like a Cuban, she was dressed like a tourist, but she was obviously Cuban. They tell me that after Raul Castro took over from his brother Fidel in February 2008, Cubans are now allowed to come and go as they please in tourist hotels, but that wasn't the case when I was first with Heidy. The bribe was 100 Convertible Pesos. I had to bribe him every time we spent the night together.' For Scott, it was money well spent. 'I felt like I was twenty-one again and I had a new lease of life.

'When she saw me off at Havana airport I told her this is more than a holiday romance. I bought her a mobile phone so we could stay in touch. As I went through security I said, in the words of General Douglas MacArthur, "I shall return".'

Scott returned the following month and then the next February. Their relationship had the blessing of Heidy's mother, Ana Maria, the family house in Santos Suarez now boasting perhaps the most expensive roof in the district, thanks, according to Scott, to a £10,000 donation from Lady Bountiful. 'It was very dilapidated and crumbling. What you don't want during the rainy season in Havana was a crumbling roof so my mother sent £10,000 for a new one.'

He had also been sending Heidy money through credit he put on a Post Office travel card and posting it out to her. This was done, according to Scott, to make her life easier.

On his February visit he went to his usual hotel, the Meliá Cohiba, in his usual suite, 1084, which cost $500 a night. 'They knew me as a VIP, that sort of thing, and I intended to stay there all the time. But there were problems this time coming back to my room.

'You would get the police parading outside the hotel just looking for irregularities or making sure the tourists were safe from muggers. On one occasion a policeman with a gun stepped in front of us and asked for identification. I showed him my British passport and Heidy showed her ID card. He spoke to her in Spanish saying "why is this man with you? Why do you need him?" It wasn't very pleasant.

'So I said what we needed was *una casa particular* – a private house or villa – which I could rent and we can be together without being in a tourist hotel and without all the hassle of her leaving in the morning.

'I didn't have any experience of hiring a villa in Cuba as I usually go through Thomas Cook and the holiday brochures. Heidy said she knew someone in charge of security at the Hotel Nacional to which the Cabaret Parisien where she worked was attached. His name was Denny.

'He was to transform my life,' Scott said.

Odeiny 'Denny' Perez was, according to Scott, a former bodyguard to Fidel Castro. 'This is not fanciful. I've seen photos of him as one of the bodyguards, who were dressed in white, while the Ministers wore green, a throwback to the time when they were guerrillas.' Denny rose to the rank of Major before retiring to spend more time with his young family and was given the security job at the tourist hotels run by the Government's Cubanacan.

'Denny knows people who know people. He knows everybody worth knowing in Havana. He was a larger than life character who when I first saw him reminded me a bit of Brian Glover, the late much loved Yorkshire actor and wrestler who was in the movie *Kes*. You wouldn't want to get on the wrong side of Denny but like all true hard men, he's just a pussycat. His mother-in-law's the boss, he's frightened of her and I used to tease him about it.'

Denny had access to a villa in the plush Siboney area of Havana, near Miramar where Scott took Heidy shopping, and offered it to Scott at the going rate.

As he had already booked in the Meliá Cohiba, he stayed there for a week before moving to the villa in time for his fifty-first birthday on February 12th 2008. A party was held and it was one of the most memorable nights of Scott's life.

Heidy was there with her mother and some friends, and Denny was there with his wife. 'There were about 30 people. The tables were filled.' They drank, talked, danced and partied long into the night. The atmosphere was heady and Scott recalls the Brazilian ambassador, whose residence backed onto the villa, poked his head over the surrounding fence to have a chat.

'He said it was like the Rio carnival in Brazil. We told him to come and join us and he did. I talked to him about Pele, Garrincha and Ronnie Biggs. The celebrations went on into the wee small hours.

'There I was, Raymond Scott, talking to the Brazilian ambassador – who had come to my party – about football. It was a magical night. I didn't want it to end. I didn't want to go home because this felt like my home.'

He said there were several big parties at the villa for which he footed the bill. Or rather, his mother did. But even at, according to Scott, a reasonable £2000 a week for the villa, he couldn't afford to stay forever. Lady Bountiful's purse was not bottomless and he was having problems with his creditors. To augment his cash flow he was running up huge debts on credit cards and when they were maxed out, he simply switched to another one. By the end of his spending spree he had run up debts of around £90,000 and the avenue of credit card cash had been closed to him. If he wanted to continue enjoying the jet-set lifestyle, he needed to find an alternative source of money.

The villa wasn't the only thing Denny had access to, said Scott. Denny's mother had left him a collection of 54 antique books, all in Spanish, apart from one they called *El Libro Viejo En Ingles* – The Old English Book.

Scott was at first a bit vague when I asked him when he had first heard about it. Initially, he said it was during his actual birthday party at the villa, then after a few moments thought said, no, it was on his next visit in June. Eventually, he was to say to police that, yes, it was in February.

What he was clear about, is that after Denny told him of the books, he went round to Denny's apartment with Heidy for dinner and to have a look at them. 'He showed me what I now call "The Cuban Copy", the First Folio, but when I saw it, it didn't look anything special. It had no binding. At that particular time I didn't know much about the Shakespeare First Folio, though obviously I knew about Shakespeare.

'I looked through it for a date of publication but I couldn't find one. The quality of it didn't seem that great, either. I've only been interested in antiquarian books since 2000, so I wouldn't have known the difference between a First Folio Shakespeare and a paperback Jackie Collins. I asked Denny for more information.' He said that Denny told him the book could be traced back in his family to around 1870, when it was in the possession of his maternal great-grandmother. They kept it in an old bible-box. It was the only English book they had.

Denny's great-grandmother taught English and had an interest in the theatre. The maternal side of the family included doctors, dentists, pharmacists and teachers. On the paternal side there were army officers, both before and after the revolution. 'Further back than 1870, when his great-grandmother was born on Cuban soil, he could not go,' said Scott.

The great-grandmother died when Denny was about eleven. His family shared a house with her and the book passed down the line to the grandmother, Denny's mother and, then, with her death, onto Denny himself.

While Scott said when he first saw it he wouldn't have been able to tell a First Folio from a Jackie Collins and that on first inspection it didn't look much, he sensed something about it. 'Although my interest was best described as a hobby I had a feeling it might be interesting. I'm not trying to be boastful but it was like the feeling I have when I taste Cuban cigars and fine wine. It just reached back through the centuries. And like the feeling I have for cigars and wine, it had the same sort of frisson, the same sort of thrill when I handled it.'

However, he added: 'I fell in love with it later. It wasn't instantaneous, like falling for Heidy, it was to take a while. I had a book in my library, it's written in Latin and is about the same size as the First Folio and is basically to do with ecclesiastical literature. It was presented to the Duke of Wellington, so the inscription said in fine copperplate-writing, on his leaving Eton. That looks more impressive than the First Folio. But still when I held the book in Cuba to my left breast and felt my heart beating against it, I thought it might be something special.'

So he decided to do some research into it and all three of them went to the El Capitolio – the National Capitol Building. Ordinary Cubans have easy access to it by producing satisfactory ID, but it is more difficult for foreigners to get in. However, with Denny in tow, it didn't prove to be a problem. 'He showed them his credentials and that opened some doors,' Scott said.

With a bank of computers available – a bit of a luxury as personal computers are not commonplace in Cuba – they went online. The more they learned about the book the more excited they became. He said that after several hours study they came to the conclusion that it might well be a First Folio. And its possible worth made Scott's heart beat as fast as when he first held it to his breast and sensed it contained a special something that reached back over the centuries. 'It felt like we were holding a winning lottery ticket,' Scott said.

And it was in the National Library that he chanced upon the name of the Folger Shakespeare Library. He said that he, Heidy and Denny formed what he described as a 'triumvirate', and it was agreed that Scott should take the book to the Folger for authentication. If it was a First Folio as they suspected, it would be sold and the money split three ways. 'We decided that was fair, as Heidy had introduced me to Denny who had the book, and as I was the person in charge of trying to sell it.'

Scott said he bought a ticket to fly from Havana to Washington. It is not a straightforward journey. While there are some direct flights from Havana to the US, these are limited to special charter flights which have to be given the OK by the US Treasury and must only be for humanitarian or religious reasons.

Scott said that he had to fly via Nassau, carrying the First Folio in a 'rather tatty' Louis Vuitton holdall. 'It was of 1980s vintage. You can tell old money from new by the state of their Louis Vuitton luggage. Only aristos would have such tat, while the vulgar nouveau riche have the latest pristine LV. It's great for getting upgraded.'

Even so, he said the trip got off to a shaky start. 'I carried the book in my hand luggage and when I went through customs, officials asked me to open my luggage and saw it. It was rather nerve wracking.

'I also had some Cuban cigars in there and it turned out they were more interested in them and didn't look twice at the book. They asked for a receipt for the cigars to make sure I had bought them legitimately and not on the black market.'

And so he said he flew onto Washington via Nassau, landing at Ronald Reagan Airport, where security was tight. The customs official who opened his bag expressed more interest in the book than the cigars this time. 'He said "what is this?" and I said I'm not sure, that's why I'm on way to the Folger Shakespeare Library. It might be something, it might be nothing. He said "good luck".'

And with that he stepped out into the city.

Chapter Five

Mr Scott Goes To Washington

In mid-June, 2008, Scott booked in at the Renaissance Mayflower Hotel, known as the second best address in Washington – the White House was beyond even the resources of Lady Bountiful. It was nicknamed the 'Grande Dame of Washington' at its opening in 1925, and was said to contain more gold trim than any other building in the city except the Library of Congress.

Scott strolled out of its historic entrance into the early morning sun. He was wearing what he described as his 'Cuban holiday outfit': a favourite pair of Tiffany sunglasses, his Gucci rings, a white Vivienne Westwood T-shirt, white trousers by Y3, white jacket and, to support the *ensemble*, white sandals bought from the Vincci shop in London's fashionable Jermyn Street.

'I was a man on a mission. It felt like the first day of the rest of my life. I felt deliriously happy. I was in love. I had enjoyed a beautiful bottle of vintage Bollinger the night before – I don't waste my time on non-vintage champagne – and I could see a beautiful future mapped out in front of me. It was like being a young man all over again, but this time happy and not lonely.'

His destination, the Folger Shakespeare Library, was about a 20-minute ride away in the centre of the US capital, located next to the Library of Congress and near the Capitol Building and the White House. Since being left as a gift to the US by Folger and his widow, Emily, it had become home to a rare collection of Renaissance books, manuscripts and works of art, and is a world centre for literary study and the renovation of rare books.

Most importantly to Scott however, was that it was home to the largest and finest collection of Shakespeare's works, most notably the First Folios.

'I walked in the door and there was a black security guard. I introduced myself as Raymond Scott from England and said I have a book of Shakespeare plays which I have been trying to research, one which I think might be of interest and could I see a librarian?'

He said "yeah, sure. I'll get Richard to come and have a look at it".'

Richard J Kuhta was the head librarian at the Folger, a post he would hold for a decade-and-a-half until his retirement shortly after the man he was now about to meet for the first time came to be arrested for possessing the book he was about to present.

Scott said: 'He came along the corridor and looked like someone right out of central casting with his pink bow tie on. I introduced myself and showed him my British passport. I gave no false name or alias. I put my cards on the table and said I have come here because I know you're world experts and I want to know, have I got something of value.'

They went to Kuhta's office and from his case Scott produced the book that he said had been entrusted to him by a friend in Cuba. Kuhta noted that the volume was unbound – without front- and back-boards, nor a backstrip on the spine – but it appeared at first glance to be a Shakespeare First Folio.

However, some identification markings were also absent. Missing were the engraved portrait of Shakespeare by Martin Droeshout, Ben Jonson's poem 'To The Reader' – usually found on the page opposite – and the final page of *Cymbeline*, which included the colophon on which the printer's mark is contained.

Scott recalled: 'He said I think it's a Second Folio and if you leave it with me I'll get my experts to look at it. I said that's exactly what I wanted.'

Kuhta gave Scott a receipt, and Raymond left the Folger in high spirits. If Kuhta's initial impression was right, he was well on his way to becoming a millionaire. So he decided to celebrate the moment that Monday in style and returned to the Mayflower hotel to crack open another bottle of vintage champagne. And wait.

Over the next couple of days Folger members of staff, Dr Georgianna Ziegler, head of Reference, and Dr Steven Galbraith, Curator of Books, examined the volume and agreed that it appeared to be a First Folio. Kuhta rang Scott at the hotel to tell him they had preliminary, very exciting news.

'He told me they couldn't find any objections to it being a First Folio. I said that's fantastic; can we go to the press? I suggested the *Washington Post* as it was the only American newspaper I knew from watching *All the President's Men* with Robert Redford and Dustin Hoffman.'

Scott remembered that Kuhta was not enthusiastic. 'He said it was a bit premature for that. They had an international reputation and wouldn't like to jump the gun.' Scott was invited to return the next day for high tea and he decided to have a special cake made. 'I asked the *Maître Chef de Cuisine* at the Mayflower hotel to bake it. I said I'd like a lemon drizzle cake in the shape of a book on which was written in icing "The First Folio Shakespeare 1623".'

He took it to the Folger, as well as a gift box of three bow ties worth $190 and two boxes of Cuban cigars for Kuhta, and was shown the experts' report. The paper and ink had been analyzed, and they corresponded with that used in the First Folios.

The atmosphere, said Scott, was celebratory. 'They said they wanted to make me an honorary member of the curator's circle because I'd brought the book to them and offered to take me on a conducted tour of the vault.'

However, staff later said Scott had in fact enrolled as a member of the Folger's Renaissance Circle off his own back, handing Kuhta an envelope with twenty-five $100 dollar bills for the privilege. But the tour did take place. According to Scott, the books are stored on three levels, the lower the level, the rarer the books. They wound their way down via a couple of lift rides and after pushing through a series of doors they arrived at the vault, which Scott described as 'the holy of holies, the inner sanctum'. 'It's where the Presidents and the Senators and Royalty are shown round,' Scott said grandly.

His eye was drawn to the wall at the end of the inner sanctum. It was there that the Folger held its collection of First Folios. At a conservative estimate the collection would be worth around £100 million. They compared his to those already held there and, according to Scott, even showed where it would be stored – in a wooden box next to a book with almost as much historical worth as the Folios, and of greater beauty – Elizabeth I's Bible.

The Bible was given to Queen Elizabeth by Matthew Parker, Archbishop of Canterbury, in October 1568. Bound in red velvet, with silver-gilt bosses of decorated Tudor roses, she kept it in her chapel. This was the book she had held when praying for forgiveness after signing the death warrants of her sister, Mary Queen of Scots, in 1587, and the Earl of Essex, in 1601.

'They handed me the Bible and I opened it,' Scott said. 'It was a very large book with such beautiful detail. Compared to it, the Folio is nothing special to look at – no illuminated letters like, for example, in the *Lindisfarne Gospels* or the *Book of Kells*, very mundane. I could see fantastic treasures there, a first edition of Spenser's *Faerie Queene*, a first edition of *The Canterbury Tales* – a near perfect copy – and the only surviving quarto of *Titus Andronicus*.' Scott added archly: 'They bought it from a Swedish postmaster who could not explain where it had come from, other than it had been in his family for years.'

They went back upstairs for high tea. Scott, in his element, was, as ever, in expansive and generous mood. 'I said if it turns out to be the First Folio I will make a provision for $10,000 each year to be donated to the Folger in perpetuity. Kuhta said that was very generous and I said it was the least I could do because of the expertise they had given me free of charge.

'Kuhta said they prided themselves on not being a museum or stuffy institution. "We are a living library," he said. They have people coming in all the time with books for them to look at for verification and people like me were grist to their mill. He said he was privileged as a librarian when I came in with an un-catalogued First Folio.'

It was then Kuhta sprung a bit of a surprise on Scott who had expected it would be the Folger that would complete the book's verification. 'Kuhta said we can't tell if it's 100 per cent genuine or not and that he wanted to bring in a friend called Stephen Massey, an independent book expert, for a second opinion.

'I said I thought I had come to the feet of the Gods, what with their seventy-nine other copies and their world experts. It was like going to a specialist hospital which tells you I think you've got stomach cancer but I'm not sure, so I'll have to bring in a friend of mine.

'He said trust me, Stephen Massey will know about this as he used to work for Christie's in London and New York.' Massey was later to become Scott's *bête noire*, but Scott recovered from his initial surprise with another extravagant offer. 'I said, well, will he want help with his travel expenses? I even offered to put him up in a suite at the Mayflower. I was very naïve.'

As they prepared to cut the Folio cake, Scott said to general amusement 'Let's hope it's not like the pie in *Titus Andronicus*'. At the climax to perhaps Shakespeare's most gruesome play, Roman general Titus Andronicus feeds Tamora, Queen of the Goths, a diabolical pie containing her two sons Demetrius and Chiron. Scott quoted to me:

> Why, there they are both, baked in that pie;
> Whereof their mother daintily hath fed,
> Eating the Flesh that she herself hath bred.

'Not exactly one of the comedies but it could have been if Tamora had asked for seconds,' he chuckled.

Before he left, he handed over $300 for Massey's train fare and a $700 deposit for his two-day stay at the Mayflower – in a marginally less-expensive suite than Scott's. Leaving the book behind with his contact details, he headed back to the Mayflower.

Exiting the front door, he paused on the front steps and breathed in the air on that balmy summer afternoon. 'I had been lionized and fêted, treated like a VIP. I didn't have a care in the world.'

Unbeknownst to him, alarm bells were already ringing. Just a couple of hours before Scott had arrived at the Folger that day, Daniel De Simone, the Curator of the Rosenwald Collection at the Library of Congress had been asked by Kuhta to examine the book and De Simone had expressed his suspicions because the binding appeared to have been recently stripped.

But Scott continued on his happy way and when he got back to his suite he celebrated in customary fashion. 'I decided to open a bottle of Dom Pérignon Rosé '96. I would have probably opened it anyway, but it tasted all the sweeter.'

As he sipped his champagne, he called Cuba where Heidy and Denny were waiting for news. He told them all was well in a short, ecstatic conversation, and returned to his $300 bottle of champagne. He dreamed of never-ending holidays in Monaco and the South of France with Heidy on his arm. Perhaps St Moritz for some winter skiing. No kids – 'Too many responsibilities – I don't do the "R" word'.

Scott said he then flew back to Cuba via Nassau, touching down at Havana airport where Heidy and Denny were there to meet him. 'It was a joyous meeting, like long-lost friends. It was a great reunion.' They headed back out to the villa in Siborney where the next few days were spent partying.

'I was thinking of a world of starvation and death and how incredibly lucky I was. I've got Heidy; I've come across a Shakespeare First Folio which had been verified. I began talking about the future with Heidy. Obviously, we talked about getting married and she wanted to go to the forbidden land she'd heard so much about, the land of Gloria Estefan – Florida. We talked of travelling the world, going to glamorous places. She just wanted to live the dream.'

Always a fitful sleeper, he would often get up in the early hours to walk in the grounds, smoking a cigar and having a drink. 'There wasn't Cristal or Dom Pérignon or Château d'Yquem, but I didn't mind roughing it with non-vintage champagne.

'I would see the security people outside patrolling the perimeter with their dog. I would invite them in but they would say, no, their job was out there. I would offer them a cigar and something for the dog.'

He said he spent about another 14 days at the villa enjoying an exuberant existence, but that occasionally his mind would stray to what was happening in Washington DC. He hadn't heard from Kuhta and yet he knew that by then Massey should have arrived to complete the authentication of the book. 'I wasn't unduly worried as I was having a ball at the time. Communication with the rest of the world from Cuba could be problematical.'

What he said he did next was as predictably unpredictable for this Quixotic character I was learning about. He went off on another little adventure. 'I decided to go to Paris to lay 12 long-stemmed roses at the Alma tunnel to commemorate the upcoming anniversary of the death of Princess Diana.'

As he couldn't get a direct flight, he travelled via Madrid to Charles de Gaulle airport in Paris. And he said he didn't stay at any old hotel, but the Ritz where Diana was staying with her lover Dodi Fayed when they died in a car crash in the Alma tunnel. 'I only stayed for a few nights. The pound was very good against the euro so I was getting value and it was worth it, staying where she had stayed. I had a nice double room overlooking the Place Vendôme.'

Scott got a bit sniffy about the scene at the Pont de L'Alma. 'It was bit undignified there. People had written "Diana we still love you" in felt-tipped pen. It looked a bit like The Westoe Netty.' (A painting of The Westoe Netty, a public toilet in South Shields, by artist Robert Olley has become a cultural symbol of North East working-class history)

Diana herself is perhaps a more surprising icon to the people of Cuba who, according to Scott, included President Fidel Castro among her admirers. In Havana you can find The Princess Diana Memorial Garden, where Scott planned to marry Heidy. 'It was opened by Fidel and the British ambassador and I had spent many happy hours there. It seems strange Fidel pandering to Royalty but he seemed to recognize genuine human decency. On the plaque it says "her ways were always gentle".'

After his sojourn in the French capital, he headed home to his mother, both of them ignorant of the storm that awaited him, and with Scott already planning his next trip to Cuba to see his beloved Heidy.

Little did he know then that he would never see her again.

Chapter Six

An Inspector Calls

There is of course much to connect Washington, Tyne and Wear with Washington DC, as a brief look at the North East town's history reveals.

Around 1180, William de Hertburn moved from his land near the River Tees to Wessyngton – the Norman French spelling of Washington – on the north bank of the River Wear. As was the custom, he took the name of his new estates, becoming William de Wessyngton, and building the Old Hall there. By 1539, when his succeeding family moved to Northamptonshire, the spelling 'Washington' had been adopted.

William was a forebear of George Washington, the first President of the United States, and the area has given its name to the US capital and many other American cities. The Old Hall is regarded as the family home of George Washington's ancestors and the present structure still incorporates small parts of the medieval home in which they lived.

American Independence Day is marked with a ceremony each year in Washington, Tyne and Wear, and former US President Jimmy Carter famously visited the town in 1977. Ironically, the area's curious design of being divided into a number of self-sufficient 'villages' had been adopted from a blueprint used by many towns in the USA.

One of these villages is green-and-leafy Albany and it was here in Wigeon Close, a pleasant, though plain, cul-de-sac that Scott lived with his mother, Hannah.

When he had left Washington DC on June 20th 2008, everything, in Scott's words, had been 'hunky-dory'. However, his mood was to soon change. After calling the Folger for an update on the verification of the book, he was told that Massey wanted to speak to him directly. It proved to be an uncomfortable conversation.

'He said he had good news and bad news. The good news was that it was a First Folio Shakespeare and a very fine copy at that. The bad news was that it could be the Durham Copy that was formerly at Durham University.

'I asked: "Had they sold it?" He said they hadn't sold it; it had been stolen along with other priceless books in 1998. I said it was the first I've heard of it and how could he be sure? He said he was sure, as he was a world expert and that its measurements matched.'

However, Scott contends, Massey went on to say that all was not lost. 'He said I know a man in Philadelphia who wants to buy your book who is a friend of mine. Are you standing next to a pen and paper? Take this number down. As soon as you get off the phone, ring the number. Go on, go on, go on, he said, like Mrs Doyle from *Father Ted*.'

'I didn't pay it much attention at the time. We talked about what was the greatest secular book in the English language. I said the First Folio. He said what about the King James Bible? I said that wasn't secular. He then said what about Chaucer? Then he asked have you got any Chaucer?'

On reflection, Scott decided that Massey had been on a trawling expedition for information at the request of the FBI. Amongst the items stolen from Durham University in 1998 was a fragment of a poem written by Geoffrey Chaucer. This could also explain the Philadelphia ruse, probably involving a law officer, who, if Scott agreed to sell the book to, would incriminate him.

The net was tightening. While Scott was oblivious to the exact nature of what was going on, he was disturbed by the turn of events. 'I got off the phone about 9.45 p.m. I must have looked sufficiently crestfallen, as my mother asked, "Is something wrong?". I gave her a brief explanation and she asked, "What are you going to do about it?" I said I felt like going to the police and she asked, "The police in Washington DC or here?" I told her about a book 5,000 miles away entrusted to me.

'I was virtually on the point of going to Washington police station and she asked, "Do you think that's wise? If you told them that story, the first thing the desk sergeant would do was to check his calendar and make sure it's not April 1st." So I slept on it.'

Scott said he woke early the next morning and sent two long text messages to Massey. 'I said I didn't think he gave me enough evidence about the Cuban copy and the Durham copy being one and the same, and I reiterated there was no way I was going to participate in selling the book off cheaply.'

That was in one text. In the other, Scott claimed that he decided to act as an *agent provocateur*, feigning interest in selling it to Massey's Philadelphia contact in a bid to expose the independent expert's possible criminality.

Massey saved the text, which he later showed to police. It read:

> Stephen from Raymond Scott after our conversation yesterday I talked to the other two principals in Cuba and all three of us unanimously and unreservedly very much desire you to join us as an equal partner so the Triumvirate will be a group of four equals one for all and all for one as we are keenly aware we need an expert of your experience to go to the market let me reassure you that precisely two people namely you and I are privy to the information you imparted to me last night as I merely told the two Cubans it was in our best interest to have you on board and they agreed. I do hope Richard is ignorant to the extent of your knowledge and remains that way although I accept auction is not the venue I wish to discuss alternatives
> Raymond.

The police concluded it showed how desperate Scott was to sell the book. Scott later admitted his pretext of sending the text was, in hindsight, unwise. For now, he awaited a reply. And waited. 'I set myself a mental deadline that if he didn't receive any reply by 4 p.m. – 11 a.m. his time – I would go to Durham police station and tell them the saga.'

He idled away the day, distractedly picking up books to read from his large personal collection, including JB Priestley's *An Inspector Calls*, then setting them down again, listening to snatches of his favourite Italian operas, and periodically checking his mobile for messages from Massey. But none came.

At 3 p.m., on July 10th 2008, he was pruning roses in the back garden when two Durham police officers arrived to arrest him. He was questioned long into that Thursday night and records show he provided a written statement in which he denied being responsible for the theft of the Folio and other items taken in 1998.

He did admit to being the person who visited the Folger with the book – 'how could I not?' he asked – but stated unequivocally: 'I have not knowingly received any stolen property.'

They said don't you find it a remarkable coincidence that you live only 12 miles away from where the Cuban Copy was stolen?

Scott replied: 'While to all intents and purposes that is true, when it comes to 1998, particularly the December of '98 when the theft took place, there's a good chance I was in London or in Switzerland because at that time before the Christmas holidays I used to go skiing in St Moritz or Pontresina.

'I asked are you saying I'm guilty by proximity? If at the time my mother lived in the centre of the country would I be half-innocent and half-guilty. And if we lived at Land's End or John O'Groats, would I be entirely innocent?'

And there was of course the central plank of his defence against the suggestion he was the man who stole the First Folio. 'I said to the interviewer I do not consider myself an unintelligent man. So why would a person take what he believed to be a stolen Shakespeare First Folio and walk into the Folger library and present it to them for verification?

'It was like somebody walking into the Louvre with the Mona Lisa under his arm a decade after it was stolen. He might as well have just surrendered himself to the Gendarmes. To carry on the Mona Lisa analogy, I might just have walked round the corner to the J Edgar Hoover building in and handed myself over to the G-men.

'I identified myself correctly with my passport; I gave all my addresses. It just didn't make sense. It's a riddle, wrapped in a mystery, inside an enigma.' Winston Churchill had used the phrase in 1939 to express his consternation at Russia signing a non-aggression pact with Germany. And the Stalin theme didn't end there, as Scott described his upset at the confiscation of property from his house, much of which he said belonged to his mother.

'I can safely say without fear of contradiction this has very much changed mine and my mother's attitude towards the police. I didn't think I was living as a citizen of a country like this. I thought what was happening towards me as far as the seizure of property was concerned was something that would happen in Stalinist Russia or Nazi Germany. I didn't know the police had the authority to arbitrarily go in and seize anything they wanted.

'They put me in a position that I had to prove the items in my possession had been acquired legally rather than the other way round where they had to prove they had been acquired by illegal means.

'We – or rather my mother – bought the Ferrari, without question. The paintings on the wall, Picasso prints, very nice but not particularly valuable. Jewellery that belonged to my late father they seized and every single book, many of which were my mother's, they simply seized. They didn't even inquire "can you produce a receipt".

'I find it quite wrong, very heavy handed, the power they have. They basically stripped my mother's house of which I am a tenant. I don't think the majority of fair-minded people realize the country they are living in. What the police have done to me and my mother, they have the power to do to any person in the country.'

It wasn't only the microwaved lasagne he found not to his taste at Durham police station. 'They were trying to browbeat me into a confession. The vast majority of questions were trying to trick me. They were asked in such a devious and cunning way but I kept my presence of mind. They couldn't pull my fingernails out as the law doesn't allow them to do that.'

He was eventually bailed, fingernails intact, and allowed home. But it wasn't just the police who had been asking questions about him. The story had generated interest around the world and it was now going to be introduced to the man who came to be dubbed, amongst other things, Bling Lear.

Chapter Seven

Bling Lear

The word 'eccentric' is synonymous with the English and when the public caught its first glimpse of Raymond Scott via newspaper and television reports, he fully lived up to the stereotype. His penchant for designer clothes, ostentatious jewellery and flash cars, his mixing of highbrow Shakespeare quotes with lowbrow *Carry On*-like comments such as 'the only thing I don't like as antiques are my girlfriends' and, of course, the bizarre nature of his alleged crime, all caught the public's imagination.

Most people, as Scott claimed of himself up to a few months before, wouldn't have known a Shakespeare First Folio from a Jackie Collins, but its estimated worth – variously reported between £1.5 million to £15 million – certainly grabbed attention.

Even the name of the street on which Scott lived, Wigeon Close, gave the whole affair a kind of Reggie Perrin feel. There were pictures of him in Cuba wearing his Tiffany shades, a shiny suit that could have been a Miami Vice cast-off, glittering Gucci rings and Rolex watch, whilst standing, it seemed, on tip-toes to kiss the cheek of his beloved Heidy, the beautiful Cuban showgirl.

After his arrest, far from lying low, he basked in the limelight. Pictures taken at home were published showing him drinking his vintage Dom Pérignon Rosé champagne from £100 Swarovski crystal glasses, a Cuban cigar between his fingers, and looking very pleased with himself.

When he spoke to reporters, often at restaurants, he ate dishes he believed signified wealth and a certain culture: langoustines, lobster, the most expensive items on the menu, afterwards giving big tips. Oscar Wilde's epigram 'The only thing worse than being talked about is not being talked about' got frequent airings.

Any defence solicitor would have shaken his or her head in despair. Raymond Scott was a middle-aged man living with his mum in a three bedroom semi-detached house in the North East of England. But he didn't seem to care – or comprehend – that a man who revelled in the trappings of conspicuous wealth, yet had never held down a full-time job in his life, might be digging a hole for himself.

He maintained that he was innocent and that he had nothing to hide. He either did not, or could not, grasp the concept that sometimes it is wise not to reveal too much.

When he was released on police bail pending further inquiries, his passport was taken off him and he was now trapped in England, thousands of miles from Heidy and the life he yearned for.

The charges he faced – theft and handling stolen goods – were serious. While to the layman, the charge of handling stolen goods might seem the lesser offence, it carried a stiffer sentence – a maximum of 14 years in jail. It seemed that sometimes Scott's protestations of innocence were imbued with a hint of desperation or self-reassurance, given that the possibility of a long jail sentence might have been a sobering thought for a man who enjoyed a champagne lifestyle.

Nevertheless, as the police conducted their inquiries, Scott went about his own with some gusto. After his arrest, the Folio continued to be held at the Folger and he sought access to it for renowned expert, Anthony James West, so as to get his opinion on whether it was indeed the stolen copy from Durham.

West, as previously mentioned, wrote the critically acclaimed, *The Shakespeare First Folio: The History of The Book – Volume I: An Account of The First Folio Based on its Sales and Prices*. It charts the number and distribution of copies at the beginning and end of the twentieth century, surveys the nineteen facsimile editions since 1807, and assesses earlier listings of the work since 1824, including Sidney Lee's Census in 1902.

More importantly, he has followed this book up with *Volume II: A New World Census of First Folios*. It lists 228 copies and gave descriptions of each, covering the condition, special features, provenance, and binding. It traces the search for copies, deals with doubtful identifications, describes the tests for inclusion, and presents details of missing copies. It also indicates the history of the ownership of each copy – ranging from a country parson to Henry Folger.

On the recommendation of Mary Jordan, London bureau chief of the *Washington Post*, who had written two articles about Scott – 'A Man Walked Into A Bard One Day' and 'Missing Shakespeare Knocks On Folger's Door' – he contacted the prestigious Washington DC law firm, Williams & Connolly, for legal help in gaining access for West.

While he was impressed with Ms Jordan's Pulitzer prizewinning pedigree – the top award for US journalists – he was not so impressed, in one respect, with those he approached at the law firm. 'Although Kevin T Baine and Kevin Hardy gave me gratis, good legal advice, I was bitterly disappointed at their names, far too mundane for Yankee attorneys who I think should have monikers like Spiro G Gnatpole IV – one of the South Carolina Gnatpoles, of course.'

Scott said he had spoken to West on the phone in July, and West had told him that he had examined the Durham copy in 1994, four years before the theft. 'Although he was understandably guarded over the phone, he asked me if the Cuban copy bore any significant ink-blots and if the Folger had examined it on the light table under ultra-violet light, intimating that could yield some notable features, but refusing to expand on this.

'The Cuban copy does have a number of inkblots, but in a book of almost 1,000 pages I can't recall their shape or page number. The Cuban copy, I told West, does have a significant dirty tidemark that West said the Durham copy lacks. As for marks or stamps only visible under specialist U.V. light, I have no idea only having looked at the Cuban copy by daylight and ordinary light bulbs.

'Also, our copy has Ben Jonson's verses in the preliminaries to the plays in original, where they are only later facsimiles in

Durham's copy, apparently. We know this because Georgianna Ziegler at the Folger and her colleague put the loose, unbound leaves from the beginning of the Cuban folio on her light-table and as world experts declared in the report "the paper definitively checks out as Folio 1 with a distinctive crown watermark".'

However, despite West pointing out this potential discrepancy which could favour Scott's contention the Cuban copy and the stolen Durham copy weren't one and the same, he went off the idea of employing him. 'In this cosy old-boy – not to say incestuous – world of rare books, West and Stephen Massey are firm friends of many years standing. West told me they had collaborated in the examination of a First Folio in Chicago, amongst other projects.

'Of necessity, West also knows Richard J Kuhta very well. Naturally my initial enthusiasm to get West to travel to the Folger at my mother's expense to inspect our copy rather cooled.'

Then Scott decided on a change of tack. As the weeks went by and with no word on whether he was going to be charged, he launched his 'Free the Books' campaign. It started with a letter to *The Journal* newspaper in Newcastle upon Tyne in which he claimed Durham University's priceless archives were nothing more than 'redundant relics' and should be sold off and the money ploughed back into the local community.

He wrote: 'Sold on the open market, these redundant relics would raise billions which could benefit the University itself and the people of County Durham, which is still a deprived area.

'I think any fair-minded person will find this morally repugnant. It has been said that it is essential for scholarship that these books are under one roof, but I and many others dispute the relevance of this when, these days, everything can be recorded electronically. Indeed, the very physical handling of these fragile keepsakes is strongly discouraged. I say, "Free the Books".'

Then, in a sideswipe in his battle for ownership of the Cuban' First Folio, he continued: 'Durham University just want another rare book to salt away in their ivory tower, for no one who is not part of the university can enter its hallowed portals. Apparently, the £15 million Shakespeare book is just the tip of a gargantuan iceberg of rare books hoarded by them, miser fashion.'

Professor Chris Higgins, Vice Chancellor of Durham University, responded, saying: 'Bishop John Cosin established his library at Palace Green in the 17th century with the aim of making his books available to the public and this continues to be the case. Durham University is custodian of many priceless treasures and we ensure they receive the specialist care and attention needed to preserve them for future generations, including residents of the North East. Thousands of scholars and members of the public have access to our libraries and archives every year, whether through private study or by visiting our regular exhibitions.'

Despite the opportunity, Professor Higgins made no mention of the fact that Scott stood accused of attempting to sell the First Folio, not for the greater good, but for his own personal benefit to enable him to live it up with his Cuban girlfriend.

In an attempt to head off in the future this presently unstated criticism, Scott said, a bit vaguely, that he had reached agreement with his fellow members of the 'triumvirate', that if they were to gain ownership of the Folio and then sell it as planned, they would distribute a third of it, split equally, to benefit sick children in Durham and Havana.

Then, in October 2008, the Folio was moved from the Folger to Durham University. Before its arrival, Bill Bryson, US author and anglophile who wrote an acclaimed book on Shakespeare and is Chancellor of Durham University, said: 'This is not only wonderful news for Durham University but for all Shakespeare's scholars and fans around the world, of which I am definitely one. Like Shakespeare himself, this book is a national treasure giving a rare and beautiful snapshot of Britain's incredible literary heritage. I'll certainly be joining the crowds who will be eagerly welcoming it home.'

One noted Shakespeare fan who was incensed by the development and would not be eagerly welcoming it home was Raymond Scott. While Scott's bail conditions did not stop him from visiting Palace Green – with the caveat that he could only do so if not dressed like Che Guevara as he had done on a 'Free The Books' demo – the whole tenor of the reporting on the return of the copy, no doubt inadvertently, undermined the central plank of Scott's defence.

Scott said, with justification, that as yet it had not been proved in an open court of law that it was the Durham copy. He maintained that what was being returned to Durham was a copy of the First Folio, not necessarily the University's copy. Scott launched a civil action against the Vice Chancellor of Durham University, Professor Christopher Higgins, to obtain access to it so he could get an independent expert's opinion.

The case was heard at a High Court hearing held in the chambers of district judge Peter Pescod at Newcastle Crown Court in January 2009. Scott chose to represent himself and cut an unorthodox figure – dressed in one of his Cuban holiday outfits topped off by a Michael Schumacher signed Ferrari cap – among the ermine-robed and be-wigged learned counsels.

It was a very short hearing. He was told he couldn't have access because it was being kept at the University on behalf of the police as they continued their investigation.

Bruce Walker, the barrister representing Professor Higgins, said: 'The wrong defendant has been sued. It is needed for the police investigation and retained by Durham Police, but it is in Durham University's custody in their climate-controlled facilities and it cannot be examined without the police being present.'

Scott, somewhat nonplussed, said: 'If I have made a mistake in naming Professor Higgins I apologize. Learned Counsel say I want the Folio's return, but that is not in fact the case. I only wish for an independent expert to be given access to the First Folio. I understand police have virtually monopolized the experts capable of examining the First Folio. I have to agree they are not in a position to release it to me. It does appear as if I have mistimed this.'

Scott later said, 'I was a bit impetuous when I went to the county court. I suppose my blood was up to a certain extent, by the very fact it had been returned to Durham University. The police investigation is into its seventh month now. Rather like the Prince of Denmark, I have borne the whips and scorns of time, and the law's delay.'

Judge Pescod formally rejected the claim against Professor Higgins. He ordered Scott to pay the costs, and asked him how he felt about paying the fee, which he reduced from £8,111 to £5,000.

Quoting from Shakespeare's *Merchant of Venice*, Scott replied: 'They are entitled to a pound of my flesh so long as they don't take any of my blood.'

Chapter Eight

All the World's a Stage

It was around the time of his civil suit in January 2009, that I approached Scott with an idea for a book, one that would tell his story. He was very keen on the project and we arranged to meet for the first time in Gateshead, where I lived. On a cold, blustery January evening I awaited his arrival with some anticipation.

We had agreed to meet in a hotel car park near my home. He stepped out of the Kia Picanto driven by his mother, Hannah, who was told to come back to the car park at 9 p.m. to collect him.

Scott was hard to recognize at first, earlier pictures taken after his arrest had shown him to be clean-shaven. He now sported a beard. Wearing a tan leather jacket, silver trousers and his favoured crocodile-skin shoes, he adjusted his Tiffany sunglasses before shaking hands. 'You are the scribe, I take it.' He held up a Sainsbury's shopping bag. 'Refreshments,' he said, and we walked to my house.

He'd barely poured himself a glass of champagne from one of the two bottles in the bag into one of my less-than-grand Ikea champagne flutes when away he went, a blizzard of information.

Straightaway it was obvious I was the audience and as I sat down and reached for a pen, he remained standing, glass clasped to his heart in-between sips, staring at a point on the wall above my head. As he told his story, he prowled about the room, his eyes occasionally flicking down at me to make sure I was writing it all down.

I learned of his stays in Cuba, the discovery of the book, his time in Washington, his arrest, and heard various libellous comments about Stephen Massey; he spoke of Lady Bountiful, his arthritis-suffering mother he received a carer's allowance to look after – and, of course, of the transcendental beauty that is Heidy.

Always there was my nagging thought, 'Did he do it?' He swatted away each subtle approach on the matter and, as the evening progressed, the less than subtle ones.

His mobile phone rang – the tone one of those old-fashioned telephone rings. His lifted his sunglasses up to inspect the number of the caller, then answered. 'I'm still with the journalist, Mother,' he tutted.

I checked my watch. It was 9 p.m. and obviously she'd arrived to pick him up. 'She'll have the car heater on,' he assured me. For a moment he paused in silent thought. He sipped from his glass then clasped it to his chest.

'The police would have you believe there are two Raymond Scotts. The first Raymond Scott is the doting son who looks after his mother, though she would give you an argument about that. Then, there is the exaggerated notion of him being an international art-thief, a guy who goes jet-setting off to Cuba, Monte Carlo, Paris, who buys expensive clothes and jewellery in London. As Shakespeare wrote: "All the world's a stage. And all the men and women merely players; They have their exits and their entrances; And one man in his time plays many parts."

'I say there are more than two Raymond Scotts. Imagine a misfit wandering round Durham in cold weather and rain who sought refuge in Durham University Library. Just wandering around and not looking out of place.

'Maybe, like the Earl of Carnarvon and Howard Carter who discovered Tutankhamen's tomb in Egypt, he came across "wondrous things". Maybe, with no one around, no security, he decided to help himself to these wondrous things. And then nothing happens for a decade. That person has blended back into the background.

'Maybe that person just decided to provoke a revolution of his own. What was the point of it? In a way it was like stealing the *Mona Lisa* or Van Gogh's *Sunflowers*. It's not an asset, it's a liability and you can't sell it but who knows, that's what billionaires do. Their ultimate goal is to buy Van Gogh's *Sunflowers*, to possess it; it's priceless.

'But then the lonely boy, a misfit, goes into his bedroom while his mother is downstairs, watching *Strictly Come Dancing*, *Emmerdale*, or whatever. Meanwhile, the son is upstairs with the finest copy of the greatest book in the English language in private hands. Reading Shakespeare. Touching a book that came off the printing press in 1623.

'We live in a material world. So often people are defined by what they have, what they possess. I can see some logic in having the greatest secular book in the English language. It's not a fact that can be publicized, but just to hold it, feel your heart beating against it; for some it would be an orgasmic experience.

'I suppose the best analogy is a committed Christian, not someone who pays lip service but a truly committed Christian, who hears the voice of Jesus. That would be a mind-blowing experience.

'Or, let's get venal, temporal, mercenary. You have Miss Universe on one side, Miss World on the other – three-in-a-bed. The phone rings and it's the National Lottery people saying you've won the Lottery, which has been on rollover for weeks. Maybe that would come close. Certainly it would be very pleasant.

'Why would a person want to part with this thing which is so precious to him, his *raison d'être*, that defines him, that says your whole life has not been without purpose? Maybe for the first time the person might realize the venal, the economic value which had never been known before. For this person, who has lived a solitary life, discovered human failure.

'Maybe the person, who is getting on and ageing, got bored with 10 years of possession of this trophy and thought we live in a material world. I've thought about this case a lot, it's multi-faceted, like Janus the Roman God, it has two faces.

'Perhaps this person decided to live one day as a lion rather than spend the rest of his days as a lamb. Maybe there's more important things and he tried to sell it. Take the money and run. To live life to the full in Havana, London, Paris. Can't do this without money, without a lot of money.

'Pandora's box is opened. Then the person who would never

have parted with a book because it was the cornerstone of his life, a symbol of achievement, thought – what have you really done with your life?

'I once possessed the greatest secular book in the English language. It wasn't kept in a bank vault; it was openly kept on a bookshelf and lovingly cherished. For a decade this person was very happy and never dreamt of selling it, anymore than you would dream of selling your dog for vivisection. Then maybe the person fell in love and thought it's time to realize an asset.'

Then Scott's glass shattered in his hand, cutting a finger. He looked at the glass, and then the finger as the blood began to flow, before concluding. 'This is just a fairy story, of course. A fantasy.'

He stood stock-still, contemplating the broken glass then looking in some puzzlement at the blood dripping down his finger onto the floor. I got a kitchen towel for him to staunch the blood. It was 10 p.m. and his mobile phone rang again. He answered it, his tone exasperated. 'I'm still with the journalist, yes, I'm coming now.'

The next day I called and offered to hold our second meeting at my house again, but Scott declined. Perhaps Lady Bountiful, not surprisingly, had got cheesed-off parked up for an hour waiting for him. Instead, he suggested Durham. At first I thought it was just handily placed, equidistant between my home and his, but as time went on it seemed he was drawn to the city.

I travelled by train from Newcastle arriving just after 6.30 p.m. Commuters hurried along the platform, heads down, past a strange guy standing at one of the exits holding a framed picture he presumably wanted to sell.

There was no sign of Scott so I checked my mobile, but there were no messages. The station had cleared now and the only two people left were me and the guy by the exit, still holding the picture, looking out expectantly onto the platform.

I looked closer and noticed a red Ferrari cap and leather jacket. It was Scott, minus beard and with the 'tatty' Louis Vuitton bag at his feet that he had carried the First Folio around in. I walked up to him. We shook hands and he showed me the picture – a framed front cover of the Shakespeare First Folio. 'This is what the fuss is about. It's a facsimile copy in case you're worried I've purloined another one.'

He had a venue in mind, the Fallen Angel Hotel in Old Elvet, a Georgian Grade II listed townhouse that had been turned into a hotel with 10 themed-rooms.

Scott, who was to reveal a nous for stage management and presentation that PR guru Max Clifford might have been proud of, had used the venue before. He had previously staged a photocall with journalists in the 'library room', deeming it wholly appropriate for the nature of his case, as well as arranging to be interviewed there by a film crew making a documentary.

He'd taken a liking to the hotel's eclectic design and the varied rooms. 'I like hotels with a bit of character. Much more interesting than your Travelodge places and worth paying that bit extra for.'

We stopped off at the Oddbins wine store on the corner of Old Elvet for refreshments en route. Two bottles of Lindauer Special Brut Cuvée for him – 'Just say Scott bought champagne, for appearance's sake,' he said – and a bottle of Pinot Noir for me. He paid for these in cash.

In reception, the manager was dealing with some new arrivals but appeared to remember Scott well. As we waited for him, we made idle chat until Raymond received a call on his mobile from his mother. 'I'm with the journalist. We're at the Fallen Angel. It will take a few hours so I'll stay here tonight. He's paying, don't worry.'

I raised a quizzical eyebrow and he shook his head reassuringly at me. He hung up and said, 'I'll try get a good price from him because of the publicity I've given the place.'

The manager returned and Scott turned to him. 'You may recall I have availed myself of your premises in the company of the world's media. We were in the library room, which I have to say I found very impressive. I am now here with another reporter and he is writing a book about my case in which, of course, the Fallen Angel's part will be duly noted. Are you busy tonight? Is there a room available for our chat and how do we stand if our conversation should proceed into the night?'

The manager smiled pleasantly but with a hint of confusion. I asked: 'If he stays the night can he get a discount on one of your rooms for a plug in the book?'

'I'm sure we can come to some arrangement,' the manager said.

The library room was taken so he offered us a tour of the others available. There was the Cruella suite, a Gothic-style black nightmare. Scott ran a hand down the black-velvet sleigh bed, considered the dark panelled walls, the black-silk screen, the black velvet seats and the black curtains.

He said. 'Have you anything more cheerful?'

There was the New York suite, the door opening to reveal a graffitied street-scene, then down a set of stairs into the room proper offering a montage of Manhattan scenes on the wall, a diner kitchen, a juke box and, for some reason, a three-speed bucking bronco.

It was certainly brighter than the Cruella – a coalmine would have been – and after a bit of consideration Scott went for this one. The manager knocked £100 off the price. Scott seemed to think the £150 left to pay was a snip and handed over the cash. From out of his case he produced a crystal glass and he cracked open a bottle of Lindauer.

'I can't bear to stay in ordinary places,' he said wafting his glass around the room as he paced the floor. He was in an expansive mood, but soon there arose more than a hint of melancholy.

'It's coming up to my fifty-second birthday. It won't quite be as joyous as my fifty-first.' It had been months since he'd seen Heidy and Scott was by his own admission a bit of a loner in England. To relieve his boredom in the past, he had merely to get on a plane for another adventure. Without his passport, still in the hands of the police, he felt trapped.

From an early age he had always seemed to be on the move. An only child, his father, Raymond, was a Scot from Govan, Glasgow and a Roman Catholic. His mother, Hannah, was Jewish and from

Gateshead. Both, according to Scott, were atheists and communists, too. A rare couple they made.

He was educated at the Royal Grammar School in Newcastle. Founded in 1525, it gained its Royal Charter from Elizabeth I. It has a number of famous ex-pupils including Cuthbert Collingwood, Admiral Long Collingwood of Trafalgar fame, the Victorian industrialist Sir William Henry Armstrong, the poet Basil Bunting and Lord Justice Taylor who wrote the Taylor Report into the Hillsborough football disaster.

The RGS is a fee-paying school of noted academic achievement, where Scott felt an outsider. He did not look back at his schooldays fondly.

'Heidy went to a local neighbourhood school. She speaks near fluent English as well as her native Spanish as well as some French and a bit of Italian. For five years I learnt French in a totally unimaginative way although *donnez moi un cognac monsieur* and *donnez moi une bouteille de champagne* has come in useful. The people at the RGS were supposed to be the cream of the cream, but the teaching techniques weren't good.

'And Shakespeare! Englishmen won first prize in the raffle of life to speak the tongue the Bard wrote in. But the unimaginative teaching techniques I came across were truly lamentable. There was no effort to stimulate your interest. They drummed it into you by rote.'

He kept himself to himself, always bookish, his free-time activity limited to long stints in the library and at the chess club. At that time, the chess world champion was US Grandmaster Bobby Fischer. Even in the world of paranoids, schizoids and the generally unhinged that made up the chess world, Fischer was a class apart. After winning the world title against Boris Spassky in Rejkyavik in 1972, he never defended it and became a nomadic recluse, involving himself in weird religious cults and becoming increasingly anti-Semitic, despite his Jewish ancestry. He was described as a 'genius and a monster' in chess circles. Scott was a fan.

Scott's first attempt at romance at around the age of eighteen came, appropriately enough, after a chance meeting in a library. Not the RGS, as it was then an all-boys school, but at South Shields reference library where he had taken a shine to one of the librarians.

'One Friday I waited until the library was closing and I got to chatting her up. I said would you like to come out with me? My face was beetroot.'

Unlike the strikingly exotic Heidy, he said she was quite plain and had her hair up in a bun. Somewhat taken aback she said yes, and they arranged to meet at Pizzaland in South Shields.

'My ideal woman back then was Farrah Fawcett Majors and I hoped when she turned up she would be totally transformed, with the bun out, some sort of elegant nighttime wear, but she arrived virtually identical to how she was in the library.'

After enjoying a night of intellectual discussion at Pizzaland, it was time for them to head towards the family home, which was then in Harton Village. The girl, whose name escaped him, lived nearby.

'We got a taxi back. I was still a virgin then but managed to pluck up the courage to go to a chemist's shop in Harton Village in an attempt to buy some prophylactics. I was hoping and praying for a male chemist but it was my worst nightmare, a woman and a very glamorous woman at that. She looked like the actress Honor Blackman. I asked for some aspirin.'

With the clock ticking and the meter on the taxi running, he tried again. 'I asked if there was a male pharmacist. She sort of looked at me strangely and said "I'm the only pharmacist".

'It's a horrible word prophylactic, condom. I made my excuses and left. Anyway the condoms would have remained in the packet even if I had bought them, probably until their expiry date. We didn't even kiss. We just shook hands. I never went into the reference library at South Shields again.'

He took a long drink from his glass then took a folder of photographs out of his case. Most were from Cuba and many taken at his birthday party. It didn't appear as mobbed as he had described it and looked more like a dinner party, a group of 8–to–10 people sat around a table full of food and a few bottles.

'We had a suckling pig on a spit. Obviously I didn't eat any of that, not that I'm religious. But it's pork. You can't really get away from being Jewish, or even half-Jewish. I'm actually Jewish in the sense that if your mother's Jewish, you're Jewish. It's transferred through the female line.'

Everyone seemed happy enough in the photo, and the exotic flora and fauna that bedecked and surrounded the garden room identified it as a world away from chilly, huddled-up, wintry Britain.

He flicked through some more of the pictures. One was of him looking sheepish in a bookstore, a dead ringer for a young John Major, but with dark hair.

Then another of him standing alongside a pretty, fair-haired woman, quite glamorous in a wholesome way, her Silvikrin hair and her floral, floaty, short-sleeved dress firmly placing her in the early 1980s. Her name was Vivien Stamp, one of two women before Heidy who Scott said he had loved.

'She was from exotic Cullercoats. She was so gorgeous, head-turning: Miss Tiffany, Miss Wansbeck, Miss Middlesbrough, runner-up in Miss Great Britain, I just sort of had to get engaged to her. If you want to call me self-serving, she was just a trophy girlfriend. You'd hear people at parties saying I do this, I earn that, I live here, I go to holidays there, what do you do? Well, I go out with Miss Newcastle.'

Their families met, he said, and a happy future was mapped out in front of them. But this wasn't to his taste. 'I was about twenty-three or twenty-four then, living off my parents. I was buying and selling antiques then. We were born in the same year, she on February 1st, slightly before me. But older is older,' he said with a sly smile.

'What she wanted was to settle down. Have a nice little bit of semi-detached suburbia with children and a swing in the garden. It wasn't for me, this dilettante, this playboy.'

His other love was called Perla, a Colombian dancer he met at Raymond's Revue Bar in London in the mid–1990s. 'I wasn't a constant patron of the establishment, I have to say. I liked the name, of course. She was a dancer, very exotic. Her English wasn't good, my Spanish was then non-existent, but we made a connection.'

They enjoyed a heady nightlife and spent days when she was off, shopping. They also spent long periods apart, she returning home to Bogota whilst he stayed in London or returned for brief stays in the North East. After eighteen months together they got engaged, but the relationship fizzled out and a few months later they split up permanently.

'It's a proud boast of mine that I've never had an ordinary girlfriend,' he said. His mobile phone rang again and it was his mother. 'I'm still with the journalist. The room's nice; we got a good rate. You can pick me up tomorrow at about 2 p.m. We can go shopping in Durham and we'll go to that place you like for lunch.' He hung up.

I asked how his mother was dealing with the situation.

'Fine, fine,' he said vaguely. 'She just thinks it's all a little strange, though I suppose she's used to that with a son like me.'

Chapter Nine

The Tempest

We met a few days later on the Saturday, again in Durham. This was three days before Scott was to answer bail at the city's police station and find out if he was to be charged. After being dropped off by his mum outside the Fallen Angel, we decided to take a stroll around the city, as it was a surprisingly warm January day.

Scott was in a tan leather jacket, silver trousers and crocodile-skin shoes. He also wore the ever-present designer shades and Gucci rings which glinted in the winter sun.

Our first port of call was Oddbins on the corner of Old Elvet, where he again bought two bottles of Lindauer Brut Cuvée. We strolled over Elvet Bridge and detoured down some stairs out of public view.

He was carrying a plastic shopping bag out of which he took empty 500ml bottles of Lucozade and Pepsi Max, topping up one and half-filling the other with the sparkling wine. 'It's best to be on the safe side as there are probably some bylaws preventing the consumption of champagne on a public street.' Scott also took out a huge Montecristo cigar from the bag. 'There's nothing like having a nice nine-inch Cuban in your mouth. Have I ever told you that?'

We spent a frustrating few minutes until he eventually managed to light it, then ventured back onto the old cobbled streets of Durham, Scott sipping from his Lucozade bottle and pulling on his cigar. As we passed groups of students and tourists, we got more than a few askance looks. We headed along Saddler Street then up Owengate to Palace Green, the scene of the theft of the First Folio in 1998.

Palace Green is a small area of grass in the centre of Durham flanked by Durham Cathedral and Durham Castle – together they form a UNESCO World Heritage site.

Surrounding the Green are a number of historic buildings including Bishop Cosin's Almshouses. Cosin was a noted theologian and liturgist whose scholarly promotion of traditional worship, doctrine and architecture established him as one of the fathers of Anglo-Catholicism in the Church of England in the 17th century.

He had been named Chaplain of Durham Cathedral in 1619, and subsequently wrote in 1627 the famed Collection of Private Devotions at the request of King Charles I for a daily prayer book at court. In 1634, he became Master at Peterhouse, Cambridge, but was exiled in Paris during the Puritan Commonwealth Government under the Lord Protector, Oliver Cromwell, then after his death in 1658, by Cromwell's son, Richard.

After the Monarchy was restored in 1660 under Charles II, Cosin was made Bishop of Durham. He founded the Almshouses around 1668 with a yearly endowment of £70. They were traditionally occupied by eight poor people – four men and four women – six from Durham and two from Brancepeth.

Scott puffed on his cigar then took a swig from his Lucozade bottle. 'It's now a restaurant for your prawn-sandwich brigade. It would obviously be too unsightly for the great unwashed to be seen shambling around while the great and the good take in such architectural splendour.'

Also on Palace Green is Bishop Cosin's Library, founded by him in 1669 as an endowed public library for local clergy and people of scholarly interests. The Library is still housed in its original building.

It predominantly contains Cosin's personal collection but also includes gifts from other benefactors, especially medieval manuscripts from George Davenport, who died in 1677, printed books from Bishop Richard Trevor (1707-71) and medieval manuscripts from Bishop Shute Barrington (1734-1826). The University used the building from 1834 and became trustee of the library in 1937. In 2005, the Library was in the first group of libraries and archives awarded Designated status under the Museums, Libraries and Archives Council Designation Scheme.

It is believed that Cosin purchased The First Folio before 1632. When he was exiled to France, the book was incorporated in the Peterhouse library, and on his return in 1660, he recovered it and took it with him, as Bishop, to Durham. After the library was built the Folio remained there, making the Durham copy unique in that it has effectively been under one ownership since its publication.

'Perhaps we should go in and ask to see it,' said Scott as we paused outside the library door. We idled a few moments as he considered the prospect.

I could imagine this causing quite a stir, and a fleeting image came to mind of Scott with Lucozade bottle, Montecristo cigar and First Folio legging it across Palace Green as fast as his crocodile-skin shoes could carry him.

But the moment passed. Scott was hungry and he had a two-for-one coupon for meals at Bella Italia, an Italian restaurant in nearby Silver Street. Located with views of the River Wear, it had a mezzanine floor overlooking the ground floor below. Both were almost full of diners and Scott turned down a window seat with a scenic view of the river, wanting to wait for a table to become available on the mezzanine level.

This was to prove an affectation of his, wanting to be in a position to observe his surroundings, one which would cause him to stroll out of restaurants or bars if he could not achieve it, particularly those where he didn't have a two-for-one meal coupon.

As tables cleared on the lower level, Scott remained steadfast in allowing other diners to be seated as we waited until, at last, a table became free on the upper level.

He said he was paying and urged me to buy the most expensive item on the menu if I so wished. However, there was no lobster, langoustines or *foie gras* here, just your usual pasta and antipasto fare as well as steak and burgers. I chose a humble, salmon pasta dish, which seemed a disappointment to him, while he zeroed in on the priciest steak. He asked for a bottle of water for form's sake that he ignored throughout the meal in preference for his Lucozade bottle.

'I used to be about 17 stone 15 years ago,' he said in-between mouthfuls. I've always liked my food. Until I was about thirty, I could eat very large meals and drink so much and at first I put no weight on. I used to go to the gym in the early days and try and burn it off. I suppose I let myself go. I was 17½ stone at its peak, the nadir, the lowest point, then I just decided that was enough. I was getting bored with the drug of food and, to a lesser extent, alcohol. I went on a crash diet. I am a person of extremes.

'The ironic thing, when I used to go to bed at night hungry, even though the cupboards were full, I actually felt good about going hungry because I denied myself the food.

'There's a world of difference in not doing something because you haven't got the means and not doing it because you choose not to. After a couple of weeks I lost my appetite. This went on for about six months and I virtually didn't eat anything. I was taking multivitamins. My weight went down to 10 stone, which for somebody of my height, 5 feet 10 inches, and build, was pretty sort of anorexic.

'Then I had to get professional advice and gradually got back eating again. It was a manifestation of my obsessive-compulsive disorder. It has been diagnosed. When I get to like something then it's very difficult for me to know where to draw the line. It has become less difficult with maturity but that maturity has taken a long time.'

We ate for a while in silence then, not surprisingly, his mind drifted to his impending date at Durham police station. 'I am confident they won't charge me. What with? Theft? I've never been to Durham library. I've got absolutely no connection with Durham University or its library. I've never been a student there and never known anyone who has been a student. They wouldn't have allowed me in. The only people I can imagine entering the hallowed portals are people on official visits or with business there, and I've no connection whatsoever with it.

'I've researched this and the exhibition from which the books were stolen in December 1998 was a private exhibition and seminar on English literature. The great and the good had been invited to some sort of symposium, as a sideshow, charting the course of English history. It was not open to the ordinary public so it's ridiculous to suggest I would, or could, have stolen it.

'If I was ever to be charged with anything it would not be theft but having it in my possession knowing or believing it to have been stolen and of course I think this flies in the face of the facts that I went openly into the Folger library, using my own name. I don't think that Durham police have anything. It required no fantastic detection to find me. I left my name and address with the Folger library in Washington. Don't let them claim any false credit for tracing me. I was in the back garden pruning my mother's roses when they came to arrest me. No Sherlock Holmes them!'

Much had been made of comments in the *Mail on Sunday* by Denny concerning the book he had given Scott. Denny had been shown a cover of the complete First Folio by a reporter and Denny said it was not the book he had given Scott. 'I have never seen it before. My book was called *Tempest* and had the front and back covers missing. Some of the pages were also missing,' he was reported to have said.

Some articles in the press had hinted that either the partners in the alleged crime were falling out and trying to pass the buck, or it was proof Denny had been used as a dupe in the master plan of Scott.

Scott shook his head and tutted. 'As I told the police it is a disbound copy. The front page is missing, the Shakespeare portrait. The majority of First Folios do [have it missing], and most have a facsimile portrait. With the whips and scorns of time they are going to become detached. That's what happened with the Cuban Copy. I think *The Tempest*, a comedy, was the last play to be written by Shakespeare but it turns out to be the first in the First Folio, at the head of the Comedies. When you look at the dis-bound Cuban Copy you see *The Tempest* on the front page. That's where the confusion comes in. That's why he said "the book I gave to Raymond was *The Tempest*".'

Scott paid the bill with his two-for-one coupon and cash, and we left the restaurant. We paused outside the door for a couple of minutes as he re-lit his cigar, then headed back into the city centre by St Nicholas's Church. Compared to the crowds who thronged the market stalls, shops and pubs, we seemed to move in slow motion, stopping every now and then as Scott re-fuelled from his Lucozade bottle. He was much taken by the scene and the possibilities it offered him.

'It's like the Forum in Ancient Rome. I have an idea after the successful conclusion of the case. I will launch my campaign to get the Cuban Copy back here. I could stage a happening. I see myself in a Roman toga, addressing the crowd. Friends, Durhamites and shoppers, lend me your ears. I will of course be accompanied by a group of similarly clad young ladies. That should grab their attention.'

Scott seemed supremely confident, on the surface, that on the Tuesday the charges would be dropped and his only struggle would be getting the book back. 'When I spoke to Massey on the phone and if he had said it had a library stamp which read Durham University, I would have told him to take it to the police. I asked if with his expert eye he could see any evidence of an attempt to obliterate any means of identifying it. If he had said yes, I would have, again, said take it to the police.

'It bears no library stamps. Not only that but unusually it bears no annotations in the margins. One was sold in Bond Street, I think in 2005, which was much inferior to the Durham Copy and the Cuban Copy. It had copious annotations in the gutter and in the margin done in italic sepia-ink, which usually used to happen to what was a library book. It's only books that have been in private hands for a long time that do not, and the Cuban Copy, as far as I can tell, was devoid of these annotations and library stamps. Most unusual.'

We retraced our steps back over Elvet Bridge and onto New Elvet where Durham City Police Station is located. He decided to go there to double-check what time he was to answer bail on Tuesday.

Apart from the police blue lamp over the front door, it could have been an elegant Georgian-style townhouse. Inside, the reception area was empty except for a group of youths sat by the window taking part in a variation of paper, scissors and rock – their version included a gun. They gave us a stern once-over, Scott getting the most attention. With his rings, ostentatious watch and designer shades he must have looked like a walking bank to them.

We rang the bell for attention and a woman officer poked her head round the door at the back of the office and told us to wait, and then disappeared.

As the youths began to nudge each other and look at us, their game temporarily suspended, we rather too deliberately took great interest in the posters on the wall. Scott said, 'They say that New Elvet police station is my *pied à terre* in Durham. The room service and meals are probably not what you get from a five-star hotel.'

With no sign of the woman officer or any of her colleagues, he began to get fidgety. 'The actual resources they have spent on this case is out of all proportion to the effect on the community, which I would say is negligent. It's a once in a lifetime investigation for them. A feather in their caps. They can say "I was one of the detectives who put Scott away for the great Durham book theft", then they can go back to their mundane duties of arresting people who have robbed gas meters and things like that.'

His mobile phone rang. 'Yes, Mother,' he answered, to sniggers in the corner. 'We're in the police station. No nothing like that, I was just checking what time I should arrive on Tuesday. You can pick me up soon where you dropped me off.'

With still no sign of any officer coming, Scott decided to head out. It seemed an odd diversion, as all he had to do was ring them up on Monday to double-check. Perhaps he wanted to re-acquaint himself with his '*pied à terre*', or had some vain hope he'd be told not to bother coming as the case had been abandoned. Or, maybe, it was just done for me, a minor theatrical moment; Scott facing down his accusers – unafraid and prepared.

As we walked towards Old Elvet to meet up with his mum,

Scott glanced briefly over his shoulder back at the police station. 'If they expect me to turn up on Tuesday with my tail between my legs, skulking through their doors like some common criminal, they've got another thing coming. I'll show them.'

And show them he did.

Chapter Ten

Cranky Noodle Dandy

On a crisp, clear January morning in 2009, seven months on from Scott's initial arrest, his big day had arrived. It had been nearly a year since his fifty-first birthday in Havana which he had celebrated with Heidy, Denny, and their friends and family, not forgetting the Brazilian ambassador.

With his passport confiscated, and his movements tracked, Scott had the notoriety which in many ways he craved, but it had proved a double-edged sword. He was in a goldfish bowl of his own making, through folly or unforeseen circumstance, depending on what you believed.

Over the preceding months, investigations had continued while Scott kicked the heels of his crocodile-skin shoes at his mother's home. He had been quick to assert his innocence and never seemed to waver much from his determined stance that he had done nothing wrong and that in time he would be proven innocent.

Now the time of reckoning had arrived. The morning began with an early call from Scott to my mobile phone as I made my way to work. 'Do you know how I can get my hands on a stretch limousine?' he asked, more direct and to the point than usual. He sounded excited and I could hear at the other end of the line him pacing up and down.

I played along. 'Any particular colour?'

'I'm undecided. Maybe pink or white. Something with a bit of pizzazz. At a discount rate of course, that sort of thing.'

'Why do you want one?'

'I want to arrive at the police station today in a bit of style. I see myself decked out in my finery surrounded by friends, drinking champagne and smoking Cuban cigars. You could join me. It would be an exclusive for your newspaper, you arriving with Scott as he meets his accusers.'

I told him I'd see what I could do. Five minutes later as I sat down at my desk to formulate a plan to get a cut-price stretch limo, Scott rang again.

'I just spoke to a chap in Bishop Auckland. Regrettably, he said they didn't have my specified type and colour available but he offered me a Hummer. I said no thanks, I just need a car. It's quite a substantial vehicle by all accounts. I got a good price and who was I to turn it down?'

'Exactly how big?'

'Oh, it will certainly make an impression. I'm looking forward to this. It all brings to mind Rousseau. You know Rousseau?'

'The French guy,' I fudged.

'Your eruditon does you great credit. "You are undone if you once forget that the fruits of the earth belong to us all, and the earth itself to nobody." That sort of thing. Will you be joining me?'

'I'll ask my editor.'

I hung up and googled Rousseau in an attempt to work out what he was on about. The quote was from Rousseau's *Discourse on Inequality and Theory of Natural Man*.

> The first man who, having fenced in a piece of land, said 'This is mine,' and found people naive enough to believe him, that man was the true founder of civil society. From how many crimes, wars, and murders, from how many horrors and misfortunes might not any one have saved mankind, by pulling up the stakes, or filling up the ditch, and crying to his fellows: Beware of listening to this impostor; you are undone if you once forget that the fruits of the earth belong to us all, and the earth itself to nobody.

It would make a novel defence, I thought. A variation on property is theft, or maybe a philosophical take on his 'Free the Books' campaign. However, Scott had seemingly convinced himself there would be no need for a defence, bolstered by Rousseau, or not. He believed there was no case to answer, or at the very least the police had nothing to pin on him, and that his liberty was around the corner. Maybe even today.

It seemed to escape him that the higher the profile of a case, the less likely the authorities are to drop it without a fight. And Scott's case had gone global.

My first experience of a stretch limo would have to wait, as my editor gave an unequivocal 'no' to my joining Scott. However, I was sent to cover the hearing and it was to prove a colourful day.

On the previous Saturday afternoon the streets had been fairly empty outside the police station. Today was different. The road was full of slow moving traffic edging into and out of the small city centre. Parking spaces were at a premium as those along the street had long been snapped up. Outside the station there was a yellow-boxed area for police vehicles in which a police van was already parked. There were three film crews and a dozen-or-more reporters and photographers waiting for Scott.

Pedestrians began to gather on the pavement opposite, looking at us and wondering what was going on. Those walking down our side stopped to ask. It took a bit of explaining.

Detective Inspector Mick Callan, who was heading the case alongside Detective Constable Tim Lerner, came out of the station. Callan, solidly built with grey hair, had a don't-mess-with-me look.

You could imagine the eye-rolling interviews he must have conducted with Scott, the self-styled dilettante, but when asked directly he just said, 'It's an interesting case.'

He was equally non-committal as to what was going to happen today, playing it by the book, just saying wait and see. Scott was due to answer bail at 11 a.m. and I gave him a call.

'Where are you?'

He said he was parked just round the corner close by the Fallen Angel Hotel.

'Is everybody there?' he asked.

'Ready and waiting,' I replied.

A couple of minutes later the nose of a gold-coloured Hummer emerged tentatively into view from Old Elvet to make the left turn into New Elvet. It's a fairly tight manoeuvre for an ordinary car, but for a triple-axled 48ft-long stretch limo it proved more than a little troublesome. Cameras whirred, traffic stopped and people gathered to watch as the vehicle edged out, reversed back, then, after three attempts, eventually managed to move serenely towards the waiting throng, causing traffic chaos in its wake.

DI Callan gave a wry smile, shook his head and went back into the station. The Hummer glided to a halt on the double yellow lines outside and the chauffeur opened the door. After a brief pause Scott stepped out. He'd certainly dressed for the occasion and later in great detail itemised his clothes for me in a letter so I would get it right.

> Full length Russian Sable fur coat from Zilli, New Bond Street, London, Mayfair WI. Raw silk trousers by Brioni (James Bond's tailor i.e. used to dress Pierce Brosnan and this current 007 whose name escapes me) of Rome. Belt by Vivienne Westwood. Vintage silk shirt by Gianni Versace at the height of his florid creative powers, similarly grey crocodile-skin shoes vintage Versace fresh out of the tissue from a salon in Old Bond Street (where Elton John would spend £100,000 a visit). Watch: Cartier Santos Dumont Steel and 18-carat gold bracelet, 18-carat yellow gold Rolex President Bracelet with 4-carat of round brilliant diamonds. Rings: Both Versace Gold (18 carat) with diamonds. Underpants: Marks & Spencer but better to say Calvin Klein. Cigar: Montecristo. Pot noodle: Sweet and Spicy.

He forgot to mention the designer Tiffany shades that he adjusted before stepping out to meet the cameras. Carrying a bottle of Dom

Pérignon 1996 vintage rosé champagne, the cigar and the Pot Noodle, he commented about the latter, 'A much underrated delicacy.'" Scott posed briefly for the photographers and cameras crews before entering the station.

DI Callan said to Scott: 'Your solicitor will have told you what is going to happen.'

Scott replied: 'Yes I'm going to be awarded the Queen's Police Medal.'

Alas, the QPM would have to wait and 20 minutes later Scott emerged from the station. Pausing on the steps outside he said: 'I have been charged with the theft and the handling of the Shakespeare First Folio. I will of course be pleading very much not guilty and I will relish my day in court.'

His day in court was to be in a fortnight's time on February 10th 2009, when he was bailed to appear before North Durham magistrates. He climbed back into the limo. It was big enough to carry most of the reporters and film crews who were then taken on a brief ride around the block as he conducted further interviews. In-between sips of Dom Pérignon he rubbished the non-existent prosecution case – 'a criminal waste of taxpayers' money' – and gave a run down on his wardrobe.

The vehicle parked up again outside the station and, after a couple more TV interviews, the limo set off again on a more pressing engagement – to find a cash point for more funds to pay for another hour's hire as Scott had overrun his two-hour deal.

I headed off to my car, a humble Vauxhall Astra, and texted him to say we should meet up later. I watched as the Hummer eventually disappeared from view, taking him not much more than a stone's throw away from Bishop Cosin's library where the First Folio, be it the Durham or Cuban Copy, was being kept.

Chapter Eleven

Snackbeth

Despite his ebullient mood on the day he answered bail, it wasn't long before it dawned on Scott that he was going to be in for a long haul. Somehow, he had managed to convince himself that the charges would be thrown out and the fight would not be over his liberty, but for the right to ownership of the First Folio.

His indictment had thrown up some surprises. In all, he faced six charges, the first two relating to the First Folio – its theft between December 10th and December 18th 1998, from Durham University, and that of handling stolen goods. The remaining charges included two further offences of theft and another two of handling stolen goods, concerning ordinary members of the public.

The first involved a filofax taken in 1988, the other a handbag containing a cheque book, cheque card, driving licence and photographs stolen in 1991. These were discovered in his home during the police search after his arrest for the theft of the First Folio, but there seemed to be no suggestion that he had tried to use them.

A quick telephone conversation the day after he answered bail revealed Scott in quiet, introspective mood. His mind was elsewhere, his answers vague. 'It very much feels like the morning after the night before during which too much champagne has been drunk and you're left with the bill and an empty wallet,' he said to me.

Scott, as if to himself, wondered out loud as to the motives of the prosecution. 'They have nothing, but to be seen to back down now would embarrass them.' He railed against 'fair England', which, to him, had revealed an uglier side, as an unjust persecutor of the innocent. Scott agreed to meet that Saturday but in a tone of voice that suggested such an arrangement would be forgotten the moment he hung up.

I texted him throughout the week, but he didn't reply. On Friday night, I was not so much worried about the meeting, but as to the welfare of Scott himself. I recalled how down he had sounded and feared the worst. My fears were allayed a bit earlier in the day than I would have preferred when he eventually texted back at 8 a.m. on the Saturday.

> What light thru yonder window breaks? It is the east Arise! And kill the envious moon eat 3 shredded wheat don running attire and jog for 10 kms (just like I've done) If you survive c u at R. County H. DURHAM high noon u can arrive in motorised luxury as parking will be free in hotel carpark and outside as I will bring mother's blue badge – my ultimate secret vengeance weapon against the evil apostates of Hell (traffic wardens) i ll treat u 2 working lunch and we'll take it from there need I bother 2 sign it.

There proved no need to use his secret vengeance weapon to evade the apostates of hell. I picked him up in Durham and we headed to Lumley Castle, a 14th-century building overlooking the River Wear in County Durham, which has been converted into a hotel and restaurant. Popular for wedding receptions, when we arrived there was one in full swing with self-conscious men in frock coats, waistcoats, starched collars and cravats, and the women in impractical salmon-pink silk dresses, which had to be hitched up to enable them to walk any distance.

They were attended by staff in historical garb, possibly Tudor. We paused as the cavalcade walked past us, the bride at the front. 'If we're being polite she could be described as Rubenesque,' observed Scott.

Her rather more rangy husband trailed in her wake. Noting the Tudor attendees, Scott added: 'Of course if it doesn't work out he could have her head cut off. Although, judging by its girth, it would take some doing.'

We headed into the restaurant. Inside it was almost empty of guests. Staff members were busily washing and drying glasses and there was a definite end-of-service feeling. We approached the bar and, adjusting his pair of Gucci shades this time with a bejewelled hand, Scott politely coughed as an introduction and addressed the eldest looking member of staff.

'Good afternoon, my good lady. My friend and I are hoping to avail ourselves in these most pleasant of historical surroundings of some of your victuals.'

The woman paused as she dried a glass and eyed him suspiciously. 'The restaurant's closed, she said. 'We're still doing sandwiches.' She nodded at a menu card on the counter. We made our order and headed into a lounge area. The only other patrons were an elderly couple sitting in convivial silence.

We briefly went over the events of the previous Tuesday. He, again, registered his surprise at the turn of events, but consoled himself with the fact he was a big fish they wanted to fry.

My first question wasn't about the case. Knowing already that there was some thought, no matter how 'out there', behind everything he did, I wondered out loud about the relevance of the Pot Noodle.

'Do you know who invented the sandwich?' he asked, by way of reply. 'The Earl of Sandwich. Why? He was an inveterate gambler. In Crockford's gaming house – still a casino in Curzon Street – he didn't want to leave the table so the waiter, or his footman or valet who was attending him would say "My Lord, your meal is ready" and it would, for example, be a steak. And he would have to go to the dining table and leave the gaming table.

'So he said, "Bring it to me" so the waiter said "How are you going to eat it? You're playing cards and you need a knife and fork," so he said put it between two slices of bread. That was after Shakespeare's time.'

And the Pot Noodle? I persisted.

'Shakespeare wrote very fast. Feverishly. I've heard the British Museum has some of Shakespeare's manuscripts and you see very few corrections. When he was on the job he stayed on the job. So he was like a spasmodic workaholic, he would compose – and this applies to the plays and the sonnets – very fast and intense.

'Obviously, like the Earl of Sandwich, he couldn't leave the desk and didn't want to lose his train of thought. I can't think of anything more appropriate than a Pot Noodle that if it had existed back then, he wouldn't have been anything other than a devotee. Everybody thinks that Shakespeare's blank verse is the ultimate. Who knows, with the aid of a few sweet-and-spicy Pot Noodles, or a beef-and-tomato Pot Noodle, he may well have been able to compose even better blank verse. I expect the idea will be pooh-poohed though.'

He was back on form, his mood upbeat. Whichever demons he'd been wrestling with before had been vanquished. For now.

Scott continued, 'I think a good way to approach this is – the Cuban Copy, question mark. Is it or isn't it? Is Scott a hero or a villain or is he an anti-hero? You must remember that in all of this no violence was used, nor was there any threat of violence. The evil of the Great Train Robbery was not the fact the men stole millions of pounds from the Royal Mail train, money that was to be incinerated. The evil was the fact that an ordinary working man, Jack Mills, the train driver, was coshed. That turned it into a venal crime of violence.'

He then turned his attention to the police and the forces of law and order, which he was convinced were conspiring against him. He wasn't going to go down without a fight.

'The police have thrown the full book at me, done somersaults backwards and forwards and jumped through hoops to bring the prosecution. Everything they put up will be challenged in a court of law to the nth degree. I will not countenance briefing a counsel who will permit or allow any reading of statements to the court. A person's testimony can be read out in court without cross-examination. But one of my privileges in fair England is to have that person brought to court to stand in the witness box to reiterate what he said in police statements and then be cross-examined. Then we'll see how sure they are of their ground.'

Interestingly, while he promised every prosecution witness

would be quizzed at length, he wasn't going to return the favour and take the witness stand himself.

Scott, a fan of Oscar Wilde, particularly of his epigram 'There is only one thing in the world worse than being talked about, and that is not being talked about', had taken on board a bitter lesson learned by the famous Anglo-Irish dramatist, poet and author at his trial for gross indecency. He had been caught out under cross-examination by Edward Carson QC and ended up being sentenced to two years hard labour.

Scott said: 'Maybe on this occasion I will learn a lesson from history. I have absolutely nothing to hide. I know I am entirely innocent of both charges, but much though I'd like the chance to protest my innocence, I must just stay silent. The golden thread that runs through English jurisprudence from Magna Carta has, in recent years with various criminal justice acts, become seriously frayed, but fortunately it has not been severed. I hope in fair England it shall ne'er be said a man needs to prove his innocence. There is no need for an accused to take one step out of the dock towards the witness box.

'I'm not sure of the strength of the prosecution case. It is intriguing but it's not going to stand up in a court of law. There's a highly distinctive inkblot on the first page of *The Tempest*, the first play in the First Folio at the head of the Comedies. As I recall, it's shaped like two testes and a male penis either circumcised or with prepuce retracted. Or if you prefer a non-male anatomical description it looks like a banana with a damson on either side. Yet there is no mention whatsoever of it in any record of the Durham Copy. How is that possible? Tell me that.

'The inkblot to me looks ancient as does a sepia, or red-dish brown, stain or tidemark running through much of the Cuban Copy. This watermark is not merely confined to the gutter or margins but invades the text obscuring the actual words which makes it a serious flaw. Again no mention of this in the Durham Copy. How can this be? My defence accordingly are endeavouring to find a world ink expert to ascertain their vintages.

'You know the police with their nasty, suspicious minds and their devious Machiavellian lawyers, will suggest they've been added after the 1998 theft – it's their only explanation, but I welcome expert analysis.

'Bringing the case to court is ridiculous. It's just to justify the vast amount of money and resources spent by this backwater provincial police force wanting to make a name for themselves. I think in this particular case they have over-egged the pudding. Yes that's the phrase, they have "over-egged the pudding" to get a charge and hopefully a conviction.

'But once the evidence is examined, it will be seen that the people who have made these statements have been selective as far as the questions. They say there's lies, damned lies and statistics – you can get any kind of answer you want from a survey depending on how you ask the questions.

'This is why I will not countenance any barrister who will say "oh, we'll let this one go through on the nod. We'll just let the prosecution read out their statements". I will say thank you, but you are no longer my legal representative.

'Everyone who has made a statement will be physically brought to the trial. They will be cross-examined vigorously as to the veracity of it, not so much the truth but the collective nature of what they've got to say. I feel passionately and fervently about it. I would feel it about anybody.'

At the time, many concerned with the case thought it would stand or fall on whether the First Folio was the Durham copy or not. However, that was to change over the coming months, thanks to the admission of someone who was to prove very tricky to get to the witness stand.

Chapter Twelve

Bombay Bad Boys

Consett is a small town to the northwest of Durham. In the early 19th century it was a small village of about 150 inhabitants, but that changed when coking coal, blackband iron ore and limestone were found under the ground there, the three ingredients necessary for blast furnaces to produce iron and steel.

Boom years resulted and over the next century it became one of the world's leading steel-making towns, providing the steel to build everything from Blackpool Tower to nuclear submarines. In the 1960s, at its peak, the steelworks there employed 6,000 people and it was renowned for a pall of iron-oxide red dust that hung over the town. Due to increased competition from Teesside and abroad, the steel works were closed in 1980, creating then one of the worst unemployment blackspots in Britain, even in the dole-hit country at that time.

Today, the red dust has long since gone revealing the beautiful surrounding landscape of the Derwent Valley and it is increasingly attracting commuters from Tyne and Wear and County Durham looking to escape to the country.

It is also the home of North Durham Magistrates Court and it was here, two days before his fifty-second birthday, that Scott arranged his second happening, revealing another, perhaps surprising side to the carefully cultivated aesthete – a liking for Boss Hogg.

He arrived at the single-storey prefab in a chauffeur-driven white Ford stretch limo dressed all in white, he said, as tribute to the villainous glutton of the 1980s TV series the *Dukes of Hazzard*, who also had a fondness for cigars.

Scott's look was completed by a sable-lined brown jacket from Zilli to stave off the cold from the recently fallen snow. 'If my enemies see me shiver they will say it's out of fear rather than from the cold. Didn't Charles I wear two shirts on the scaffold for the same reason?'

Accompanying him was a pretty blonde 'researcher' he introduced as Claire Smith. Inevitably, he was smoking a cigar and brandishing a Pot Noodle. 'A Bombay Bad Boy,' he said. Glancing briefly at his researcher, Scott grinned: 'I wouldn't like you to draw the wrong conclusions from that of course.'

Pausing on the steps before he entered the court, he chose to read an extract from the opening scene of *Richard III*. 'Now is the winter of our discontent, Made glorious summer by this son of York …'

His researcher, dressed in a thin, short-sleeved white shirt and black skirt, bravely ignored the cold as she held the book up for Scott to recite from. 'I knew the whole passage by heart but Claire had to have something to do,' Scott explained later.

Concluding the monologue with: 'He capers nimbly in a lady's chamber, To the lascivious pleasing of a lute,' he headed towards the magistrates chambers, to the pleasing of the local JPs.

During the ten-minute hearing, prosecutor Michala Glass outlined the case against Scott, and asked for the matter to be transferred to Crown Court.

Clive McKeag, representing Scott, told the JPs: 'The defendant will not be putting in a plea today. The defendant does not agree with everything that has been said from a factual point of view, but now is not the time to raise it.'

The magistrates declined jurisdiction and adjourned proceedings until April 14th when the case was to be transferred to the crown court. Scott was released on conditional bail and on leaving court, he invited reporters to join him in the limo alongside his researcher and two local lads he had recruited as his bodyguards, dubbing them the 'Bombay Bad Boys'.

He told the reporters: 'Like Hamlet, Prince of Denmark, I have had to suffer not only the whips and scorns of time, the oppressor's wrong, the insolence of office, but also the law's delay. Once again nothing has happened, absolutely nothing has happened. The case has been adjourned for nine weeks until April 14th. Again the police are not ready to proceed.'

Unable to join him at court, I texted to ask how it went. He soon texted back:

> Well its not for me to say how it went but we had fun. My research assistant is Claire or sometimes Chlöe but whats in a name? A rose by any other name would smell as sweet!! I recruited her for her assets – she has a very rich indulgent daddy and she came up to me in a nightclub and said (and I quote) 'I've fallen truly madly deeply in love with you and want to have your babies! Do you think you could get to like me?' So I said yes because life's too short and not just Heidy should experience the pleasure of my body! No honestly it's a strictly platonic relationship her biggest asset is a B.'A.HONS in English Lit. (NORTHUMBRIA) – she wrote a dissertation on Lady MacBeth as a radical feminist! She has a husband doing 7 years for GBH with a bit of a jealous temper and yours truly would like to keep his kneecaps not to mention the uncircumcised shamrock in my Y Fronts. I really don't know where all this bullshit comes from – it just spews out of me.

Later in the week I phoned to wish him a happy birthday. It was a short, maudlin conversation. I asked how he had celebrated and I could virtually hear a resigned shrug on the other end of the line. 'I was in bed all day. The lumpen man was here; it was a long, black day. My last birthday was of course fabulous with Heidy, her family and the bonhomie of the fiesta at Siborney. The only fiestas round here are of the battered Ford variety. Not my choice of conveyance.'

When we eventually met at my home he had pulled himself around, re-living the events surrounding his court appearance. His explanation for Claire's appearance was a little more prosaic than he had insinuated by text. 'I got her out of the Yellow Pages. One of those thingy-grams and a single mother. She has a child to look after. I wanted to liven things up, Consett isn't the most exciting of places at the best of times.'

He'd made up the bit about a psychopathic ex-husband and, as for the 'Bombay Bad Boys', he first met them as he entered the court. 'They were local lads, nice lads, in their twenties or late teens, called Barry or Larry or Gary, maybe Mephistopheles and Nigel, how is one to know? They had turned up because their mate, whose offence escapes me, might be sent to prison. They weren't allowed in court, they said, and were a bit bewildered at proceedings. Kindred spirits I thought, so I made them my bodyguards.

'Bodyguards are very useful in the antique books world; it's not as genteel as you may think. Some dealers make Arthur Daley look like a paragon of virtue. Ever watched *Lovejoy*? No less than the truth. They said they were from Stanley and asked if I could drop them off and I told them to tell the driver where they lived. So there was me, my researcher and these two local lads in the back of the limousine, drinking champagne.

'They behaved like perfect gentlemen, watched their Ps and Qs – not to mention their Fs and Cs, without my prompting, ordinary working-class lads, not unemployed through any indolence but because the work isn't there. Previously they would have been miners or employed in the steel works.

'At least they were free – I think their friend got sent down – free to make a conscious decision to leave a room, walk down to the end of the street, not to go and spend any money, actual physical freedom, speaking to me in this motor car, people who have never been deprived of it don't realise just how rich they are in their freedom.

'We went to a run-down council estate; we altered our vocabulary so we didn't use big words, and dropped them off. They asked if it was OK to take pictures and I said sure. A rent-a-crowd came around, it was just one of those things. We were drinking three types of champagne, a Dom Pérignon Vintage Brut 1999 and, because I knew Claire was coming, I got a bottle of Cristal Rosé and a Nicolas Feuillatte Cuvée Rosé Champagne, blended for the Cannes Film Festival in 1995. I think the chauffeur may have been getting a bit nervous; there were a lot of wheels on view to be possibly pinched after all, so we drove off.'

I asked again about his dark mood on his birthday and he spoke of suffering from manic depression. 'Not bipolar disorder,' he added hastily. 'I dislike the term as it suggests I alternately embark on expeditions to the Arctic and the Antarctic for no good reason.' Sufferers swing between abnormally high and depressed moods. He said he'd had it for years for which he had been prescribed a number of drugs, including lithium.

'I had lithium implants in my arm. It was absolutely appalling, reminding me of the days in the Soviet Union. In her poem 'Grey Is The Colour Of Hope' about her time in a Soviet psychiatric "hospital", Irina Ratushinskya described how major tranquilisers were used by evil Soviet doctors to control their thoughts, to make them less creative, more malleable and "socially manageable".

'I had asked for tablets but I was told they don't work on people like you because you just won't take them. So I had a slow release capsule in my arm and they said I was going to feel a lot better. It was like a month of complete and total purgatory. It was like someone had poured fast-drying cement into my head. There was an impenetrable wooliness, like being a robot. I never had an original idea in that time and was so malleable that any suggestion I would have complied with.

'I had it just the once and refused further treatment. It had been voluntary on my part. They said without it you will be getting into trouble. But it was like castrating Casanova; removing the vocal chords of Caruso; chopping off the hands of Mozart; reducing somebody to a zombie, one of the living dead.

'Just as Amy Winehouse said, they tried to make me go to rehab and I said "no, no, no". If I had another implant in my arm I'm more likely to commit suicide. It's just one of those things you've got to learn to live with.'

He took another drink of champagne from his ever-present Lucozade bottle, and warmed to the subject. 'It's no secret that creative people, whatever their field of endeavour, painters, writers, comedians, are much more prone to bipolar disorder or manic depression. Their most creative period is when they are high, then they weather the storm of their low periods. Spike Milligan was a classic case. He could never have written all those Goon scripts or the ground-breaking comedy Q8, unless he had those highs, but he had the lows as well which later were controlled by lithium, which I'm not sure was such a good thing. Raymond Chandler the author, was another and then of course, Ernest Hemingway, whose typewriter and manuscripts I have seen in the Havana hotel room where he wrote *Death in the Afternoon*. It was necessary he had a bottle of booze and fags in front of his typewriter when he wrote. It's unthinkable that he would have been able to create when he was as sober as a judge.

'Francis Bacon always had several bottles of Bollinger to hand when he was painting. The best rock music and that sort of thing, wouldn't have been written it if these people had been smoking menthol cigarettes and drinking soda water. They had to be fuelled by stimulants like coke or heroin to increase their intensity. Would Jimi Hendrix have written 'All Along The Watchtower', 'Voodoo Child', 'Purple Haze' and 'Hey Joe' if he had been teetotal?

'My drug of choice is alcohol because I can get a crescendo effect from it. I've never injected myself with any kind of drug. With the crescendo effect it takes a while to build up, you can savour it as it develops. It's one of the reasons I drink champagne. I don't get drunk too quickly.'

Instead of the Jimi Hendrix Experience, it was the Raymond Scott Experience today, which meant a goody bag he had brought from Marks & Spencer – Peking duck, spring rolls, Coquille St Jacques and lobster thermidor with a salmon mousse.

As we ate, I asked about his relationship with his father, Raymund. According to Scott, he was a bit of a firebrand communist from the East End of Glasgow, not a place big on sales of lobster thermidor. Of course, not unless it was deep fried.

'It was a difficult relationship. 'Have you ever seen the film *Long Day's Journey Into Night* by the "American Shakespeare", Eugene O'Neill about a family tearing itself apart? The definitive version of course starred Katharine Hepburn, Spencer Tracy and Jason Robards. That was my home life.

'Rows would start out of nothing over trivial matters. There were three people with their own opinions; she argued with him, him with me and I with both of them. Not even a United Nations peacekeeping force could have maintained tranquility. Things might have been different had I had brothers and sisters. When they rowed I always had the last word. You didn't consult me before you had me, I'd say.

'I consider bringing a child into the world to be the epitome of selfishness because a child has no say in the matter. I said to them your decision to bring a child into the world was dictated by social convention because it was expected. You get married, your peer group are all having children, so you have children. There is no doubt that people love their children but their creation is clearly a selfish act.

'They were law-abiding people. They believed in the system and that ordinary people could change it by helping to fine-tune things through political pressure.

'I didn't want anything to do with this system. We had one blazing row when we lived in South Shields and my father was going to vote for Labour. It was an ultra-safe Labour seat, a donkey wearing a Labour rosette would have been returned, although that might be a little unkind on donkeys. Anyway, I said "why vote?" My mother said people had fought and died to win the right to vote. Remember the suffragettes? They said people should be fined for not voting.

'I said if that was the case I'd get a dog and wait for it to have a shit outside the polling booth. I'd spoil the ballot paper and wipe the dog's backside with it then put it in the ballot box. I suppose that would be a bit unfair on the people who counted the votes, but there you are. That's what I think of politicians of any colour.'

Scott also couldn't understand how his mother and father, former communists, didn't share Stalin's dim view of the British Labour Party. 'After the Second World War Labour were voted in under Clement Attlee. Churchill was voted out and of course it was Churchill who had been dealing with Stalin. When Attlee went to Moscow to meet Stalin, he expected a warm welcome.

'But Stalin could understand Churchill – born in Blenheim Palace, grandson to a Duke – Stalin knew where he was coming from. But Attlee got a very chilly reception; in fact, the delegation was treated very badly, very shabbily, because Stalin couldn't understand why there hadn't been a revolution in Britain. He later wrote in his memoirs that he saw them as social traitors. I have my own morality. Laws made by man can be broken by man.

'It's not as if I'm exploiting anybody. You've got to be prepared to do your own thing. "To thine own self be true." Somebody who works nine-to-five, pays their taxes and never steals anything, I've never criticised them. But people are always having a go at me for my lifestyle. They call me a leech, a parasite, it's just water off a duck's back, I don't say they're petty bourgeois, I say horses for courses.

'To them I would say, yes, my life is more colourful than a person who works at the DSS at Longbenton, a nine-to-five civil servant. There's nothing wrong with that. My mother still receives benefits. But you can picture the stereotypical person who works in the DSS and that sort of thing. I don't criticise that person but so many times in my life I have been criticised because the mainstream consider my life to be adventurous, eccentric.

'I think it is born out of jealousy. They're going to criticise me for being a colourful character. If I was doing something demonstrably wrong I could understand the criticism, but this has come from conventional people who didn't have the nerve or the verve to be colourful like me.

'You're way out there, they say, you're eccentric. I can't see the reason for the herd instinct. There are good laws to protect the majority but so often people just become hidebound. Creativity and individuality is stifled just because people don't want to appear different, they don't want to put their head above the parapet. I have never done a day's work in my life. I have never received a wage in my life. It's a very proud boast of mine.

'Why? Suppose you work in the Nissan car factory in Washington. At the end of the week you've made a car and the owner of the factory sells the car for £1000 profit, he doesn't give you £1000 he gives you £500, or £100 or less, then you're being exploited, you're not getting the full value of your labour. It's what Marx and Engels expounded in *Das Kapital*.

'My mother has said to me on many occasions "don't judge everyone by your standards. Your life is fundamentally unhappy, but don't assume that everybody else's is. People with not a fraction of our money are content".

'I can't be happy without money. I had a psychiatrist who asked me, "Did you have a happy or unhappy childhood?" I said, compared to whom? Compared with some slum kid from Bombay or Mumbai or whatever it's called, my childhood was very happy.

Then he said, "Oh, you're confusing happiness with material possession." I said it was easy to do that but how can you be happy if you are a slum child in India or the Third World? If you want to compare it to some fairytale childhood from Hans Christian Anderson then I don't suppose it was. Although it could be "Grimm",' he laughed.

'It's comparative. We're sitting here eating and drinking very well compared to poor people. Yet, sixty years after the introduction of the welfare state here, despite being one of the richest countries in world, there are large areas of endemic poverty not far from where we're sitting right now.

'That was the thing about Gandhi, and this is all relevant to my point. If the Tories had got in after the Second World War there wouldn't have been any sort of Indian independence. The ruling class thought it was their divine right to colonise and rule. It wasn't anything to do with Gandhi starving himself and his non-violent resistance. It was just that the Labour Government decided they weren't going to hold onto the empire and we were going to become a Commonwealth. The Establishment doesn't change unless the Establishment wants to. The system won't change me unless I want it to. I say fuck the system, *viva la revolution*! Have some more lobster, it's delicious.'

As we polished off the wine and champagne, his mobile rang again. He lifted his shades up and squinted at the number. 'Mother, I'm still with the journalist. Can you pick me up at Durham ... Yes, I'll be all right.'

He hung up. 'She's a bit worried because it's getting dark. Presumably for herself not me, although with mothers you never know. Anyway, I'm giving you *carte blanche* to write anything you want apart from if you said Scott went up on the Cumbrian moors and had anal sex with a sheep. I'd object to that, because it's not true and I haven't done that for a long time.

'There are two other things you can't say. One, I've never committed incest and two, I've never participated in Morris dancing, both upon the advice of Noel Coward. In the final analysis I believe if I was to meet Saint Peter at the pearly gates I would give him a good argument to get into heaven although he'd probably like to go through a few moot points with me.

'I think I am fundamentally a good person and I belong up there rather than down there.'

Chapter Thirteen

Crime and Punishment

Whilst the Folio case was ongoing, Scott appeared before Gateshead magistrates where he pleaded guilty in a separate case involving the theft of two books. They were not in the Folio league – worth about £50 for the pair – but they were an interesting choice.

The first was *The Cannabible* collection by the renowned pot-grower Jason King and the second was *Enclosure* by Andy Galsworthy, a British sculptor, photographer and environmentalist.

He had taken them from a bookshop in Gateshead the previous September while he waited to answer bail for the theft of the Shakespeare First Folio. He had been spotted by two security guards acting suspiciously in the store, which he then had left without paying for the books.

For the Gateshead hearing, Scott had dressed soberly – jeans, T-shirt, a mustard-coloured leather jacket and a navy baseball cap. Prosecutor David Mayhew said Scott was stopped as he left the store and when challenged removed the books from a House of Fraser bag and admitted he hadn't paid for either of them. 'He was asked if he intended to permanently deprive the shop of the books and he said he didn't know what his intention was,' said Mr Mayhew.

Magistrates were told that Scott, who had previous convictions for similar offences, was the subject of a pending inquiry into a much more serious matter – that concerning the theft of the Durham First Folio.

Defending, Judith Curry said as a result of the other matter, Scott had been under stress and pressure. 'And there is a question as to his psychiatric mental health at this time and at the time that this offence was committed,' she said.

The magistrates fined him £90 with a total of £165 costs.

When we met up again, this time in Newcastle, and walked into the city centre, he produced a plastic bag from his case that contained an inch-thick sheath of papers. Scott puffed on a cigar and nodded at the contents of the bag. 'As *Minder* would put it, my previous. You see I have nothing to hide.'

As we stood in the street, I took out the notes and flicked through the top few pages, which were solicitors' letters and then a computer read-out of his antecedents – or previous.

There were 24 convictions in all, dating from 1977, when he was nineteen, through to 2007. The majority of them were thefts although, in 1989, a firearms and threat-to-kill offence caught my eye.

As I took that one in, Scott, almost sniffing the air, said: 'I'm in a good mood today. Energised. You know when you feel you have a purpose. Sometimes I do get into a terrible fug but I feel today is going to be one of my good days.'

And off he went at pace, heading towards the Books for Amnesty shop in Westgate Road. Once inside he went straight to a glass cabinet by the side of the counter. Scott gave the door handle of the glass cabinet a try but it was locked. 'It's where they keep their valuable items. We could jemmy the door, grab the books and make our escape,' he smiled knowingly.

'Old habits, eh?' I joked, and he laughed.

One of the staff came over to us and Scott turned his attention to him. 'Good afternoon, young man. You might recall I was on the premises the other day and was particularly taken by a few splendid examples in this cabinet. Might I have another look?'

The man unlocked the door and Scott pointed to three blue volumes on the top shelf, Shakespeare's *Histories*, *Comedies* and *Tragedies*. He gently caressed each book as he held them in turn. Scott managed to knock the price down slightly to £75 for the lot. After he paid in cash, Scott commented, again with a hint of knowing, 'It's amazing the bargains you can pick up if you know what you're looking for.'

He appeared further energised by his purchase and next we headed for nearby Blackfriars, a restored 13th-century friary behind the city's Chinatown. After years of neglect the buildings were restored and now are home to a restaurant and various craft shops. We walked into one of the shops containing a motley collection of metal and wood sculptures, paintings and ornaments, with just the odd bit of Newcastle and North East franked tat as a nod to tourists. Scott struck up a conversation with the woman shopkeeper who ran it with her husband.

Most of the work on display was their own. Again, Scott had been in before when he had been particularly taken by a Rembrandt self-portrait painted by the husband, an impressive copy of the famous 1665 original. After a brief chat – haggling would be too vulgar a word for it – he offered £160, which was accepted and, after handing over the cash, asked to pick it up at a later date.

'I like to see myself as a patron of the arts although it's a good job I didn't have that hanging on the wall when the Inspector called,' joked Scott.

With £235 spent, it was time for food and he produced another two-for-one meal voucher, this time for La Tasca, a Tapas bar on the Quayside which we walked down to. As we ate, I asked him about his previous.

'I've a lot of convictions for shoplifting but only a few concerning books and those were new books. They intend to use that against me as an example of bad character. Because I've been convicted on numerous occasions for stealing books – which I consider to be a revolutionary act – they want to equate that with the theft at Durham University library, even though I've never been convicted of stealing a book from any library, nor a remotely old book.'

I asked how the thefts were a revolutionary act. 'I suppose Robin Hood was my first political role model. Robin Hood rebelling against the oligarchy which came over with William the Conqueror.

'I'm not like Fidel and Che who fought in the mountains and started a revolution with 28 men in the Sierra Maestra. What was I supposed to do? Put on a uniform and foment rebellion in the Cheviot Hills? Chairman Mao said a revolutionary has to be like a fish swimming in the sea of peasantry.

'I've never ever and never will steal from a corner shop off a Mr Smith or a Mr Singh. All of my thefts have been off chain stores, supermarkets and multinational corporations. I consider them to be revolutionary acts of an urban rebel. Often, I would donate liberated items to charity shops.'

The revolutionary mood had obviously taken him as he spoke of turning up at his next court appearance dressed as Che Guevara with attendant camouflage-clad bodyguards. 'Or I could turn it around. I could turn up in court in the clothes I did the gardening in. Arrive in a rusty old minicab. Scott in through the back door of the police station, which was offered to me.

'You have to be careful when police start offering you things like that. It looks as if I've got something to hide. Quite the opposite. I suppose I went extremely in the opposite direction, arriving by limo, well-dressed and through the front door.'

He paused for a drink from his Lucozade bottle and slumped back in his seat for a moment. 'I would have preferred that none of this had happened, really. But now it has, well, it's just happened. The sting in the tale is the possible 14 years of imprisonment at the end of this.' But he didn't intend to go with a whimper.

'If I can provide a bit of entertainment, a bit of colour, a bit of a carnival, that's fine. The only problem is when you wake up in the morning, usually with a hangover; the original problems are still there. It's why you have to party to forget.

'I'm a rebel with a cause. What cause?' he asked of himself. He paused again. 'I'm a bit of a Robin Hood, Heidy my Maid Marion and Durham Police the Sheriff of Nottingham. Maybe I'm a Krug Communist, keeping a bit back for myself. I'm quite easily seduced by luxury.'

His quest for luxury, the good things in life, and no obvious lawful means of paying for them were obviously a constant source of friction with his parents who seemed to have both indulged and castigated him for his foibles in equal measure over the years.

His father in particular, whose hard-working, industrious and frugal life was a polar opposite to that of his son's. Sometimes Scott gave the impression that his feckless lifestyle was in part to dishonour his father. On the face of it he disparaged him, but at times there was almost a contradiction between the dislike he was trying to express and the words he used to express it, which revealed a certain respect for him.

'At least I went out and stole off the rich *à la* Robin Hood and donated things to charity shops. When did their intellectualism ever achieve something?

'The only significant socialist thing I can point to with my father was when he was a full-time electricians union official of Reyrolle in Hebburn. I think it was the early 1970s, a time of high unemployment. He persuaded the men to accept a ban on overtime. At that time they were working weekends and late shifts to get a delivery completed and he argued and persuaded the management, backed up by the threat of strike action, that they should abolish overtime and take on more men.

'They took about 50 off the dole queue and gave them back the dignity of work. It meant that those workers already working got less pay because they weren't working overtime, but it was a sacrifice they were prepared to make because of my father. I can just picture him now up on the soapbox like Peter Sellers in *I'm Alright Jack*, addressing the brothers. Commissar Scottski.'

I said that was an achievement to be proud of.

He replied, seemingly begrudgingly. 'I suppose it was an achievement in a way. Something I can say I'm quite proud of as his son, that he achieved that.

'He offered me the opportunity he never had by sending me to the RGS. He left school at fourteen and started his apprenticeship as an office boy. He said I don't want you to forget where we came from but you've got to take advantage of these opportunities.

'I think my parents wanted me to become a doctor and then do medical missionary work in the Third World. For a while I toyed with the idea of going to medical college – I was good at sciences – but not to give my services free to the sick in an underdeveloped country. I thought of emigrating to America and making a pile being a VD doctor in LA. Or opening a chain of abortion clinics. Who knows, by now I could have been rich, eminent even.

'But I was just a frivolous hedonist, a playboy. During arguments my father used to say "you're a disgrace, you're frivolous, a dilettante, a flunkey, a dabbler. You disgust me".

'In later life we were reconciled. I looked after him when he had Alzheimer's.'

He took out a packet of tablets out of his pocket. 'Sticks and stones, you know,' he said dreamily, popping a couple of pills in his mouth. 'When you mix codeine with alcohol you get a nice detached feeling of floating away.

'I would have liked to have different parents; unfortunately I had no say in the matter. Rich people, more cultivated, urbane, sophisticated. A French castle in the Loire. Wouldn't we all? I didn't win in the birth stakes.' Scott paused for a moment and chastised himself with a line from King Lear:

> How sharper than a serpent's tooth it is,
> To have a thankless child.

Then he continued: 'Well, perhaps I didn't lose. Millions are worse off than me, but I didn't hit the jackpot. I came to realise that all of his life, he and mother who started as revolutionaries weren't really revolutionary, they were just sort of like nine-to-five people and the revolution was in their head.

'It was all theoretical, they didn't do anything practical. My father resigned from the Communist Party after the Soviet invasion of Hungary in 1956, my mother in 1968, after the invasion of Czechoslovakia and they both joined the socialist Labour party. I think what I've done with my life has been more significant. I've been more revolutionary.

'If I had been born in Cuba as a contemporary of Fidel I would have been one of his men in the mountains. In this country I think of Arthur Scargill as a revolutionary. I've never been down a coal mine; I've never done a day's work in my life. I'm not exactly a horny-handed son of toil. The circumstances weren't right for me; I was born in the wrong place at the wrong time.

'I would have been happy there in mountains in the Sierra Maestra. Seed can only grow if it has the right soil, the right conditions. I was totally bereft of that sort of thing. A misfit, born out of my time. My parents just talked. Don't get me wrong, I love my country, I just hate the things that have been done in its name. I haven't reverted yet to armed struggle, but I'm no pacifist.'

Which reminded me of one of his previous charges, sticking out like a sore thumb in a sea of petty thieving, his 1988 offence of making threats to kill. He was given an absolute discharge, but the mere appearance of it seemed somehow out of place.

In his own mind, Scott was a wannabe revolutionary, eager to find a cause to take up arms, but this didn't quite ring true. The thought of him trudging round the rugged Sierra Maestra in non-designer fatigues with the forces of President Batista in hot pursuit was an unlikely one. He was more Don Quixote, tilting at windmills, than Castro and Guevara, launching an attack on the Moncada Barracks that nearly wiped the revolutionaries out.

Scott proved evasive when it came to giving details of what exactly happened in 1988. 'It was merely a reciprocation. You attempt to do this to me and I will to do it you. Montague and Capulet stuff transferred from Verona to South Shields, a bit of personal enmity and it has no bearing whatsoever on this particular case. It was twenty-odd years ago.'

Pushed further, he still remained vague.

'It was just a simple case of I am not going to sit back and let him do what he did without reciprocation. It was getting on towards being a personal vendetta. His, not mine. There was vandalism to my mother's car and it ended in a catharsis. It was another case when the police went overboard towards me and when the full circumstances were explained to the Judge at Durham Crown Court he decided it was all a storm in a teacup and he released me.

'The maximum sentence I believe is 10 years for threats to kill. Three years was the going rate. He released me because of exceptional, extenuating circumstances. I'm not a black-and-white person. I am full of complexities but this hasn't got anything to do with the matter that is pertinent and it's ancient history.'

I tried to push more.

'I don't want to come across as a knight in shining armour. I want to come out as the person I am, which is a complex but fundamentally decent individual, not hidebound by petty laws and restrictions. You have to remember what the Nazis in Germany did was not against the law. Everything they did was within the law of their country at that time as these were laws made by them.

'When they put the Nazis on trial at Nuremberg they had to come up retrospectively with laws to try them – crimes against humanity.

'Before Adolf Eichmann was hanged in Israel – Eichmann was the architect of the final solution – he said, "I was only following orders". Laws made by man.

'I have never ever had a sleepless night over the deeds I have done. I've never had my conscience pricked as a result of any of my actions and that from someone who is fifty-two is a very proud boast.'

Chapter Fourteen

Measure for Measure

Was Scott's conscience clear about the theft of the Durham Copy of the First Folio? Even if it wasn't, the police seemed to be encountering difficulties in firming-up the case against him.

Despite having been arrested 10 months before, and with a number of court appearances behind him, Scott had yet to be asked to plead to the charges. This meant the prosecution's case was not complete; investigations were continuing, and, despite the tenor of reports in the media, it was not an open-and-shut case.

At the root of Scott's defence was his claim that the book had belonged to Denny and that it had been in his family in Cuba for over a century. Even if the First Folio was the one stolen from Durham in 1998, and the evidence to that end was very persuasive, it was not conclusive that Scott knew it to be one and the same.

Ironically, one of the reasons for an element of doubt about whether they were the same book formed part of the prosecution's argument. Pages which could have definitively identified it as the Durham Copy had been removed, and this had been done so fairly recently, the prosecution claimed. Who else would have done that but someone who wished to conceal the identity of the book? But who?

Over the centuries a number of Folios had been stolen and others were yet to be accounted for. How could it be proven it wasn't one of these?

It was a complex case with additional difficulties. The chief one was Durham police actually getting to interview the two other members of Scott's so-called 'triumvirate' – Denny and Heidy. Up until this point, the Cuban authorities hadn't granted permission for officers from England to travel there to question them. All the police had so far on this matter were notes taken by news reporters who had interviewed the pair after the case had broken, and Denny's description of the provenance of the book, which had been translated by Heidy for him, and sent to the Folger.

Written on Hotel Nacional de Cuba notepaper, it said:

> I Odeiny Moreno Leon inherited the Shakespeare book together with 53 other books all in Spanish when my mother Mirian (born 1940) died of cancer in April this year. Ever since I was a boy I remember the book as it is today in my family home in Holguin, Oriente. We called it *El libro viejo en ingles* (the old English book) and kept it in a wooden bible box in a bookcase. As far as I can recall it was the only book in English my family owned. My maternal grandmother Aleyda (born 1906) now deceased since 1980 lived with me, my late father Agustin and mother and she told me that the old English book had belonged to her mother Mirta (born 1877 died 1932) further than that I cannot go. I am a white Cuban of pure European descent principally Spanish from Galicia who emigrated to Cuba where my maternal great grandmother was born.
>
> After my birth it was not possible for my late mother to have any more children so I have no brothers or sisters. In May 2008 I brought the books and other things of my late mother to my home in Habana.
>
> Three years ago I retired from the Cuban Armed Forces with the rank of Commandante (Major) to spend more time with my wife Ima daughter Danielle and son Alejandro. I then went to work for Cubanacan, the Cuban National tourist board and now have responsibility for security in tourist hotels. Through Heidy I met Mr Raymond Scott at the start of November 2007 and we became friends. Because his first tongue is English I invited him and Heidy to my new house to see the Shakespeare book and ask him if it was of any interest.

I speak some modern English but read it less well (my late mother and grandmother spoke only Spanish). The book looked in bad condition with no covers and pages loose as I always remember it.

Raymond said it was a book of Shakespeare's plays (which I knew) and that he was without doubt the greatest writer ever in English (which I did not) so it could well be of note. The family of my mother were principally scientists, doctors, dentists and farmacists [sic] while that of my father army officers both before and after the revolution in 1959. We could find no date of publication so next day all three of us went to the National Library and learned of the First Folio at the Folger Library. As Cuban nationals me and Heidy cannot visit the USA so Raymond said he would take it and left me a deposit of 10,000 cuc (convertible Cuban pesos or approx $11,000 US). We saw him off at Jose Marti airport as he flew to Nassau. I know that without Heidy and Raymond the Shakespeare book would not have been found during my lifetime.

This account was exactly as Scott had described how he came to be in possession of the Folio. On the face of it, it seemed hasty for him to have been charged with its theft when police had yet to interview the very person that he said he had gotten it from.

The conundrum, as Scott freely admitted and in a way incriminated himself, was that Denny had never travelled outside of Cuba, let alone visited England. If he didn't get the book as he described, then how did he?

The obvious answer to this would be that Scott had given it to him and it was all part of an elaborate story to create a false provenance to cover up its theft. But what difference did it make where Scott said it had come from when he walked through the doors of the Folger? They were always going to check out its provenance.

And even if he had somehow deluded himself that the Folger

would be taken in by the alleged deceit and he had stolen the book himself, why would he have involved Denny and lose a third of the potential proceeds of its sale?

It didn't help his case that he had opened a bank account in Vaduz, Liechtenstein at the HQ of the Landesbank, where money from the proposed sale of the First Folio was to be salted away.

Like everything concerning Scott, nothing was straightforward. While he took every opportunity to declare his innocence, he was not averse to, in keeping with his penchant for leggy, young dancers, showing a bit of leg himself to tease you into doubting him.

In his 'fairy story' he talked of the police having people believe there was more than one Raymond Scott: the overindulged mummy's boy and the international 'Raffles'-type thief. They had that impression because he had given it to them. His ostentatious court appearances did nothing to dissuade them from the conclusion they had drawn. Not many people living on a carer's allowance and benefits travel about in a limo while smoking £25 Cuban cigars and drinking £200 bottles of vintage champagne.

Any holes in the prosecution case were equally as deep as the holes Scott was digging for himself. What did they have, other than Scott arriving at the Folger with a book that might or might not be a First Folio?

He certainly had previous for book theft, but they were exclusively petty thefts. He lived 12 miles from Durham University when the theft took place, but then, quite a few thieves do. There must have been a degree of inside knowledge of the Durham University theft, enough to know where and when the Folio was on display, and the best time to take it.

Not only did Scott say he had never been into Durham University library, which is hard to prove one way or the other, he also seemed to have no connection with it. And, it was hard imagining him doing such a thing; it wasn't his usual style. He was more of an impulse thief and not a very successful one at that, as on many occasions he had been arrested within minutes outside the premises, looking 'shifty'. He did not cut an inconspicuous figure.

This was something that struck Richard Kuhta when Scott had first walked through the door of the Folger, his actions there and those subsequently being the foundation of the prosecution case. 'The appearance was of someone who just came from the Caribbean or something like that. Lots of jewellery, big rings, sun glasses that he never took off, not the kind of usual figure that we would have coming to the Folger. I didn't judge him. The fact he didn't make an appointment, it just struck me as odd.'

Kuhta talked of his reaction when Scott took the book out of his briefcase and put it on the coffee table between them. 'He took out an unbound copy of what he said was the First Folio. When I say unbound it means that there were no boards on it. There was no spine on it, it is what we call a text block, in other words, it was just a thick book of printed pages.' Despite this, Kuhta said he suspected pretty quickly what the book was. But it was Scott's attitude towards it that first sounded alarm bells.

'I didn't touch the book. I looked at it and there were pages missing. He said he believed it was a First Folio and, you know, I have to say my heart was pounding a little bit because we know what the book is and the first thought in my mind is: but where did it come from? So I tried not to say too much.

'And the first moment that really sort of alarmed me was that he sort of immediately became insistent that it was a First Folio. So here's a book that's unbound with pages missing that someone who professed a kind of naïvety in these issues was suddenly asserting that it was a First Folio. That gave me pause and made me wonder again what happened, where's the book from? There are no unrecorded copies of the First Folio for the last hundred years. So Mr Scott's insistence that it was a First Folio, you know, although I couldn't show it, I felt was slightly alarming.

'He didn't say whether he wanted to sell it, he didn't say whether he wanted to donate it to the library, he didn't give me any indication of what he wanted to do with the volume.'

Another matter which alarmed Kuhta was Scott's almost cavalier handling of this most rare and valuable of books. 'The First

Folio is idiosyncratic in the way that the Table of Contents was printed before the compilers knew that they would have the play *Troilus and Cressida*. There's no First Folio that has *Troilus and Cressida* printed on the Table of Contents. There was room made for it in the book, the play was added later, and the first thing that Mr Scott did in sort of insisting that it was the First Folio, he sort of thumbed through the book in a kind of rough way. We would never handle the book that way.'

Scott went straight to *Troilus and Cressida* and said that the place it appeared in the book confirmed his case that it was the First Folio. So much for Scott's 'naïvety'. Kuhta said: 'That made me even more uneasy because that was the sort of moment I say well, yeah, it looks like a First Folio, now where did you get it from?'

Before he had a chance to ask the question, Scott volunteered that it had come from Cuba and gave him the story of its provenance that Denny, with Heidy translating, was later to commit to print on the Hotel Nacional de Cuba notepaper.

In their conversation, according to Kuhta, Scott had created a wealthy family background for himself, a fantasy life. 'He told me that his father had died in the 1990s and he had inherited the business, a business of construction and building supplies, and he told me that he was a millionaire many times over. He told me that his mother lived in Monaco and he gave me quite the impression of a wealthy man, independently wealthy, free to travel and indulge himself in his own way. He presented himself as someone who it didn't matter to whether the book was valuable or not. That he didn't need the money.'

The only thing that was missing was the castle in the Loire valley.

Kuhta said his first meeting with Scott had lasted between 30 and 50 minutes and that his overall impression afterwards was not a comfortable one.

He arranged another meeting two days later, the time in between used by experts at the Folger to study the book, at the end of which they, too, came to the conclusion it was a First Folio. It was during this second meeting, as previously revealed, that Scott suggested going to the *Washington Post* to publicize the discovery, only to be cautioned against it by Kuhta.

Scott also had handed over the $2,500 dollars in $100 dollar bills to become a member of the Folger's Renaissance Circle, produced the celebratory cake and offered Kuhta a gift of a box of cigars and the gift-wrapped bow ties.

Since Scott's arrest, Kuhta had given these gifts a bit of thought, so by the time he was interviewed by police he had come up with a darker reason for why they were offered other than generosity and joy at the potentially historic discovery.

'I don't know if I should say this – but it never occurred to me in my business, it never occurred to me, that the money was a bribe. One of our trustees recently told me … Richard that money wasn't to be for membership of the Renaissance Circle, that money was for you.'

The police assured Kuhta they didn't think it was a bribe, that perhaps he was flashing the cash around to prove he was affluent. Having got to know Scott over these recent months, I knew there was a simple, even mundane, explanation for his gifts. He just liked giving them as a token of friendship. It's his way of cementing relationships.

Over the months he had given me several bottles of top quality red wine, a couple of electronic gadgets, a signed (by the author, not Scott who wasn't quite that vain) copy of a first edition JG Ballard and a remote-controlled boat, the final gift saying much about him. He had seen a similar boat being piloted on a lake near his home, took a shine to it, bought one for himself, used it once and got bored with it. Rather than throw it out he gave it to me for my kids.

However, Kuhta went on to explain at length why his colleague, Daniel De Simone, was convinced the book had recently been stripped to get rid of identifying marks. 'He said it looked like a couple of the sewing supports had been cut … mostly because of the cleanliness of the pages. The pages are very clean. The front pages are very clean. If this book had been out of its binding for a hundred years the pages would have been very soiled because it would have been knocking around. Even on a shelf it would have been soiled.'

Kuhta didn't share his suspicions with Scott who, when he left, thought the Folger had called in Stephen Massey for definitive authentication of the book. 'He sort of happily departed the next morning for what he told me was Bahamas or Cuba.'

A couple of days later he received a letter from Scott on Mayflower Hotel headed paper about the confirmation of the reservation and, for the first time, information about his 'triumvirate' with Heidy and Denny.

'Now it's clear that he's looking to sell the book,' said Kuhta.

As Scott went on his merry way, Massey arrived and it took him barely a few moments to confirm Kuhta's suspicions. Kuhta explained: 'He measured it. Stephen arrived with the measurements of [those eight unaccounted for copies along with the Durham Folio.] He came with the measurements and the first thing he did was to measure the text in millimetres and within minutes he identified it as the Durham copy. He was categorically sure, based on that one bit of physical evidence. 'It seemed now my sort of darkest suspicions about us being in possession of a stolen copy was ringing true.'

They had a question to ask themselves. What would they do now? 'We huddled in an office, we meaning Stephen Massey and myself. I called the Director of the Folger Shakespeare Library, Dr Gail Pastor, and we had a conference call with the Chairman of the Board of Governors, Mr Paul Ruxin. Mr Ruxin advised us we needed to disclose the information. So we contacted the field office of the FBI in Washington DC, we contacted Scotland Yard in London, we contacted the British Embassy here in London and later I contacted by e-mail, Dr John Hall, the University Librarian at Durham.'

Of all the people connected with the case, Scott retained most of his bile for Stephen Massey, a person he never met until his trial, their contact restricted to one brief and one long phone-conversation and text messages.

Massey is an independent rare book appraiser, born in England but now a resident in New York. He is an international consultant for Bloomsbury Auctions located in London, Rome and New York, as well as being a consultant for Peter Harrington Books in Fulham Road, London. To add to an extensive CV, he also appears on the American version of *Antiques Roadshow*.

Among the artefacts he has sold are two copies of the Guttenberg Bible and four copies of the American Declaration of Independence. In 1994, he was responsible for the sale of the Codex Leicester, a collection of largely scientific writings by Leonardo Da Vinci, to Microsoft billionaire Bill Gates for £30.8 million.

In keeping with Kuhta's rather sniffy assessment of Scott, Massey's view of him was that he looked like 'a tanned footballsupporter', not 'a person who would be wandering around with a deeply serious scholarly book like a Shakespeare First Folio'. An interesting comment bearing in mind they'd never met. But however disdainfully he viewed Scott, it didn't prevent him from accepting his largesse with the payment for his stay at the Mayflower Hotel and travel fees. Not only this, he kept four boxes of the finest Cuban cigars – worth about £2,500 in the UK – which Scott had made a gift of. For some reason, Massey at first omitted to mention the cigars to the police.

As Kuhta had said, it had taken moments for him to come to the conclusion Scott had presented the Folger with the Durham Copy of the First Folio. Massey, with no excess of modesty, explained how. 'I measured it up … looked at it and said this is the Durham Copy and they sort of applauded and said that must have taken you fifteen seconds. It was pretty much a no-brainer.'

To reach the conclusion on the measurements, he had placed a pre-cut piece of card over the Folio. However, other than that positive identification, the other tell-tale signs were negatives – what the First Folio didn't have.

'The last leaf had an identifying mark, identifying it with Durham University or Cosin, Bishop Cosin, I believe [it's] gone. Well, in my mind that's proof. As well as the back leaf missing, there should have been a pasted letter from the Deanery Norwich, 1914, and that leaf is missing; then the title page with the Peterhouse Pressmark stamp, that's missing; and then the large repaired hole in the colophon, that's the last leaf, that's missing; so you've got 1, 2, 3, leaves that are missing and each would comprise or contain a piece of positive evidence. The binding was an 1845 calfskin, called Morocco binding, and that was missing. Four distinguishing features have been removed.'

A second positive identification concerned the play *Troilus and Cressida*. As Kuhta had pointed out, it didn't appear in the earliest issues of the First Folio but was added later. In the Durham copy, its inclusion was noted by a hand-written notation in the Table of Contents. The First Folio Scott brought to the Folger, Massey spotted, had this distinctive notation.

When Kuhta said he was going to call Massey in to help authenticate it, Scott claimed he had wondered out loud to them why he was needed, believing the Folger was the last word on identifying a First Folio. As Massey later revealed, it was not a question only Scott had posed.

Kuhta said: 'John Wilson, a great friend of mine who is curator of rare books at the Globe Theatre and is widely known in Shakespeare scholarship quipped to me on many occasions … "what on earth is the world coming to, why would the Folger need anyone to tell them what a First Folio Shakespeare was"?'

The reason was that Scott didn't just want it authenticated, but appeared to want to sell it. Massey explained: 'The Folger, because it's an institutional American library, doesn't sully its hands with murky trade, to coin a jokey phrase, and they needed a professional to do that.

'Because I know Richard, he approached me and so my position wasn't to go in and say "oh that's a First Folio", my role was to go in there and say "yeah that's a First Folio and it's worth so and so and I'd love to sell it or – you know – whatever".'

It was not just that Massey had been the one to confirm the First Folio as the stolen Durham Copy to the authorities that had irritated Scott. He thought Massey a bit of an Arthur Daley of the book-world. While there is no suggestion of criminal intent on

Massey's part, he did provide an enlightening insight into how the First Folio could have been altered to ensure it could not have been identified as stolen.

'In this case what would have made my job a lot more difficult is if he'd taken a circular saw and trimmed all the binding, trimmed the leaves down. By three centimetres at the top and two centimetres in width, then you'd have different measurements. If he'd gone further and removed the contents [page], if he'd taken away all those things you could sort of say, well, it might be the Durham Copy, but I wouldn't have been so certain. The other thing he could do, some mischievous sprite told me, he could have broken the whole thing up and sold it play by play. And, in fact, that might have been, you know, wearing the devil's hat, that might have been the way to realise some money on it.'

Massey had also given Scott the impression he was 'hot for a deal'. This was based on a conversation between the two in which Scott had been told by Massey the he had a friend who was interested in the Folio. Scott later figured out that Massey was acting as an *agent provocateur* for the FBI.

However, what was in no doubt was that Massey knew the kudos he would have received if he had helped identify the Folio and the money he could have made if he had handled its sale. 'I can think of maybe ten books I'd love to handle for sale and get some money from. If I put that through Bloomsbury book auctions they might pay me a little more than the small retainer they pay me. Or if I went to Pom Harrington [of Harrington Books] … do you think we've got a client for this, he'd say yes, and he'd say I'll see you all right too.

'And there's all the kudos of it … Massey's uncovered the Cuban First Folio, marvellous, wonderful and I'd have my name up in lights and that would be a tremendous thing for a rare book specialist. 'I'd love it not to be the Durham [Copy] in one sense, but it so patently is … that I wouldn't go near it with a ten-foot pole.'

The damage done to the First Folio, he said, was 'tragic', slashing its potential sale price. The removal of the last leaf alone had lowered its value by $200,000. As a result, far from the £15 million it was mooted as being worth after Scott's arrest, Massey put now put the value at between $1 million and $1.5 million.

Scott had contacted Massey by phone but it was a very brief chat as Massey was busy with a colleague at Bloomsbury at the time. Massey then contacted an FBI agent in Philadelphia, as he had been told to do if Scott tried to contact him. He was advised to ring Scott and, getting voicemail, left a message. That was July 2nd. They eventually spoke on July 9th.

Massey recalled: 'It was a long rambling conversation where I said how pleased I was to handle such a lovely book and he sounded as if he'd had a bit to drink. Two-thirds through I said well ... I'd love to help you sell this but I can't because I'm certain it's the copy that was stolen from Durham in 1998.'

Massey then explained why he had come to his conclusion. He said Scott listened politely but continued to reiterate what he believed was its Cuban provenance and talked of Heidy and Denny. 'He was obviously wishing it wasn't the stolen copy all the way through but he certainly didn't say "oh it is stolen".'

'I said that there wasn't anything I could do to help him commercially. I said I'd love to, but I'd be swinging from a beam, I'd be dead meat in the book business.'

The conversation ended and Massey hoped he would have time to liaise with the Folger to issue a statement about the matter. But the next morning any hope of this was shattered when he was contacted by the FBI field agent in Philadelphia.

He was told 'they've got him'.

Massey asked: 'What do you mean they've got him?'

'"Oh, the Durham police swooped on his house, it's in the newspapers, it's on the TV, the university is saying the book's worth £15 million," at which point I started to feel very, very, very angry. I felt that the Folger and I had done a huge favour for Durham and that they might have had the courtesy to say they were going to announce.'

Massey was almost speechless. 'They just, they just, you know it was all over the papers. Lies and rubbish. I mean, well, not lies, but rubbish.'

He was incredulous that Durham University had referred to the First Folio as a manuscript – a manuscript being a handwritten document. Massey was absolutely fuming at the £15 million price tag, not just because it was inaccurate, he felt it hurt him professionally. And with some reason.

'I'd gone to the whole length of explaining to Mr Scott and writing this report to Kuhta about what I thought the value of the book was, which was why I was called in in the first place and to have all this exploded.' He said he was going to give Durham University an earful but now, on reflection, he commented: 'I'm glad I didn't.'

Instead, after getting the OK from the Folger, he contacted a number of friends and acquaintances in the book world to prove it wasn't him who came up with the £15 million price tag.

After their phone call and the arrest, Scott, according to Massey, 'bombarded' him with the texts. 'Yes, he pestered me, if you'll excuse the vulgarity of the expression, after the shit hit the fan.'

However, Massey said he didn't read any of them, just deleted them unseen, but did reply saying he was happy to speak to him again if he wanted.

The police showed him the one Scott had sent shortly before his arrest, previously referred to, in which he invited Massey to join the triumvirate.

Massey was asked about his briefing by the FBI to let them know if there was any contact on the phone with Scott. Strangely, at first Massey appeared a bit evasive. 'Yes, but I mean, I don't, I don't consider this contact on a phone. I think in terms of a phone call as a phone call. This is the first time I've read this.'

Probed what could be read into the text, Massey replied: 'It looks to me as if he's asking me to participate in the sale of a book that I have previously identified to him as the Durham Copy stolen in 1998.' After further questioning he insisted: 'I've deleted all text messages from him. They were a nuisance to me.'

One thing that didn't prove a nuisance was two gifts from Scott.

They were an 18th-century Spanish book and a box of Havana cigars, passed on to him at the Folger by the original recipient, Richard Kuhta, because he didn't smoke.

'I had not disclosed the cigars; I disclosed them to you now. So I feel half honest.' He went on to say: 'You can appreciate that is a huge weight off my mind.'

Massey appeared as irked with Scott as Scott was with him. 'He says can I sell this book and I tell him you can do whatever you like but guess what? It's the stolen book and I cannot help you. And I thought if he was an innocent man I had provided him with some very, very, very useful information because the guy was so off the wall that one had no idea whether he was deeply involved himself or just some stooge who'd been put up to it.'

It was a thought that was later to cross the minds of the police, thanks to an unlikely source.

The First Folio title page, in all its glory.

Sheila Hingley, Head of Heritage Collections at Durham University, holding a copy of the First Folio – the copy that was stolen is in the glass cabinet in front of her.

Raymond and Heidy living it up in Havana.

The 'Triumvirate':
Raymond Scott, Heidy Rios and Odeiny 'Denny' Perez.

Raymond launches his ill-fated 'free the books' campaign.

Raymond in the back of the rented limo after his first court appearance.

FROM: RAYMOND
SCOTT
SATURDAY 5TH JULY
2008.

Dear Richard
& Stephen.

Ritz Paris

I have returned to France because my mother Mrs. Hannah Scott has travelled from Monaco in a wish to see me. I first visited Cuba in 1996 because at that time I smoked Havana cigars and was paying high tax inclusive prices in Europe where the freshness of the tobacco leaf often left a lot to be desired despite the premium prices. I loved the prices and the freshness of the Habanos but on medical advice I stopped smoking during 2004 but continued to visit the lovely island two or three times a year. In late October 2007, while staying at Hotel Nacional de Cuba I met señorita Heidy Garcia Rios working at

The handwritten note on Ritz Hotel stationery sent to the Folger.

(Left) *Raymond after his failed County Court bid to gain access to the folio.*
(Right) *One of the many faces of Raymond Scott.*

Chapter Fifteen

Guns and Poses

Meanwhile, the criminal justice system creaked slowly on. Scott was getting a bit cranky, sending texts which, if not replied to as soon as he wished, took on some dark meaning for him. 'R u still speaking 2 this dangerous menace 2 society…' began one.

I had gone away to the Lakes with my kids for a brief holiday. Before going, I had spoken to Scott about his next court appearance. I tried to advise him that, while the limos, the researchers, the champagne and the Pot Noodles had been entertaining, perhaps a lower profile would be prudent now.

'But when you're hot, you're hot,' he argued.

I again tried to point out it would be for his own good. Arriving at each court hearing like some soap star on a publicity jaunt, merely drew attention to the fact he was throwing money around, of which no one could work out the legitimate source.

He grunted his acknowledgement which I took as his agreement and I went away feeling quite the media sage. A couple of days later, as the rain bounced off our holiday cottage roof like bullets, he sent another text. He'd obviously checked the weather reports:

> Hi I bet u just love school hols! Just checked and The Queen graciously desires my attendance at Consett Magistrates 10 a.m. Tuesday April 14th after Easter Monday and despite being a republican I might as well turn up.

I didn't reply, it was my holiday after all. The weather didn't improve and after a few days we headed back to Gateshead, where I checked my texts. Sure enough there was one from Raymond.

> Hi Mike long time no c or hear (has some lousy grass whispered in your shell like and said – hey guv this Scott's not nearly as nice as he looks). Ah time cannot wither nor custom stale the infinite variety of the English language. Sent u text about Consett Mag. Don't know if u got it. Going 2 book fair in Harrogate. Full of bibliomaniacs who want to lionize and fete a person who once had in his bookcase the greatest book in the English language.

I booted up my computer to find out what had happened at the hearing by googling 'Raymond Scott First Folio'. I clicked on the story and up it popped. 'Fuck,' I thought.

It was the picture of Scott that first grabbed my attention. He was dressed in combat green complete with hat, dark shades and brandishing a rifle and a handgun. The headline was: 'Gun drama as Shakespeare accused arrives at court.' Then the story:

> Dressed as Che Guevara, the man accused of stealing a priceless first edition of Shakespeare's work triggered a gun drama when he arrived at court.
>
> Eccentric Raymond Scott made his dramatic entrance at Consett Magistrates Court, charged with three counts of theft and three of handling stolen goods. Not forgetting his trademark Pot Noodle, which was tucked in a pocket, Scott, formerly of Washington, stepped out of a stretch limousine. He was followed by an entourage of three women and a man dressed as guerrilla fighters, carrying a placard stating 'Blockade kills Cuban children' and waving a Cuban and a Union flag. Scott was stopped by staff after trying to enter the court with a hand gun and a rifle. He was forced to hand them over.

So much for Scott being low key and for the persuasive powers of this media sage. I scanned the story again to see if he'd been arrested and faced further charges for turning up in court armed to the teeth, but there was no mention of it. The article just said the case had been committed to Durham Crown Court in May. Perhaps defendants turning up at Consett magistrates tooled up was par for the course, which is why they'd just taken the weapons off him like he was a naughty boy. Tough place.

I hastily arranged a meeting at my house where he casually explained his latest exhibition as a show of solidarity with his brothers and sisters in Cuba. As for the guns, they had been just taken off him by court officials who didn't appear to have made much of a fuss about it. The rifle turned out to be an air rifle that fired pellets and the handgun was a starter's pistol, both of which were later returned to him. He said: 'I'll probably sell them on eBay and donate the proceeds to the RSPCA or the NSPCC, my two favourite charities. I do a lot of work for charity, but don't like to talk about it.'

I reminded him of our conversation a couple of weeks before about being low-key. 'That was never going to happen,' he said. 'I am what I am, a bit of a showman. I can never be criticized for being mundane, run-of-the-mill. I have standards to maintain.'

Sometimes I wondered if all this wasn't as much for Heidy as for him. Showing he's a somebody with all the cameras and the hoop-la that surrounded him. They were still in communication by text, but the only time she could possibly see him was via news and TV reports of his appearances. And what she would see would be the Scott she remembered, extravagant, larger than life, a character. Now a celebrity of sorts.

He said the reason for combat garb was also a tip of the hat to *'el Presidente'*, *Fidel Castro*. 'He was a hero of mine long before I met Heidy. I was once staying in a hotel in central Havana behind the Capablanca chess club – Capablanca, who was from Cuba, was the greatest natural genius of the game that ever existed – and there was a huge cavalcade of black Mercedes outside the hotel and I wondered what's going on, so I asked someone on reception.

'He said "It's Fidel." Not the President, but "Fidel", like he was a friend. He was attending a meeting with Ramon Valdes, the interior minister, and it was all to do with tourism in Cuba and expanding it and generating more money. In my small way I have supported the revolution, of course. Money goes a long way and is one thing none of us can do without – not even the mendicant monks. So anyway I waited with my camera and then after half an hour he came back with his bodyguards. Fidel stopped and he spoke to the people, tourists, in Spanish and basically said I'd like to thank you for coming to Cuba, *La Isla Bonita*, enjoy yourselves.

'He came past me and I spontaneously yelled "*Viva Cuba libra*! *Viva La Revoluçion*! *Viva Fidel*!" and I sort of got a nod from him. This person seemed so charismatic.'

I asked Scott if he would consider living in Cuba.

'I wouldn't fancy working in Cuba, cutting sugar cane for 14 hours a day for a few Cuban pesos. I wouldn't mind living in the villas in Siborney beside the Brazilian ambassador with Heidy.'

And had he planned for their future together?

'Sure,' he said vaguely. The he perked up and treated me to a bit of William Blake.

> O there did I spy a young maiden sweet,
> Among the violets that smell so sweet.

Worth all this grief? I wondered out loud.

'It's a love story. "Everybody loves a lover", he sang. From Blake to Doris Day in a couple of sentences. What of the time he spent with Heidy, preferably in his own words? I asked.

'I remember the restaurants, the freshly-squeezed orange and mango juice. The guy in charge of the villa had two children. We played with them in the pool. It was not one of these upstairs-downstairs outfits.

'I remember going around buying her clothes, perfumes, it was very easy on the pocket compared to Paris or London. I remember buying one outfit, dress, shoes and handbag which cost the equivalent of £100, a lot of money, more than a surgeon can earn in 12 months. She just looked absolutely fantastic. Is it worth the grief you ask. *Je ne regrette rien.* I regret nothing. There are things I've done that were not the right things to do, but I just move on. What's the point in beating yourself up on something that can't be reversed?

'I think I'm one of those happy people, we few, we happy few, we band of brothers who wouldn't do anything different. I do have regrets in that I'm less conservative than I used to be. It's usually the other way round. I'm more devil may care, whereas before I was more conservative with a small 'c'.

'If I had my time over again I would do it all over again but to the power of 2 or 4 or 6 or to the nth degree. Maybe I wouldn't be sitting here. I've had a good time but maybe I could have had a better time.

'I will marry Heidy. I just got a text message from her last night. She said in the summer you have to come over here and get married in this country. What we will do is get married in Havana at a civil ceremony in the Princess Diana Memorial Garden, then have the union blessed at Havana's Old Cathedral. I wonder how much you have to bung a Cardinal Archbishop these days? What would His Eminence consider reasonable and not vulgar?

'It's not ideal. My mother couldn't come to the wedding in Havana. I promised Heidy I would marry her because I love her. Does she love me? What is love? Poets have tried to express it, as has the Bible. With Heidy it is a meeting of minds as well as everything else, no matter what people think. I love her and I think she loves me. Whether that means we would lay down our lives for each other, hopefully we will not be tested. It's a very pragmatic arrangement because I am a man of fifty-two. To be seen out with a beautiful twenty-two-year-old woman in restaurants is very flattering to the male ego and it's easy to see why I'm attracted to Heidy.

'How is she attracted to me? You have to realise we live in a material world as Madonna taught us many years ago and in many ways, in socialist-controlled Cuba, access to money and the Cuban Convertible Pesos, money means even more. By marrying me I promised her she will have a British passport as well as a Cuban passport. It will make her free. At the moment she isn't free. At the moment she can't leave Cuba without express permission.

'Heidy has a whole life in front of her. I'm fifty-two. Will alcohol preserve my body? I've got to be realistic about these things.

'She has so many talents. She speaks fluent English and is a very intelligent girl. She just wants something more than what Cuba has to offer her at the moment and I'm able to provide that route out of Cuba. Her life will be transformed. She can come and go as she pleases. Go anywhere she wants.'

Then his mind drifted to what seemed his other great love, the First Folio. The two were inextricably linked and sometimes he seemed almost torn between them. Often, as now, he would speak of one then in the next sentence speak of the other, even though the order of conversation did not follow logically.

'When I had the First Folio Shakespeare, the Cuban copy, it was a great frisson for me to look at the passages everybody knows like the Merchant of Venice: "Hath not a Jew eyes? Hath not a Jew hands, organs, dimensions, senses, affections, passions". Richard III: "Now is the winter of our discontent", The Scottish play, Macbeth, when he learns Lady Macbeth is dead: "Tomorrow, and tomorrow, and tomorrow, Creeps in this petty pace from day to day, To the last syllable of recorded time." I can recite the whole Agincourt speech from Henry V.' Which he proceeded to do.

'If it wasn't for that book in front of me they would have been lost for posterity. It was very thrilling. There is no doubt the Shakespeare First Folio is the greatest secular book in the English language. I have to qualify 'in the English language' because there are so many great writers in other languages. Pushkin in Russia. Your mother tongue has to be Russian to appreciate it, it's untranslatable.'

Then he paused briefly and took a sip from his Lucozade bottle and his mood visibly darkened. 'If this goes wrong, very badly wrong, there's a possibility it can because of a drawing together of the various strands. Thesis and antithesis equals synthesis – which proves I haven't had too much to drink to remember that and pronounce it!'

Scott explained: 'The thesis is an intellectual proposition, the antithesis is the negation of the thesis, a reaction to the proposition, the synthesis solves the conflict between the thesis and antithesis by reconciling their common truths and forming a proposition.'

Right, kind of, I thought. The thesis is the prosecution case, the antithesis the defence case and the synthesis the court's judgment. The one common truth is he was trying to flog a First Folio, which could well turn out to have been stolen.

'I know I'm an innocent man. I'm not so naïve to think that just because you're innocent you can't be found guilty and sent to prison. Fidel Castro was sent to prison for fifteen years but he never lost belief in his principles and he was a man who was prepared to die for his beliefs. History will absolve me,' he said.

'Timothy Evans and Hanratty were innocent men who were hanged. If it all goes very badly wrong, the worst-case scenario is I could get a substantial term.

'My mother is now eighty-one. She might die – lets hope this doesn't happen – while I'm in prison, my relationship with Heidy might deteriorate, if that happens I won't have any room left for warm personal relationships. I think of myself as an army of one. I don't really have sides. I'm not willing to subjugate or relegate my own interests for the majority. I don't like big groups.'

While Scott's moods could markedly change, there was a greater degree of fatalism now. Having looked at the police evidence, it seemed to me that the odds on his having turned up with a previously un-catalogued First Folio were slim to non-existent.

In an extensive report written for Durham police, the conclusions of Anthony West, who Scott said he had been in touch earlier, backed up Massey's suspicions in great detail. It was not just its dimensions, and the pages that were missing; every scratch and blemish he found seemed to further prove the book was the Durham Copy. He was dismissive of Denny's claim of how it came to him through his family who had moved from Galicia in Spain to Cuba.

West wrote: 'To my knowledge, there has never definitely been a First Folio in Spain. There have been repeated suggestions that a Count Gondomar [ironically Gondomar is a town in Galicia] took a copy to Spain. After an extensive investigation, I expended four pages in West Census failing to prove he had. France, Italy and Switzerland can boast a copy of First Folio and Germany three copies, but Spain is not in their company.

'At the same time, I find it highly unlikely that a First Folio could silently survive for a century in Cuba without coming to public notice. The Durham Police gave me the manuscript notes in which Mr Scott and two of his friends record a Spanish-Cuban Provenance. I found none of the details convincing.'

There was another point that cast doubt for me on Scott's story. On our first meeting he had said it was shortly after his birthday party in the Siborney villa that he had flown from Havana via Nassau to Washington DC to have the First Folio authenticated. Denny also referred to this trip in his note on the supposed provenance.'

It was now known that he had flown from Washington, Tyne and Wear, to Washington DC in June to have it verified. After I put this to him, he said he had flown home in the February from Cuba with the First Folio after giving Denny the $11,000 bond.

This explained comments in his 'fairy story' in which he spoke of reading the book upstairs in his bedroom as his mother watched soap operas on the TV downstairs. When I had asked him about the discrepancy in the two accounts he seemed surprised at my confusion and was happy to clarify it.

To further cloud the issue, in Denny's description of its provenance, he said he had brought the book to his home for Scott to see in May 2008 – three months after Scott now said he was supposed to have seen it. Scott couldn't answer that one, other than it must have been an error in translation.

Heidy had also said Scott had first seen the book in the February. So, if you were to accept the book at the centre of this was the First Folio, there were two possibilities of how it came into Scott's hands.

The first was that Scott had indeed stolen it from Durham University in 1998 and kept it for those 10 years. As he actually flew from England to Washington to the Folger to have it authenticated, this could mean it had never actually been to Cuba in the first place. Then, with the help of Denny and Heidy, he had concocted the Spanish-Cuban provenance story.

The second possibility was that Scott was actually telling what he believed to be the truth. He had gotten the book in Cuba from Denny, his friend, who told him it had been in his family for a century or more.

What if Denny, not Scott, was lying?

I asked if he'd heard from Denny and, if so, how was he doing?

'He's getting on with his life, looking after the tourists. He's concerned about the book which he entrusted to me. I've done my level best to get it back but Denny, living in Cuba, is totally aware of how difficult it is.'

Why did he believe Denny's story about how he got the First Folio?

Scott seemed almost outraged at any suggestion that Denny had acted in any way dishonestly. 'The alternative is fantastical. The evidence points against it.'

The alternative was that another thief had given in to Denny. If Scott was telling the truth that he wasn't the thief, then suspicion was pointing to Denny.

Scott went quiet for a while. The implication of the alternative was unpalatable. His great friend – the Mr Fix-it of Havana with whom had spent so many convivial days and nights, had introduced him to his family, had smoothed his relationship with Heidy – had spun him a yarn. The First Folio, which Denny offered up and for which Scott had handed over $11,000 as a bond had been transformed from a ticket to a new life into a millstone around his neck.

It was supposed to have brought Scott and Heidy together. Instead, with the consequences of him taking it to the Folger, it had driven them apart.

However, while Scott had been devout in his loyalty and belief in Denny, his defence team had not. They had been digging around. Working on the assumption that Scott was telling the truth and that he did indeed get the First Folio from Denny, a man who had never ventured out of Cuba. They then had to explore how else it might have come into Denny's possession.

It led them into the world of the Tome Raiders – thieves who make a healthy living from stealing rare, antique books. And one man in particular was to cast a new light on the case.

Chapter Sixteen

The Tome Raiders

The circumstances surrounding the theft of the Shakespeare First Folio at Durham University in 1998 are an example of why such crimes are easy pickings for those in the know.

As mentioned earlier, the First Folio, along with an early manuscript bearing an English translation of the New Testament dating from the 14th or early 15th century, a manuscript of the same period containing a poem written by Geoffrey Chaucer, two works by the 10th-century scholar Aelfric, a first edition of *Beowulf* printed in 1815 and a 1612 book of maps and poetry, were stolen.

These items, which had been on public show in rooms of the library, were among more than 50 exhibits charting the progress of English literature from the Middle Ages through to the 20th century. Glass-topped display cabinets had been forced to gain access to them. No alarm bells rang, no security guards or staff dashed to apprehend the thieves, because there was no alarm system, nor staff specifically designated to ensure their safekeeping. In fact, it was a couple of days before it was realised a theft had taken place simply because a light-protective cloth had been put over the cabinets.

None have been recovered, apart from, it was now evident, the First Folio, and that only because it was almost impossible to sell-on. As an article by Paul Collins in the online arts-magazine *Slate* put it, '... aside from a face-melting Ark of the Covenant, a Shakespeare First Folio is the lousiest loot in the world to steal.' The reason for this, as detailed before, is that the surviving 230 First Folios have been minutely catalogued during the past 190 years.

Collins wrote: 'Does the Folio have graffiti inviting the reader "to kiss the wrightere's arse"? Then it once belonged to theologian Daniel Williams. Were several plays used as scrap paper for loopy handwriting exercises by a quill-wielding 17th-century child? Then you're probably looking at the Sutro Library's Folio. Did your folio contain greasy food stains and crumbs fallen into the binding? Then you're in the British Library with Samuel Johnson's copy.'

A First Folio stolen from Williams College Library in Williamstown, Maryland, USA, in 1940, illustrates the book's special place in the antiquarian world. Collins detailed how, four months after gaining entry with the forged papers of a fictitious 'Professor Sinclair E. Gillingham', the thief turned himself in and identified his three fellow conspirators. The reason? 'The folio they'd stolen was hot enough to roast marshmallows over. It was unsaleable.'

Similar censuses have been made of all surviving copies of the Gutenberg Bible, Audubon's *Birds of America* and Copernicus' *De Revolutionibus Orbium* Coelestium (*On the Revolutions of Heavenly Spheres*). Few other titles have been so minutely surveyed.

Countless lucrative antique books, their locations not widely known, are being kept in sites where security can be charitably described as lax. Adding to the attraction for crooks, amazingly, is that when thefts do take place, usually from establishments of high learning and education, they are seldom reported to the public. Auction houses where they are likely to turn up aren't alerted as a matter of course – and knowledge of the theft is kept in-house. As a consequence, many books worth a fortune have gone under the hammer with no one any the wiser to the fact they'd been purloined.

There are believed to be a handful of specialist crooks who operate in the world of international antiquarian book traders, collectors and curators, making a healthy living your ordinary thief can only dream about.

One of them was David Slade. In February 2009, he was jailed for two years after admitting the theft of £232,880-worth of extremely rare books from one of the most powerful financiers in the world, Sir Evelyn de Rothschild.

Slade, fifty-nine at the time of his sentence, was a well-educated, highly knowledgeable former president of the Antiquarian Booksellers Association in the UK and a dealer who had sold internationally since he was seventeen.

He was hired by Rothschild to catalogue the family book collection. As he did his work, visiting Rothschild's house in Buckinghamshire two or three times a week, Slade discreetly removed the odd book, each of which was an extremely valuable and beautifully crafted production by one of the private presses that operated in the late 19th and early 20th century.

He took them to an auction house where his reputation was unquestioned and sold them for significant sums. It was during a routine audit that Rothschild noticed the books, 68 in all, had gone missing.

Yet, the case received no publicity and only came to light after the then president of the ABA, Alan Shelley, decided to speak out in an attempt to lessen the trafficking of rare books, urging libraries, auctioneers and dealers to work more closely together.

Jolyon Hudson from Pickering and Chatto antiquarian booksellers said: 'We all need to be a bit more grown up. [Libraries] are the curators of the nation's knowledge, and when they lose it they are somewhat embarrassed to admit that.'

Another thief was Farhad Hakimzadeh who was also jailed for two years, a month before Slade, for stealing pages from rare books in the British Library.

He was a very wealthy businessman who lived in a large property at a prestigious address in Knightsbridge, London. He was also a published author, a collector of rare books, and was described as 'evidently extremely knowledgeable' by one expert. Hakimzadeh was also a former director of the Iran Heritage Foundation, which promotes Iran's cultural heritage, and was a director of a company that publishes books in the Middle East.

Rather worryingly in hindsight, the British Library described him as 'eminently characteristic of our group of readers'. For despite his respectable appearance, he was a thief who mutilated the very precious texts he professed such an admiration for.

His activities only came to light when another reader in the library who saw that one text had had a page cut out, raised the alarm. An internal audit followed, which examined all 842 books Hakimzadeh, amongst others, had looked at between 1997 and 2005.

The list of those who had viewed these particular texts was not extensive – given their rarity – and the one common denominator of the 150 texts eventually discovered with leaves missing was the Iranian-born British national. He often used a scalpel to cut pages out, and then later hiding them in books at his home. One example was an engraving of a 16th-century world map by Hans Holbein the Younger, an artist employed by Henry VIII. It alone was worth £30,000.

Finally, one of the most celebrated – or notorious – cases was that of the grandly named Forbes Smiley III. In 2006, he was sentenced to three-and-a-half years in jail by a US Federal court for stealing 97 rare maps worth £1.6 million. Amongst them was the world famous Apian map from the British Library.

Smiley, a fifty-year-old US dealer in rare books and known for his impeccable blazers and scholarly manner, had visited the library in June 2004 with his favourite crime tool – a razor blade. He used it to cut out the world map, one of the first to show America as a separate continent, drawn by 16th-century German cartographer Peter Apian from a volume originally owned by Thomas Cranmer, the Archbishop of Canterbury.

The description and MO of all three thieves were similar. They were seemingly respectable members of society who quite easily moved around in the rarefied world of antique books and historical artefacts, with blazers and scholarly manners to the fore. This explains why the staff at the Folger Library was so sniffy about Scott's appearance – the 'tanned football supporter' according to Massey and 'like someone on a Caribbean cruise', according to Kuhta.

Most thieves in the rare-book world are well-educated, discreet and calculating, and are usually undone by chance. Scott could be accused of many things, but being discreet is not one of them. His every action brought attention to himself. He didn't fit the classic profile of this group.

And there was one more character well known to the authorities who had spent years plying his illegal activities in libraries and archives across the world – William Jacques. After being charged with the theft of numerous antique books he had jumped bail in 1999, a few months after the theft of the First Folio at Durham University.

And, to paraphrase the famous Humphrey Bogart line from Casablanca – one of Scott's favourite movies – of all the towns, of all the cities in all the world, which one did Jacques walk in to?

Havana, Cuba.

Chapter Seventeen

The Third Man

The name of William Simon Jacques, a.k.a. William Jaks, a.k.a. Mr Santoro, a.k.a. the disappointingly banal, David Fletcher, first appeared on the radar of Scott's defence team around Christmas 2008 when his solicitors had been researching the world of antique-book thefts. Over the months they had looked more closely into the case and there were several echoes with that of Scott's, and not just the Havana link.

Detective Constable Michael Elsom and a DC Burn from Durham Constabulary had questioned Jacques in November 2002 about the missing First Folio, whilst he was doing time at Ford Open prison for a series of book thefts. The purpose of seeing him was a general enquiry into the theft of rare books, thus he wasn't interviewed under caution.

He seemed indifferent to their questions. He was told of the theft of the First Folio from Durham University library, 'a place off the normal tourist trail and only people with specific knowledge of books would know about'. The officers told him that owing to the nature of his crime they wanted to speak to him to find out if he had knowledge that might help them recover the books taken from Durham.

Jacques simply replied: 'I can't help you, gentlemen.'

He was asked if he had ever been to Durham University library, but chose not to answer. He did not even reply when asked if he'd ever been to the city of Durham. Jacques then said he wasn't prepared to speak any longer but commented, somewhat enigmatically: 'I think you have had a wasted journey, or maybe not.'

Jacques is the son of a well-to-do farmer from Selby, North Yorkshire. He was an economics graduate from Jesus College,

Cambridge and went on to work in the tax accounting department of Shell UK.

He was serving time at Ford Prison for the theft of hundreds of books from the Cambridge University Library, the London Library and the British Library – from around 1991 to 1999 – which rocked the antiquarian book world. An estimated value of around £1.1 million was put on the volumes he stole, including works written by Isaac Newton, Galileo and Copernicus.

As a student at Cambridge during the late 1980s, this gave him ready access to the Cambridge University library, and he had maintained his membership there up until his initial arrest. He was also a member of the London Library and the British Library.

His involvement in the thefts came to light in February 1999 after it was discovered that he had sent books that had been stolen from the London Library to Bloomsbury book auctions in London.

Carl Williams, a 'runner' in the book trade – a book dealer who does not trade from a shop but instead picks up a volume in one place and immediately moves it to another dealer for, hopefully, a swift profit – had bought a book from Bloomsbury Book Auctions entitled *Pure Logic* by William Stanley Jevons.

He then left the book with rare book dealers, Pickering and Chatto, hoping to get a good price for it. The managing director of the company, Jolyon Hudson, examined it and found that erased markings within its pages had all the characteristics of markings found on books belonging to the London Library.

On a hunch, Hudson rang its chief librarian, Alan Bell, and suggested that he look in the political economy section for the title. His hunch was right and within hours Bell had identified the book as their copy. Carl Williams was devastated. 'I felt guilty in a way, as if I was knowingly handling stolen goods, though of course I wasn't.' Hudson exonerated Williams, 'Carl behaved impeccably.'

Further inquiries revealed that Jacques had been selling books through Bloomsbury Book Auctions for about eight years, with many of them matching books missing from both libraries.

Hudson then went back to Bloomsbury Book Auctions and asked employee Rupert Powell where the book had come from. He was told it had been 'consigned' to auction by a young man called William Jacques.

'He had been dealing with us since 1992 or 1993,' Powell said. 'He was just a smartly dressed young man. He wore pinstripe. He spoke quietly. He didn't suggest great knowledge of the business but as time passed themes did develop. Economics was a favourite subject of his. As to value, it would vary. Virtually all of them were single lots, which meant they went for more than £50. There were a couple of four-figure books, nothing above that.'

Over the years, infrequent visits had become more regular and Powell discovered that his company had sold hundreds of titles received from Jacques. 'There was nothing with hindsight that indicated anything was up. Yes, all indication of where they had come from had been removed but that isn't necessarily suspicious because there are so many ex-library books legitimately on the market,' said Powell.

Powell and Alan Bell of the London Library now looked through the catalogue for the auction in which Williams had bought the Jevons' book. All the titles consigned by Jacques had been stolen from the London Library. Powell telephoned Jacques and asked him if he'd stop by the office to resolve the issue.

'When I told him about our concerns over the the Jevons' book he was very surprised, very calm, very polite. He said he had acquired it from a middle-aged man at Portobello Market whom he'd never seen before, or since, and that he'd paid cash.'

A couple of days later, Jacques sent an unsigned fax to BBA from his office at Shell UK. With breathtaking arrogance, he laid out the terms upon which he was willing to cooperate, including that his identity should remain unknown to the libraries.

Soon, auction houses all over Britain and Europe were alerted to Jacques' past activities. Reviewing the list of books missing from the London Library, Christies in London realised it had dealt with books from Jacques on nine separate occasions since October 1996.

In Berlin, the house of Galerie Gerda Bassenge discovered they had sold books from Jacques, most of them rather esoteric German Reformation pamphlets. The London Library once had a great collection of such pamphlets. In Munich, the house of Zisska and Kistner found that they had thirteen titles on the warning list, waiting for a forthcoming auction. They also had a number of items stolen from the Cambridge University Library, as did BBA.

Jacques had first sent books to Christies in October 1996. In total he submitted books for sale in nine separate auctions up to January 1999. Again, many of these books corresponded to volumes missing from the British and London Libraries.

In April 1999, Jacques was interviewed at a police station in Cambridge. The man in charge of the investigation, DC Paul Howitt of Cambridgeshire Constabulary, said: 'I found him to be a very educated man and a very arrogant man. And a bit of a loner. He lived in a bedsit.'

Jacques said he had dealt with only one auction house and he had come by the books honestly. 'I think he thought we could never prove the provenance of these books and that was his downfall,' said DC Howitt. Jacques was released on bail to return to West End Central police station in London. He never turned up.

Later that month the man who lived in a bedsit transferred £360,000 that he held with the Jyske Bank in London to a branch in Gibraltar. He then sent a fax to Gibraltar marked 'urgent', ordering them to transfer the money to the Banco Metropolitano in Havana, Cuba and insisted that they should not attempt to contact him. Within days, he had flown to Cuba to be with his cash, firing off a letter of resignation to Shell before he went.

Later, more books would be found in a locker at the company. Despite being in a country which has no extradition treaty with Britain, Jacques appears to have thought himself too exposed in Havana. He transferred $20,000 to a bank in Santa Clara, an industrial town in the island's heartland famous only as the home of the memorial to Che Guevara. Apparently now convinced he was beyond the reach of justice, he sent a letter back to the police via his solicitors. It listed a series of safety deposit boxes that he held with banks in London, York and Cambridge.

One by one, the safety deposit boxes were taken from the banks. Those in London were removed to the London Library for opening in the presence of Alan Bell. Those in York and Cambridge were removed to the Cambridge University Library where they were opened in the presence of librarian Brian Jenkins.

Inside these boxes were more than 100 valuable titles, among them works by Thomas Paine, Galileo and Robert Boyle. But the most striking box was the one in Cambridge. Inside it were the two missing editions of Newton's *Principia*.

Brian Jenkins was so relieved they had been recovered undamaged that he kissed one of the books, much to the amusement of police.

The major works recovered included the following, with the date of publication and value:

> I. Newton, *Principia Mathematica* (1687) (two copies) £100,000
> J. Kepler, *Astronomia Nova* (1609) £65,000
> J. Kepler, *Tabulae Rudolphinae* (1627) £14,000
> G. Galileo, *Sidereus Nuncius* (1610) £180,000
> G. Galileo, *Dialogo* (1632) £28,000
> T. Malthus, *An Essay on the Principle of Population* (1798) £40,000
> N. Copernicus, *Astronomia Instaurata* (1617) £7,500
> C. Huygens, *Traite de la Lumiere* (1690) £15,000
> A. Smith, *An Inquiry into the Nature and Causes of the Wealth of Nations* (1776) £2,000
> J. Napier, *Mirifici Logarithmorum canonis Descriptio* (1614) £16,000

There was no way he could find a buyer on the open market for these books; they were just too valuable and well known.

In total, 101 books and pamphlets were recovered; 12 belonging to the London Library, 74 from Cambridge University library and a further 15 belonging to the Society of Physical Research, which had been held at Cambridge University library.

Some of the volumes were wrapped in newspapers dating back to 1993. The police also found 'a ringing kit', the tools used to disguise the books. There were sheets of old paper for use as new folios and for patches, as well as bindings and backs.

Many of the books stolen had their library identification marks removed in order to disguise their origins. However, it was noted, in the main this was crudely done and as a result many had been badly damaged, reducing their commercial value considerably.

Interestingly, the police said that while his membership of all of the libraries did give him legitimate access to the books, many of the more valuable books were held in secure areas not readily accessible to members, particularly with regard to many of the books stolen from the Cambridge library. However, this hint of an inside job never led to anyone other than Jacques being charged with the offences.

Bizarrely, a few weeks later Jacques flew back to Britain from Cuba. He has never explained his actions. During police interviews at the end of 1999 and early in 2000, he stuck to his story that he was a chartered accountant whose hobby was old books and that he had acquired them honestly.

In the course of an investigation lasting almost two years, the police travelled across Britain and Germany, following the complex trail of Jacques' books, and even flew to Cuba to track the money.

In February 2001, he was brought to trial on nineteen counts of theft. He challenged every single book that was brought up in front of him by claiming that it belonged to him and that it was honestly come by. After a five-week trial, he was found guilty and immediately sent to prison.

He appealed twice, unsuccessfully, against the verdict. After a year in jail, a second trial covering two more counts was to be held and the authorities prepared for another long courtroom battle.

However, shortly before it was due to start, Jacques changed his plea to guilty. When he appeared in the dock, his appearance had changed from the thin, somewhat delicate figure with close-cropped hair from the year before. He had bulked up thanks to the prison gym and wore his long hair in a ponytail, tied back with a blue ribbon.

The prosecution encouraged the judge to be enthusiastic in sentencing. 'Underpinning what he did was greed,' said Karim Khalil, for the Crown, 'albeit it hidden behind a shabby cloak of respectability.'

In mitigation, his defence barrister, Annette Henry, described him as a 'hugely humiliated' man who had 'shattered' his personal and professional life and stripped himself of a future career. Henry, in a phrase that could be read more than one way, added that 'the book – or should I say books – have been thrown at him.'

Jacques was sentenced to four years in prison. 'You were a man of good character,' the judge said. 'You had the benefit of a Cambridge education but you have not used those advantages. You are clearly a very dishonest young man.'

There was little sympathy for Jacques, all condemning him not only for the thefts but more for the cultural vandalism in the way the books had been damaged to cover up their provenance.

Jolyon Hudson of Pickering and Chatto commented: 'I wouldn't mind so much if they'd just been stolen and resold. It's the destruction of the provenances that distresses me. It's like taking out the crown jewels and cutting them up.'

For Brian Jenkins at Cambridge University Library, there was a further, terrible, implication from Jacques's activities; that the books weren't so much 'thrown at him', as Jacques's defence barrister had stated, but handed to him on a plate by a third party. 'That leaves only one possibility,' Jenkins said. 'A member of staff was involved and that is hugely distressing for us.'

As a final observation on this episode, Hudson offered this sanguine comment. 'I was once told that every great book has been plundered at least once in its life.' Rome's great libraries were built by Asinius Pollio and Augustus and filled with books stolen on the

Roman army's many campaigns. Henry VIII ransacked the monasteries, Napoleon stole nearly 2,400 books for his exile on Elba, and Hitler enshrined the plundering of libraries, museums and galleries in State law.

But throughout the case it seemed evident that William Jacques didn't want to read any of the books he stole, he just wanted to sell them. It was pointed out by one observer at his trial that he came to court each day with a Wilbur Smith novel.

And when he got out of jail, it was not long before Jacques was up to his old activities. He was arrested again after the theft of thirteen volumes of *Nouvelle Iconographies des Camellias* from the Royal Horticultural Society's library. The volumes, by Ambroise Vershaffelt, contain an array of coloured plates with explanatory text of camellias by the 19th-century Belgian author, and were valued at around £50,000. The thefts took place between December 2006 and February 2007 from the RHS's Lindley Library in Vincent Square, London.

Soon after his arrest he skipped bail but was re-arrested on Christmas Day 2009 in the town where he was raised, Selby, North Yorkshire, after a tip-off. His trial was set for June 2010.

With regard to the Scott case, Jacques wasn't just an isolated anecdote from the murky world of antique-book dealing. The coincidences had stacked up. He was originally from the North, which in the police rule of thumb in Scott's case of proximity to theft equalling possible guilt, and this put him on the fringes of the Durham University theft. Also, the fact that the first period of his criminal activities took place between 1991 and 1999, straddling the date of the Durham theft, was something that couldn't be ignored.

Jacques' enigmatic comment when asked about the First Folio in 2002, when he told officers they had had a wasted journey, 'or maybe not', added further spice. Then, of course, there was the crux of the link. He had fled to Cuba after jumping police bail. His habit of ripping out and/or destroying identification marks, blemishes and stamps from which the true provenance of the book could be ascertained, had been inflicted on the Durham copy of the First Folio.

And also there was the fact he did not keep the stolen items in his home, but dotted around England – York, London and Cambridge – in deed boxes in several banking institutions. While there is provision to store valuable items in Cuban banks, they were far less likely to be kept away from the prying eyes of the state. Castro, after countless assassination attempts, was not surprisingly paranoid about where the next exploding cigar, assassin's bullet, bomb or poisoned dart was going to come from.

If some foreigner fresh to the island was to deposit something of value in one of these banks, it would not be long before Castro's security forces would get to hear about it and it would be searched. So, if you were to have fled to Cuba with a valuable book, where would you store it if not in a bank?

Maybe in the safekeeping of someone who at first had been a casual acquaintance. A man who over a period of weeks had become a friend, trusted to an extent. Anyway, even if this man had the nous to realize the value of what he had, it would not be possible to sell it himself in Cuba, while travel restrictions meant he could not leave the island without official sanction and only then, no doubt, with his baggage thoroughly searched.

But how would a foreigner get to know a Cuban in such a short space of time? Particularly one, slightly gauche and a bit of a loner like Scott, who did not make friends or mix easily.

Perhaps a man who wins trust easily and could be confided in, a Mr Fix-it who knows his way round, who seems well known among the locals and can make things happen, make your stay interesting, always there with a suggestion as to the best places to visit, the best bars, the best cabarets.

Could it be that ten years before Scott, Jacques had become acquainted with Odeiny Perez Leon, Scott's friend and fellow member of the 'triumvirate'? In his home, Denny did not have a deed box but a bible box in which, when Scott arrived, he was told was kept 'the old English book' that had been in his family for a century.

For months now Scott had insisted that their First Folio was not the Durham Copy, but a new Cuban Copy. He had steadfastly stood by his story that Denny's description of its provenance was true. 'To consider otherwise is unthinkable,' he had said.

Now Scott began to think the unthinkable.

Chapter Eighteen

The Play What I Wrote

In January 2010, the English winter had stretched any romantic notion of a white Christmas to breaking point. The country was stuck in a snowdrift. A nation that had once conquered vast swathes of the globe thanks to a small coterie of adventurers and opportunists, armed with little more than a superior attitude, ground to a halt because it hadn't stocked up enough grit. And not for the first time.

Scott's case had gone similarly cold and was making as much headway as the cars buried under mounds of snow on the country's streets and motorways. In the latter half of 2009, he'd had one last hurrah, turning up at Durham Crown Court for yet another adjournment, in a horse-drawn carriage led by a Scottish piper playing 'Scotland the Brave'. Dressed in a Royal Stewart tartan kilt, a Harris Tweed jacket and cravat, and foregoing his usual vintage champagne for a bottle of Drambuie, he claimed Bonnie Prince Charlie as a distant relative. Asked by the judge if he was Raymond Scott, he answered 'Aye, that I am,' in a distinctly Highland burr.

Subsequent hearings found him more sober-suited and a trial date was at last set for June 14th, 2010, exactly two years after Scott had walked into the Folger in Washington DC with the copy of the First Folio. The trial was anticipated to last two months.

Scott and his team were going to fight every spit and comma, and had an army of experts lined up to discuss the minutiae of exhibit 1, the First Folio. The main characters from the Folger, Richard Kuhta and Stephen Massey, were to take the stand, but arrangements for the two other main protagonists had not been finalized.

Heidy and Denny had still not been directly interviewed by Durham police. Representations had begun in the summer between Durham and the Cuban authorities, but so far to no avail. It was proving a vexed issue. The chance of them being allowed to travel to Britain was virtually non-existent. There had been talk of a video link but, as far as Scott knew, that had come to nothing. It seemed, on the face of it, an impasse had been reached.

Then in January, Scott got a phone call from Denny. He said it turned his world upside down. The first I knew about it was a text from Scott. No verbiage, double entendres and concluding chorus of Vera Lynn's 'We'll Meet Again' as had been his custom of late. He got straight to the point.

'EXCLUSIVE. Denny confesses all,' it began. The rest, alluding to Jacques, I later deleted at his insistence for fear that what Denny had confessed to was part of some elaborate plot to get Scott off the hook. After Scott's explanation, it made a kind of sense, but that was to come when we were to meet up at the end of the week.

In response to my reply to tell me everything, he told me to 'expect another cheap brown envelope full of sound and fury' in which all would be revealed.

The following day it arrived through my letterbox. I'd foolishly expected all to be revealed in a conventional way, a letter detailing in totality his conversation with Denny. Instead I got a mock Shakespearian play, part comedy, part tragedy, part histrionics.

However, the prologue began promisingly. In a nutshell, it said that Denny had been interviewed 'out of the blue' by three Cuban detectives. According to Scott, Denny had been given good and bad news by them. First, the good news. He had been told he had broken no Cuban laws and would walk free. The detectives went on to tell him the book had been stolen, his *'compañero'* (Scott) was facing a long time in jail and that he had no chance whatsoever of profiting from the book.

Following the interview, Denny, an honourable man as Scott said, adding somewhat stingingly Mark Antony's comment of Brutus in Julius Caesar after Caesar's assassination 'so are they all honourable men', had rung him in England.

Scott wrote: 'His voice breaking with emotion, he gave me a sincere apology and this time LA VERDAD (THE TRUTH).'

Denny's revelation had left him in a quandary, not knowing if it was good or bad news for him. 'With time on my hands I turned Denny's confession into a play – it seemed apposite.'

And so, with an introductory nod to the Al Stewart hit 'Year Of The Cat' which music fans of a certain vintage will spot, we had the following:

Unvarnished Veracity Productions

In Association

With Credible Concepts Proudly Presents:

Shakespeare & Love In Cuba
or
My Innocent Role In Shakespeare Real-Life Drama

A comic trajedy (sic) in four acts as told to and written down by Raymond Scott (NOT a member of the RSC)

All of the action takes place in Havana, Cuba. Firstly in Old (Spanish Colonial) Havana with its warren of quaint courtyards, alleyways and backstreets where a visitor can wander until their sense of which direction completely disappears. Peopled by characters who look as if they've escaped from the pages of *The Maltese Falcon*. Indeed at every turn one expects to come across Peter Lorre and Sidney Greenstreet (complete with Fez) sitting at a pavement café contemplating some nefarious enterprise.

Siborney, the suburb where the villa is located, redolent of Darras Hall but with palm trees and the heat notched up, just to demonstrate that while all are equal in communist Cuba some are a little more equal than others.

Dramatis Personae (in order of appearance).

DENNY: A Cuban. Full-time subaltern in Cuban army and part time 'jitero' or fixer for foreign tourists who show their gratitude quite literally with gratuity in much prized hard currency (Yanqui dollars being especially cherished). He can get tourists cigars better and cheaper than at the state owned Casa Del Habanos shops, escort them round La Habana etc. Probably even get a personally signed photo of Fidel Castro. An affable fellow. Speaks English.

MR JACKS (spelt phonetically): An English tourist. Tall and thin. Brown haired and pale invariably wearing sunglasses. Nervous.

RAYMOND SCOTT: A hapless English tourist whose avocation is old books. Ignorant of theft of priceless books from Durham University Library in 1998 an edifice he has never entered. In love with Heidy.

HEIDY: Beautiful young dancer in love with Raymond Scott to whom she is engaged to be married. A Cuban but speaks excellent English.

Also various visitors to Havana, hotel staff, American librarians and law enforcement officers, British librarians, police officers and last but by no means least, lawyers and journos.

ACTUS PRIMUS SCENA PRIMA

El Floridita – a bar in Old Havana very popular with

tourists because of its rich historical associations with Ernest Hemingway. It was his favoured watering hole.

ENTER DENNY.

DENNY – Una cerveza camarero por favor! (Translation: A beer barman please!).

He spies an obvious tourist sitting nearby alone, looking dejected and miserable. Denny approaches and begins to speak in English – his only foreign tongue but very useful as it's the modern lingua franca.

DENNY – Cheer up amigo! Are you Canadian?

MR JACKS – No, I'm English.

DENNY – From London?

MR JACKS – Sort of. Yes and no.

DENNY – Do you like Cuba?

MR JACKS – Yes. But not Havana because of all the tourists.

DENNY – Maybe I can help you. I'm Denny. Everybody calls me Denny. I know a lot of people in Cuba. A lot of people know Denny.

MR JACKS – Hi I'm…well just call me Jack.

DENNY – Been here long?

MR JACKS – Couple of days.

DENNY – Which hotel are you staying at?

MR JACKS – Hotel Ambos Mundos.

DENNY – Ah! You big fan of *El Papa*! (historical note: *El Papa* is the affectionate sobriquet of Hemingway who lived at the hotel in the 1930s where he began his novel *For Whom The Bell Tolls*. His suite of rooms is now a museum housing some of his belongings notably his typewriter).

MR JACKS – Yes.

DENNY – Been in his room?

MR JACKS – Yes.

DENNY – Been to Cojimar? (Literary note: Cojimar outside of Havana city is the locale of his novella 'The Old Man and the Sea'(1952 Pultizer prize) contributing towards his Nobel Laureate in 1954).

MR JACKS – No not yet.

DENNY – Like to go? I can arrange for you to meet the old fisherman who inspired the book!! He's a very old man but still living.

MR JACKS – You can?

DENNY – Sure! When you're with Denny nothing is impossible. Is very lucky for you we meet! Several more drinks are consumed all being paid for by JACKS in American dollars.
More banter then JACKS announces:

MR JACKS – I'll see you tomorrow morning at the hotel. I'm going to walk back to my hotel now.

DENNY – Oh no my friend! Not along Obisipo at this time of night! It's not safe! (no less than the truth) I'll arrange for a taxi! (Geographical note: Obisipo is the principal thoroughfare of Old Havana on which the hotel stands but is riddled with alleyways and passages of the Spanish colonial period – *disreputibles* loiter therein)

MR JACKS – Thanks.

DENNY – My friend I think I just saved your life maybe – certainly your dollars and nice watch!!!

MR JACKS (He laughs).

EXEUNT DENNY AND JACKS TO TAXI.

ACTUS PRIMUS SCENA SECUNDA

Outside Hotel Ambos Mundos but still in taxi.

MR JACKS – I'd also like very much to visit El Papa's house and see his fishing boat and visit Hemingway Marina.

DENNY – No problem! Maybe I even get you inside the house! (Tourist note: Hemingway's house where he lived until 1959 or 1960 is permanently closed to the public – the wooden structure is fragile as is the Pilar (his boat). Alas on this occasion the undoubted fixing skills of Denny proved woefully insufficient to persuade the implacable guard but they did peer in through the window.)

MR JACKS – That would be great! See you back here at 10 tomorrow morning.

DENNY – You can bet on it!

Exeunt Jacks to hotel.
Taxi leaves with Denny alone satisfied with his nights 'work'. OK he has to pay the taxi fare but reckons what the hell it's a good investment in the future and all night, for about one hour, he only had to buy one bottle of beer! Result or what?

ACTUS SECUNDUS SCENA PRIMA

The morning after the night before. Denny waits inside the Hotel Ambos Mundos. He is early. He is challenged by reception manager (R.M.).

R.M. (in Spanish) – Can I help you señor?

DENNY (replying in his mother tongue also) – I'm looking for an English tourist, my friend Jack.

R.M. – Jack who?

DENNY – I dunno just Jack.

R.M. – We have a Mr Jacks an Englishman staying here. Could that be the gentleman in question?

DENNY – Could be.

R.M. – I'll call his room. Who shall I say requires him?

DENNY – Denny.

R.M. – No reply. Maybe he's gone out.

DENNY - No way we had a definite meet arranged! I'll check the roof maybe he's there.
(Culinary note: Breakfast at the hotel is taken on the roof terrace with its breathtaking panoramic views of Old Havana. The perfect way to begin the day.)

Denny enters hotel lift and ascends to roof terrace restaurant encountering Jacks alone finishing breakfast. He is beckoned to Jacks' table. Pleasantries are exchanged (inconsequential and platitudinous). But then Jacks remarks …

JACKS – Do you know Denny I've been unable to rent a safe deposit box in all of Havana not even at the Banco Metropolitan where I have an account. They will not allow me even to leave a box in their vault at any of their branches even if it's unlocked!

DENNY – Fancy (with raised eyebrow).

JACKS – Yes I've tried. Maybe it's because I'm a foreigner perhaps you could rent one for me, on my behalf. I can pay you.

DENNY – Unfortunately not, it's not possible here, we don't have cajas desseguridades (secure boxes) in the banks in case people hide things in them from the Government – things they should not have.

JACKS (laughing uproariously) But that's the whole point of having one!

DENNY (ignorant of the ironic content in Jacks' last

remark and not seeing the amusing side) – What's so valuable you want to stash away?

JACKS – Oh just this and that you know.

DENNY – Maybe this hotel can keep them in the safe for you

JACKS – Oh I've got a safe in my room.

DENNY – Well then ...

JACKS – It's not big enough and what happens when I leave the hotel?

DENNY – Where are they now, these valuables?

JACKS – Locked in my suitcase in my room. It's OK don't worry Denny.

DENNY – Mmmmmm ... (Denny is intrigued but can't work out all the permutations or conceive of an article which is valuable or treasured without being intrinsically valuable but of such proportions that it will not fit inside a hotel safe. I don't think I'm spoiling the plot if I say we are all going to hear a lot more about Jacks' mystery artifact later. For dramatic effect there is a long Pinteresque pause at this juncture)

Jacks completes his breakfast. Exeunt omnes pursued by attentive waiter who summons lift in search of tip alas in vain.

ACTUS SECUNDUS SCENA SECUNDA

For the next four days Denny and Jacks are constant

companions. Denny has leave from the army and shows Jacks the charms of Havana. Jacks always pays for everything from a seemingly inexhaustible roll of American banknotes. At the end of each day Jacks tips Denny well for his services. Denny likes Jacks. Jacks reciprocates. Denny takes care of him (there are a lot of unscrupulous people out there in the big bad world, some will rob you with a gun, some with a fountain pen and a smile). The relationship warms but Jacks is taciturn and monosyllabic when it comes to his life. Denny enquires what Jacks does for a living. Jacks replies that he is a 'bookkeeper', a 'keeper of books'. Could this be a pun? A cryptic double entendre perhaps? Jacks is particularly impressed with the transportation Denny lays on – a comfortable vehicle, sheer luxury when compared to the ancient Lada taxis with their inadequate suspension.

Jacks admires the way Denny arranges their visits to Hemingway's house, the Marina, restaurants and Havana's vibrant nightlife including The Tropicana and Parisien Café. The highlight is their visit to the fishing village of Cojimar outside of Havana City and an audience with the aged angler who roused Hemingway 'to pen' *The Old Man and the Sea*. I, personally, am willing to believe that they met an old man purporting to be the very same salty sea dog portrayed in the book. Enough said.

But as Denny likes to say (indeed as the French Protestant refugees of the 16th–17th centuries also used to utter) 'It's not what you know, it's who you know.' Think about it, take your time – I've never been able to crack the Times cryptic in the boiling of an egg either. Anyway, to cut a long one short suffice to say a friendship is cemented between Denny and Jacks which began with that chance encounter in El Floridita. And when

Jacks is tired of Havana and its abundance of other tourists it is Denny who suggests a sojourn in Santa Clara and smoothes his passage there. What are friends for after all?

ACTUS TERTIUS SCENA PRIMA

Outside Hotel Ambos Mundos early afternoon, a bustling street scene in Old Havana. Jacks has checked out of the hotel.

DENNY – All your bags are in back of car, Jack.

JACKS – Thanks, Denny.

The two bosom buddies get into car which proceeds to the Malacon and thence to Habana Este (East Havana). It stops outside where Denny, then still a bachelor, is residing. The duo egress the taxi. Jacks retrieves a package from a suitcase.

JACKS – This is what I wished to deposit in the bank for safekeeping.

DENNY – What is it?

JACKS (Removing it from a plastic bag) – It's an old book that once upon a time belonged to my great grandmother.

DENNY – Is it valuable?

JACKS – Not really but it's of great sentimental value. I take it wherever I go. She also bequeathed a globe and that means the world to me.

DENNY – Really you are mirthful!

JACKS – Yeah thing is I don't want to lose it in Santa Clara or elsewhere during my travels in Cuba and it's rather cumbersome. Do you think you could possibly be so gracious as to look after it for me until I return to collect it and here's some money for your trouble.

DENNY – Sure thing! Denny take good care of the book! You can trust Denny with your life – a book is nothing my friend. We are like brothers! Your book is safe with me!

JACKS – Spiffing!

DENNY – What is this 'spiffing'? I don't know.

JACKS – Esplendido! (Splendid)

The two brothers embrace (though no Gallic style kisses are exchanged) in a fraternal farewell.

JACKS – Adieu

DENNY – *Hasta pronto hermano* (see you soon brother). Jacks enters the car and after a final lingering wave it speeds towards the autopista (motorway) and an easterly direction towards the delights of Santa Clara. The book still in a plastic bag is put by Denny into an old wooden bible box which coincidentally once housed a bible belonging to Denny's great grandmother. It's a snug fit and could have been purpose made. True to his word Denny will keep the book safe and sound until Jacks' return, for Denny is an honourable man, an officer and a gentleman in fact. But Jacks does not return, no word is heard of

Denny's erstwhile comrade, no letters, no postcards, nothing. Denny cannot contact the itinerant Jacks of no fixed abode. Sleuthing elicits from the car driver the hotel in Santa Clara where Jacks was dropped off. Denny phones them. Jacks has departed for an unknown destination. Impasse.

Sedulously, Denny visits the British Embassy in an effort to trace Jacks but is turned away as the only biographical detail he can furnish is the name Mr Jacks, possibly from London. Stalemate.

The months pass into years. Denny is promoted, he acquires a spouse, she gives issue – twice. Denny moves home, several times, but always the book snug in its box accompanies him. He regards it as a talisman. He has no idea of its value. Possibly the children can use it when they grow up and learn English at school. He is resigned to the fact that Jacks will not return. He considers the book to be his. Well he would, wouldn't he?

ACTUS QUARTUS SCENA PRIMA

Fast forward to mid-February 2008. The scene is a villa in the Havana suburb of Siborney. Heidy lounges by the pool. Denny sits at a table smoking a cigar, on the table is something in a plastic bag. It is mid-afternoon.
    Enter Raymond Scott through the French windows. He has partaken of a siesta (slept it off). He wears a silk dressing gown *a la* Noel Coward.

R.S – God bless all here. Anyone for tennis?

DENNY – *Buenos tardes compañero* (good afternoon close friend). Look what I got for you!

R.S. – Not more bloody cigars Denny, I've got enough already.

DENNY – No not cigars my friend something right up your alley!!

(Denny knows of Scott's interest in old books and removes the book Jacks entrusted to him all those years before). Voila! (with a flourish).

R.S. (Inspecting the volume) – It's an old book of plays by William Shakespeare. Where did you get it? Be careful you'll get ash on it!

DENNY – It belonged to my great-grandmother it's been in the family for generations.

(In prosaic time honoured tradition – a white lie that was about to plunge R.S. into more than just tepid water).

FINIS

Chapter Nineteen

Honourable Men

It must have been one hell of a conversation. Since I'd first began reading about the case, and on innumerable occasions since we had met, Scott had been adamant that Denny had been telling the truth – that the book had been in his family for years and it was by happy chance he had come across it and 'sensed' its value. Now he had changed his tune. Was this 'revelation' really that, or another hastily concocted story, although revealed with a bit of a flourish?

The news, if true, was a double-edged sword for Scott. First, it all but confirmed – as if it was needed – that the book he strolled into the Folger Shakespeare Library was indeed the stolen Durham First Folio. But here was testimony, which I assumed Durham police must now know of, that he was ignorant of this fact. That he'd been duped by Denny. That neither was he guilty of theft nor of handling stolen goods, as he wasn't aware when he handed over the $11,000 to Denny for the Folio, that it had been pinched.

It could explain why he went to the Folger in the first place, making no secret of his true identity and then urging Kuhta and his colleagues to go to the press when they provisionally identified it as a First Folio. And Denny wouldn't have warned him not to go because he obviously believed Jacks' story that it had been in his family for generations and was probably unaware then of Durham University's existence, let alone any theft from it.

There seemed to be a sense of anger in his hastily written 'play' about his conversation with Denny, who was not viewed as the amiable Brian Glover look-alike of old. The term Mr Fix-it he used to describe him, previously one of affection and not a little admiration, was now used to damn him.

There was also a pointed insight into Denny's methods of ingratiating his way into the affections of foreigners. That he would be your best friend – if there was something in it for him. You can imagine the conversations he had with 'Mr Jacks' being repeated a decade later when Scott came on the scene. For the pair's literary tastes were similar and Scott would have as easily been reeled in.

'Are you a big fan of *El Papa*?; Been to Cojimar?; Been in his room?;'Like to go? When you're with Denny nothing is impossible. Is very lucky for you we meet.' The bitter irony was not lost on Scott who had described how Denny rang to tell him the truth, being an honourable man. Like Brutus, 'so are they all, all honourable men'. Even when he's been made a mug of, Scott reached out to Shakespeare to put things in perspective.

And the sense of him being made a mug of was palpable in the whole tone of the piece. Despite this, there was a residue of loyalty to his old friend in his description of Denny's 'white lie' in claiming the book had been in his family for years and had belonged to his great-grandmother. He'd merely passed on the lie 'Mr Jacks' had told him. It was a white lie for which he had been paying for nearly two years now which could leave him facing a maximum fourteen years in jail. Most would have given it a less euphemistic tag.

And what about Heidy? What did she know? She obviously knew Denny before he met Scott – it was Heidy who introduced them, after all. Was she aware of how Denny first got hold of the book? To be even more conspiratorial, had she been used by Denny in the past to try and find some, apparently rich, foreigner with an interest in old books he could palm it off on? Had they both hit pay dirt when Scott came on the scene? That would be the bitterest blow for Scott. He had never been so naïve as to pretend she had fallen for him just for his sparkling wit, sartorial splendour and ability to recite huge chunks of Shakespeare without prompting. But, if true, this would represent a terrible betrayal. The news meant that even he must now admit he'd lost all claim to the First Folio. It would be devastating to lose any hope of somehow ending up with Heidy when this had all played out.

And so we met in Newcastle on a freezing Friday night, the rain firing icy darts. It was 6 p.m. and the revellers were already out as I made my way to the railway station to meet Scott – me underneath three layers of clothes topped off with an oversized 'Columbo' mac. The female revellers sported miniskirts and the thinnest of tops, the men in jeans and trendy T-shirts or, those resigned to not scoring on the night, football shirts. Even the famously hardy Newcastle nightlife was walking that little bit faster because of the Arctic conditions.

Because of the weather, I'd suggested we meet in the Centurion bar, which is attached to Central Station. Scott arrived promptly, most unlike him, as he had always boasted of there being Greenwich Mean Time and Scott Mean Time, which run at least half-an-hour apart. There was much to discuss and he obviously wanted to get on with it, but not in the Centurion. He expressed surprise at it being mobbed and he wanted a little privacy. It was Friday night, what did he expect? I asked.

A church would have been our best option, but I led him hurriedly across the road to the Union Rooms, a vast two-storey place of worship to drinkers, with three separate bars inside selling cut-price booze. The icy rain was now causing the blue-skinned revellers to almost break into a trot between bars. It was packed, too. Scott didn't want to stay there either.

We went back across the road to the Destination bar. It was only two-deep at the bar and there was the odd empty foot of space to stand in which, for Newcastle, was as empty as we were going to get. Scott looked uncertainly around him. We're staying here I told him and he scuttled off to the toilet. He was holding his ever present carrier bag with his documents of the day and the inevitable bottle of Lucozade filled with Cava or champagne. A couple stood up to go and I launched myself at their seats at the head of the stampede and was settling in with notepad out, drink at my elbow, jacket off, everything but a campfire built to signify I wasn't budging. Scott emerged from the toilets a couple of minutes later and he seemed OK with the arrangement and settled into his seat.

'What did you think of the play?' he asked.

'Entertaining. But not quite what I expected.'

He smiled and took a surreptitious swig from his bottle. 'I was inflamed. I was up all night writing it. It was a pastiche of the great man, I concede, but I deemed it appropriate.'

'So what happened?'

Scott put more prosaically what he had described in his play. Some Cuban detectives had turned up at Denny's home to ask him questions at the request of Durham Constabulary. They had decided he had done nothing to break any Cuban laws, so he wasn't questioned under caution and he need not answer any questions. After several reassurances he had described how the book came into his possession.

I offered that Denny's previous position as loyal bodyguard to Castro, and his later one as head of security for Cubanacan, must have helped in the process.

'It will have done no harm, I am sure,' agreed Scott.

Then he talked of the emotional tenor of his telephone conversation with Denny. How Denny had almost been tearful as he came clean about the provenance of the book.

'He's a good actor,' I pointed out.

But Scott was adamant. Denny was genuinely remorseful and wished he'd told him in the first place. 'It was, of course, only a white lie he told me. The book, as he understood it, had been in the family of its owner from the time of his great-grandmother.'

'But not his great-grandmother.'

Scott nodded. 'There lies the rub.'

I thought about Heidy and asked if she had known anything about how Denny had got hold of the book.

'It is inconceivable that she knew anything about it. The first she had seen of the book was that February when he brought it to the villa. There is no reason for him to have told her about it. She, like me, believed it to have been in his family for generations.'

I pointed out that up until their 'tearful' phone call he had thought it similarly inconceivable that Denny had acquired it any other manner than the way he had originally said.

Scott was emphatic. 'No, she's as innocent as I am.'

I raised an eyebrow at that comment; Scott smiled and took another quick drink from his bottle. Then he became serious again, 'Sometime after I was first arrested I received an envelope in the post. Inside was a note with just a mobile-phone number. I rang it and spoke to someone who gave me some very interesting information which I passed on to the police. It involved several coincidences surrounding the theft of the Durham First Folio and other books.'

I remembered vaguely Scott talking about this some months before. The gist of it was that at the time of the theft of the Durham First Folio, there was a member of staff at the university who had been previously working at other libraries when valuable books had been stolen. It wasn't an off-the-cuff remark and he went into the matter in some detail and he mentioned a name. I thought he seemed well informed but Scott hadn't told me where he'd got the information from and had made no mention of the letter with the mobile-phone number.

It was intriguing, but at that time we were working on the premise that the First Folio he had tried to sell was an un-catalogued one – belonging to Denny's family – thus not the Durham copy.

I then asked if he believed this person at Durham University was responsible for the copy Denny had given him. He said no, viewing it as a wholly separate set of circumstances. The two copies weren't one and the same, just that it was quite a coincidence. I had left it there. If, as he said, he had mentioned it to the police, as far as I was aware, the matter had gone no further.

The previous crimes he had referred to had taken place at Cambridge University and had been committed by William Jacques. The police had noted at the time of those thefts that the university authorities had regretfully conceded that the thefts had more than likely been committed with inside help.

Jacques came from Selby in North Yorkshire. And while the man Scott said he talked to did not give his name, and asked him to destroy the number he had given him to call, Scott said he had spoken with a Yorkshire accent. 'I contacted his mother to find out where he is now being held and I have sent a letter begging him to come clean. I've heard nothing back yet.'

The bar was now absolutely heaving. I'd made my drink last about an hour and accusing eyes were looking at Scott swigging from his Lucozade bottle. We were transgressing the natural laws of bars up and down the land by, on my part, not drinking quick enough to earn the right to a seat and Scott, more heinous still, not having actually bought his drink at the bar in the first place. A semi-circle of ill-concealed scorn had gathered around us and it was time to leave.

He got on his mobile to his mother to tell her to pick him up at Durham station in about half an hour. As we walked the very short distance to Central Station for the Newcastle to Durham train, I said he must be feeling pretty good that police had evidence now that would clear him of the charges. And just in time for his fifty-third birthday the following week.

'Oh, sure,' he said vaguely, hardly doing cartwheels. Sometimes he would drift away, his mind wandering to something else, some thought, some plan. Maybe a new play. Time would tell.

We arranged to meet again in Durham the following Saturday after his birthday which turned out to be, by the sound of it, another quiet affair. We ended up, yet again, near to the place where it had all began, Palace Green at Durham University, careful not to get too close so as not to breach his bail conditions.

He'd obviously given a lot of thought about the recent twist in the case which, on the face of it, had exonerated him of all charges. Now, it seemed, he wanted to talk his way back into the hub of the matter and onto the fringes of guilt. The logic to his train of thought, if logic could sometimes be applied to Scott, was it must have irked him that while previously he had been at the centre of the story, the turn of events potentially threatened to shunt him not so much to the sidings, but as one player among a number in a larger story. Worse still, the thought of being a dupe or a patsy must have rankled someone as proud as him. He was having none of it.

'I told you I was a chess player when I was at the Royal Grammar School didn't I?' he began. 'I was the under-15 champion and I played three games against the overall school champion. He was eighteen. I can't remember his name but he was one of these methodical players. A great positional player who took few risks. 'I, on the other hand, was the opposite. I would sacrifice pieces just to spice things up.

'In my first game against him I sacrificed my Queen. I even raised my hands up and sighed as if I had made a mistake. But I had lured him into a trap. I had thought several moves ahead and foreseen a position where I could checkmate him. And so it proved. Because of his character he couldn't imagine that someone, particularly a boy of fifteen, could have sacrificed his Queen, the second most important piece on the board behind the King, and the most important attacking one, without good reason.'

His anecdote reminded me of a famous match played by his great chess hero Bobby Fischer when he was just thirteen. The so-called 'game of the century' was against the US player Donald Byrne. Fischer, as Scott claimed to be, was a master of improvisational chess. He sacrificed his Queen, which led to him capturing several of his opponent's pieces before annihilating him. It was a game that brought him to the attention of the chess-playing world.

'Sounds very like the famous Bobby Fischer game,' I said.

'Oh, that Queen sacrifice was much less obvious than mine,' Scott said magnanimously.

Then he got to his point. 'The police have this notion that I am this jet-setting, international thief, weaving a web of intrigue. Yes, a cunning, deceitful spider spinning an ever more complex web. So what if this latest turn of events is part of this web, part of my grand plan? Perhaps it was my plan in the first place.'

I said I didn't follow him.

'Let's go back to the beginning,' he continued. 'Scott walks into the Folger Shakespeare Library in Washington DC with what is claimed to be a stolen Shakespeare First Folio. He correctly identifies himself and even leaves it there for them to authenticate. It would be obvious that in the authentication process, it would be found to be stolen, if that was what it was. If a person were aware the book was stolen and that he could not sell it, how would he be able to cash in on it? How, for example, if he was like me, a man who wants to live with the love of his life, Heidy, but that life will not come cheap. So he has to cash in his assets to fund it. And he has very few assets.

Say, for example, he was aware of the dubious provenance of the First Folio and knew what would happen if he was to walk in somewhere as prestigious and as knowledgeable as the Shakespeare Folger Library to authenticate it, during which process it would, as I have said, be established it had been stolen. Imagine the notoriety the case would generate. Think of the amount of people who have said this story would make a great film. Imagine how much a film studio would pay to make that film. So perhaps we're standing here in Durham just a few hundred yards from where the Durham First Folio is, again, housed, talking at a point I had all along planned to reach. It's like a game of chess.'

'No one,' I said, 'can plan that far ahead.' Not even Bobby Fischer, arguably one of the most perceptive people of this or any age on the chessboard, whose extraordinarily complex thought processes left him vulnerable to unfounded suspicion, paranoia and, ultimately, madness.

But he was away again on another flight of fancy. 'Of course, Hollywood would put its spin on it. They'd probably have me played by Denzel Washington. I can see my eminent QC, Toby Hedworth, played by George Clooney. He won't need the hair dye to make it grey, he's very distinguished looking. As for Caroline Goodwin, his supporting barrister, his aide-de-camp if you will, Helena Bonham Carter springs to mind. The clipped vowels, the ever-so accent, the superior demeanour. A very intelligent woman.

'And of course I wouldn't just walk into the Folger, there'd be some Al Qaeda sub plot, perhaps a car chase, speeding through the streets of Washington with a ticking bomb. And there we'd be at the Folger. I'd hold the Folio up in the face of Richard Kuhta and I'll tell him if you move the Folio gets it. I'd make to tear one of its pages in front of his very eyes and he'll be whimpering "no, no, not the book".'

We both laughed at that one. Then he changed tack again. 'Toby Hedworth, I've been very impressed with. He says in a criminal case it's best that it is complicated, not cut-and-dried. There has to be that element of doubt that the First Folio is in fact the one stolen from Durham. If that was to be accepted without challenge then the charges could naturally fall into place. But if the jury is in anyway undecided and thinks "but are they really one in the same. Can they really be sure?" then that helps the defence case.'

But that was if it ever got before a jury. He was due in court the following Friday where I presumed the Denny information would be revealed and then the prosecution had some hard questions to ask of its case.'

From the outside looking in, at this stage it was advantage Scott. Denny's confession tied up a lot of loose ends about how the Folio got to Cuba in the first place. The evidence had been gathered on behalf of Durham Constabulary for the prosecution case. I couldn't imagine, if his witness statement was to be submitted to court, Scott's barrister would challenge it, unless he really wanted to complicate and confuse things by disputing the fact his client had no knowledge whatsoever of the provenance of the First Folio when it ended up in his hands.

But inevitably with Scott, nothing was going to be uncomplicated or cut-and-dried either. He'd turned up for the hearing, this time at Newcastle Crown Court, dressed as *El Comandante*, Castro himself, although Castro perhaps doesn't boast a similar fondness for designer sunglasses and Gucci jewellery. Scott had called me before and promised to spritz the assembled media with a magnum or perhaps a jeroboam of champagne if, as he'd hoped, the case were to be dropped. It was just as well he saved some money by opting for the standard sized.

Far from throwing out the case, for the first time since his arrest nineteen months before, charges of stealing the First Folio in December 1998, handling stolen goods between that time and his arrest in July 2008, and a new one, removing stolen property from the UK between January and July 2008, were put to him. In a rather too sonorous impression of Sir Laurence Olivier, Scott boomed 'not guilty' in the hushed court.

Judge Richard Lowden told him: 'Don't be so dramatic please.'

The case was adjourned until May 2010, and a provisional date for the trial was set in June.

We arranged to meet up afterwards at 'Revolution' in Newcastle again. I walked through the door and scanned the room but there was no sign of him. A waitress approached. 'Are you looking for the man dressed as a commando?'

'Highly likely.'

As she pointed in the direction of the toilet, Scott emerged and on catching sight of us stopped abruptly and gave a formal, heel-clicking salute.

'Will you be drinking or eating?' the waitress asked me.

'Drinking.'

Despite the bar being almost empty Scott led me on a circuit until a table on the upper level, located discreetly in a corner, was to his satisfaction.

'So what happened?'

Scott shrugged. 'They asked me to plead. It was quite funny. I put on my best *basso profundo* voice to plead on the first charge and it came out a lot louder than I thought. "No reason to be so dramatic, Mr Scott", said the Judge. So for the second I was quiet as a mouse. "No need to be so quiet, Mr Scott", said the Judge. Very amusing.'

'How come they've charged you despite Denny's confession?'

Scott shook his head: 'It wasn't introduced to the court.'

'Why did your defence team decide not to put this before the judge?'

'They don't know anything about it.'

Even for Scott that was a weird admission. He hadn't told the defence about a crucial bit of evidence that would surely be the central plank of their case to clear him?

Then a thought crossed my mind and I asked, 'You haven't made it up?'

Scott was emphatic. 'They spoke to him, it must be about five or six weeks ago now, and I find it fascinating they haven't given a whiff of it. Perhaps they're trying to smoke me out.'

'Smoke you out?'

'You see, they haven't told my defence team. And if my defence had raised it in court today the police would guess that that information could only have come from me. Therefore, they would have known I'd spoken to Denny and they might speculate that this was the next part of my elaborate plot to get off the charges.'

'That you'd told Denny to put another name in the frame to get you off the hook?'

'And that I'd planned this for months. The spider at the centre of the complex web. Like a game of chess. Only you, Denny and I know about the conversation.'

In Durham, Scott had been all for making out everything was falling into place in some grand strategy. Now he seemed a little nervous. It was all right chewing the fat when the only comeback was a healthy dose of scepticism from your audience. There were consequences for playing Machiavelli in court when your liberty was at stake.

'I hope you've deleted my text about it.'

I rather theatrically deleted it in front of him.

'And you've destroyed my little play?'

I sucked my teeth. 'Not exactly.'

'I trust you'll do so.'

And with that we headed for the door. Scott marched quickly off towards the centre of a drizzly Newcastle, dressed as *El Commandante* wearing enough bling to make a Premier League player envious, his future as uncertain as at any time since we'd met.

Chapter Twenty

Call of the Copse

Another day, another text and another grievance, this time about alleged shenanigans by the authorities in Cuba. Scott said he had been contacted by Heidy who told him three 'security men' had visited her at home who had attempted to bribe her and Denny into shifting all the blame of the First Folio theft onto him. One of them, it seemed, did not appear to be Cuban.

'Fucking bastard serious or what?' he summarized in a phrase not borrowed from Shakespeare or old song lyrics as was his usual habit. The use of profanity was a first.

He forwarded me a text he said had been recently sent to him by Heidy.

It read:

> Hola mi vida. Yesterday in the afternoon the mans of the security was at parisien looking for me, they want to know how I meet you, also how I meet denny and other questions about the book, I explain everything mi vida, they also try to offer money, they told me if I can convince denny to accept money if he change the history, I think my vida I'm not sure but one of the man doesn't look like Cuban, maybe not I'm not sure, they told me they will be back again. Now I have a problem at parisien with the director because you know in the hotel national the security is very hard and I can't see or talk with anybody there in the hotel, esta prohibido, this Monday I have a meeting with the director and the security boss of the hotel. Tell me what are you doing my vida. Amor y Bestos tea mo. Mua.

Scott was looking for advice so we agreed to meet in Durham at the Radisson Blu Hotel on the edge of the city centre. He claimed to be appalled about what the text contained but was, by the time we met, a little heartened. 'They must be desperate if they are trying to coerce witnesses.' The inference of the suggestion that one of them wasn't Cuban was that he was one of Durham's finest, which I said I found extremely unlikely.

Scott shrugged. 'They showed no ID. Only two of them spoke, the third man didn't. Heidy said he was fair-skinned.'

I pointed out that that if Durham police had had such grief getting to speak to Denny and Heidy in the past on an official basis, it would be strange they had managed to have one of their officers take part in an unofficial and illegal attempt at coercion. Plus, if true, his lawyers could go to town on it, as it was a blatant attempt at trying to pervert the course of justice.

Scott shrugged again. He said he had contacted the Independent Police Complaints Commission about the matter.

There was something odd about the text from Heidy. It was a curious mixture of perfect and imperfect English. She had also referred to the 'Hotel National' rather the 'Hotel Nacional'. The use and timing of the phrase '*esta prohibido*' for emphasis was similar to letters Scott had sent me in the past and when he spoke.

When I asked if Heidy had really sent the text, he frowned at me as if I was mad and showed me the original text on his own mobile phone. So I left it at that. The IPPC was later to give his letter very short shrift.

The meeting was shorter than normal and I drove him to the station to catch his train. As we headed for the city centre, I parked up briefly outside a multi-storey car park. Scott called his mother to arrange a time for her to pick him up when his train arrived at Darlington. We set off again and he pointed to some trees off by the side of the road.

'Do you see that copse over there? It played a very important part in the First Folio story.'

I glanced briefly at it, then back at Scott. 'How so?'

He gave me one of his infuriating enigmatic looks. 'All will become clear in the fullness of time.'

In the weeks running up to the trial, Scott's moods veered from bullish to melancholic. One day, he sent a jubilant text about an expert's report saying the dimensions of the stolen Durham copy and his were significantly different. He recalled one of the pivotal moments in the OJ Simpson trial when Simpson tried on a glove found at the scene of the murder of his wife, Nicole Brown Simpson, and her lover Ronald Goldman – the glove didn't appear to fit. Scott quoted Simpson's defence attorney, Johnnie Cochran, who had told the jury: 'If it doesn't fit, you must acquit.'

Scott's variant was: 'If the book don't measure up, you must acquit. Sounds good to me.'

Scott sent me the expert's report and while it did highlight the slight discrepancy in size, in all other factors it concluded the Durham and Cuban Copy were one and the same.

On one day in particular, just before the trial started, Scott's mood was to plunge. It had started off well enough when he bought a £60 Panama hat as he put the finishing touches to his proposed wardrobe for the opening day of his trial. He'd even intimated he was to accede to the request by his barrister Toby Hedworth to tone things down for the trial, keep his appearance and arrival at court more understated than previously so as to not adversely influence the jury. Although, the purchase of a Panama hat hinted that his idea of understated and that of Mr Hedworth's might not quite be the same.

We ended up in Zizzi's, an Italian restaurant in Newcastle's Grey Street and, for the first time, we had simply run out of things to talk about. 'Our conversation has reached a hiatus,' said Scott and he excused himself to go to the toilet. He was gone a good 15 minutes. When he returned he sat down, thought for a few moments, then began.

'If this goes wrong and I am found guilty and sent to jail I will have a letter prepared to send to Heidy telling her I'm dead. Complications with treatment for pancreatitis. I have thought about it and I think it only fair on her. She should not have to wait around for me. Maybe she wouldn't anyway.

'My dream of a life with her in the South of France would be gone and it would be painful to cling onto it. Perhaps she'll find another Raymond Scott; she is a beautiful woman, after all.

'Sometimes I think I've been foolish, risking everything. For what? I've lost two years of my life. Sure, I've enjoyed my fifteen minutes of fame – more like fifteen hours – but it has come at a price. Perhaps too high a price. I've had plenty of time to think about this and I believe it to be best for all concerned.'

I told him it seemed melodramatic, and unkind on her.

'She never really cared for me, it was always about money. While I'm sure she found me entertaining and we enjoyed each other's company, I've never deluded myself about my principal attraction to her. As Mrs Merton asked Debbie McGee, "What attracted you to the millionaire Paul Daniels?" She could have asked the same of Heidy about me.'

It seemed foolish also, I said, as it was something she could easily check out.

Scott shook his head. 'It's time to a draw a line under proceedings.'

Chapter Twenty-One

The Trial of Raymond S

On Tuesday, June 15th 2010, nearly two years to the day since Scott first walked in the Shakespeare Folger Library with the copy of a First Folio, the trial was set to begin. I sent a good luck text and asked how he felt.

He replied: 'I've never lived so INTENSIVELY in all my life its FANTASTICO!'

His interpretation of 'understated' soon became evident. Scott had arrived at Newcastle Crown Court in a silver Chrysler 300 limousine and emerged into the media throng flanked by four burly bodyguards. He was dressed in a tan, pinstripe suit, his Panama hat, white snakeskin loafers and Tiffany sunglasses. The summer sun glinted off of his Cartier watch, Rolex bracelet and Gucci rings as he flashed 'V' for victory signs. Everything, apart from a marching band.

The best part of the day was taken up with legal arguments over whether his previous convictions would be admissible. It was only late in the afternoon when a jury of seven women and five men were sworn in, and the hearing adjourned for the trial to start proper the next day.

Meanwhile, nearly 300 miles away and with considerably less fanfare, the trial of William Jacques had begun at Southwark Crown Court in London. Charged with stealing rare volumes of *Nouvelle Iconographies des Camellias* by Ambroise Verschaffelt between June 2004 and March 2007 from the Royal Horticultural Society's Lindley Library in London, the court heard that police found an A4 piece of paper with the names of 70 volumes of rare books kept at the library, which were listed in sequential order as to where they could be found.

The Trial of Raymond S

It was described as a 'thief's shopping list'. Notes were also made as to their valuation and whether they included maps and plates, which could be removed and sold separately.

The court was told the crime was a 'systematic, carefully planned theft committed by a man who knew precisely what he was doing'. Staff had become suspicious, as Jacques had kept turning up in the same plain tweed jacket.

I met with Scott at the end of the first day's hearing at Destination bar where a few months previously he'd spoken excitedly about Denny's 'confession' to him that he had been given the First Folio to look after by a man called 'Jacks'.

There was no sign of Scott's burly minders and, unlike our previous meeting there in the freezing rain, it was balmy and hot so we sat outside. 'It's like Cuba,' he said, wafting himself cool with the Panama hat.

'Nice understated arrival this morning,' I said, and he smiled.

'I gave it some thought but in the end, what could I do? It's just not me to skulk into court. We're in Court 10, at the top of the building. The Penthouse, just as I prefer.'

He took a drink from his Lucozade bottle. 'We had a small victory today. Well, actually quite a big one. The prosecution wanted to introduce my previous convictions but Toby successfully argued against it. They concerned modern books that had never been stolen from Durham. Therefore in the eyes of the jury I am a virgin, my record is clean. Yes, it's been a good day.'

So you've never stolen any books from Durham? I asked.

'I've never been prosecuted for stealing books in Durham,' he said with another enigmatic smile. Foregoing any battle of semantics, which no doubt would end in a chess simile, I instead asked what his barrister thought of his chances.

'He said, "Raymond, we have a mountain to climb." I asked Everest or Ben Nevis? He said somewhere in between. His concern is the lies I've told to the police about my movements and my background.'

And the following day, when Robert Smith QC, flanked by his

second, Mark Giuliani, opened for the prosecution, Scott's lies were laid out in great detail.

Mr Smith said that after arriving at the Folger library with the First Folio, he had told chief librarian Richard Kuhta he had just arrived from Cuba where he liked to go to fishing, that he had inherited a construction business from his father and that he himself was a multi-millionaire. Scott had described how he had a residence in Switzerland, that his mother lived in Monaco and gave the impression he was independently wealthy and it did not matter whether the book was valuable or not.

Mr Smith told how Scott's passport contained references at the back as to who should be contacted in an emergency. These included the manager of a Liechtenstein bank and his mother at an address in Monte Carlo. And then, with Scott sitting in the dock in all his designer glory, occasionally adjusting his Tiffany sunglasses with a heavily bejewelled hand, came the punch line.

'The truth was Raymond Scott lived in a house at 3 Wigeon Close, Washington – not DC, but Tyne and Wear – with his mother. He had written into the back of his passport his mother's address as an address in Monte Carlo in order to present a false image of himself to the Folger library staff. The evidence will establish that he was not a wealthy man by any means. On the contrary, he was living on state benefits and the evidence in the case will establish that he was living way beyond his means.

'He had incurred debts to the tune of more than £90,000 by way of credit card and bank liabilities by the time this meeting in Washington took place and he had been spending his mother's money as well. His mother did not of course live in Monaco. The address, which he had written into the rear of his passport for her, was that of a 5-star hotel in Monte Carlo and he did not have a place of residence in Switzerland. He had not inherited a construction company. He had indeed been visiting Cuba, in February 2008, but he had certainly not just arrived from Cuba when he met Richard Kuhta in Washington.'

I recalled my first meeting with Scott when he had said the same thing – how he had travelled from Cuba via Nassau to Washington to go the Folger. He'd later amended his story to say that he actually first set eyes on the First Folio in the February and had taken it home to Wigeon Close before, four months later, flying to Washington with it. But what he said first to the police counted and any amendment would be seen not as a display of inexact recall to be blamed on drinking too much champagne, but of plain deceit. I winced at the mention of his passport not containing his home address, as he'd told me so many months ago this was proof of his ignorance of theft.

Smith continued: 'The evidence establishes that he had met a Cuban woman when he visited Cuba in February 2008 and had become infatuated with her. He began transferring substantial sums of money to her which he could ill afford to do and which he borrowed for that purpose.'

He went on to detail how, after Scott left, Kuhta called in colleagues to examine the book and they concluded that it was a First Folio, and how he was 'unhappy' and 'suspicious' about the circumstances which Scott claimed to have come by it.

Then, Smith detailed, how at the next meeting two days later, Scott had handed over $2,500 in $100 bills to join the Folger Library Renaissance Group and given Kuhta two bow ties as a gift.

'Since the defendant had no assets but was heavily in debt, you may wish to examine his motives in making this payment to the library,' said Smith. 'You may wish to ask whether this donation, from monies that he could not afford to provide, was done to assist the library or was part of a dishonest veneer that the defendant wanted to portray of a wealthy man with no interest in the value of the book that he was seeking authentication for.'

Smith didn't go so far as to suggest the $2,500 was intended as a bribe to Kuhta, as one of Kuhta's friends had speculated, but he was not far short of it. Scott was being hoist by his own very extravagant petard. My impression, no doubt coloured by my numerous meetings with him and witnessing his idiosyncrasies first hand, had been of a showy man eager to impress, showering presents like confetti. The prosecution, understandably, had taken a different view – that of a con man doing his ground work, setting the scene. For a man up to his neck in debt, it appeared a spectacularly ill-advised gesture.

After agreeing to independent book expert Stephen Massey looking at the First Folio, Scott had then flown onto Cuba. Before setting off he had written a letter, on Mayflower Hotel stationery, in which Scott had made reference to Denny and Heidy and the intention to sell the book and the suggestion of a $10,000 a year donation to the Folger from each, in perpetuity. A Liechtenstein bank was identified as the bank to which the proceeds of the sale were to be credited. And on it went. Smith spoke of Massey's involvement and his identifying the book as the Durham First Folio. And of the pages and binding removed to disguise its true provenance: 'A cultural legacy that had been damaged and brutalised' but still worth about $1.5 million.

My mind flitted back again to our first few meetings when Scott had been adamant there was not one 'scintilla' of evidence to prove it was the Durham copy. How, even a few weeks before the trial, he had said that his barrister was still going to query whether they were one and the same book. That strategy – if it did exist in the first place – had been binned. The DNA of the First Folio, despite attempts to remove it, was sufficiently intact for it to be incontrovertibly identified.

Scott's problem was that not only had he been telling lies, but that they were easily disproved. The Liechtenstein bank account he had planned to put the proceeds of the sale of the First Folio in, was opened on May 15th 2008. This was a month before, as he had originally maintained to me, that he had seen the book for the first time. (He closed the account on July 31st and transferred the credit balance of £998 to his mother's bank account in England).

On May 21st, Scott booked a direct flight to Washington which was to leave London's Heathrow Airport on June 15th. As was to be the case with the vast majority of all the transactions, the people who dealt with Scott remembered him well.

There was an indisputable paper trail documenting his many purchases in England when he claimed that he was in Havana, preparing to travel to the US with the First Folio.

In January 2008, he acquired a Post Office Travel Money Card, where he put funds for himself for use in Cuba. Subsequently, he gave the card to Heidy, who later withdrew thousands of pounds from it. In May, he made three phone calls to the same travel agent asking about flights to Nassau from Washington in order to fly onward to Cuba.

In June, he went on a spending spree in Newcastle and London. He bought Hugo Boss swimming shorts, a Vivienne Westwood T-shirt, the Tiffany sunglasses he was to wear to court and our many meetings which cost £499.95, a pair of £420 shoes, as well as putting £3,000 into the Post Office Travel Money Card account. He bought boating shoes, Armani flip-flops, a pair of Lacoste shorts, and more Vivien Westwood, in the form of a blue swimwear top.

On June 10th, he went back to the Vivienne Westwood shop and presented a female shop assistant with a large hardback 'Vivienne Westwood' book. He said it had belonged to his wife but they were getting rid of books and giving them to charity as they were moving to Cuba. The book appeared brand new and unused. He bought jewellery, Hugo Boss linen shorts, a Lacoste Polo top, telling assistants that he was going to Cuba for a four-week fishing holiday.

Rather cuttingly, Mr Smith said: 'Several of the shop staff who sold these items to him remarked upon the discordance between his appearance and age and the clothes that he was buying.'

On June 14th 2008, he had begun his journey to Washington, not from Cuba but from Durham railway station, travelling first to King's Cross in London. He had checked into the Marriott Hotel at Heathrow and tried to pay with his Mastercard. The transaction was refused and he had to pay cash – £104.58. He checked out the next morning and took the British Airways flight to Washington later that day.

After the meetings at the Folger, he flew to Cuba where he remained until July 3rd when he flew to Madrid and, the next day, on to Paris. He obtained access to Ritz Hotel notepaper – there was no proof other than his say-so that he had actually stayed there – and written on it to Kuhta. He had also enclosed the letters written on Hotel Nacional de Cuba paper by Heidy and Denny and the three books in Spanish to Kuhta as well as the box of cigars and another 'worthless' Spanish book to Stephen Massey.

When he returned to Durham, he was arrested by police there on July 10th. In all, he had credited the Post Office Travel Card with a total of £10,100 between January and July 2008, all of the cash being withdrawn from ATM machines in Cuba – and all but £122 being withdrawn when Scott wasn't there.

Many attempts had been made to withdraw cash when there were insufficient funds in the account, indicating that whoever was using the card as a regular source of money was unaware of the credit balance. No prizes for guessing who was taking out the money, the lovely Heidy.

And where was the money coming from? Apart from the credit cards, Scott was getting £60 a week in Income Support and a Carer's Allowance from the Disability and Carers Service of £50.55 a week. His credit card debt had risen from £1090.19 in 2002 to £44,292.59 by the end of 2007, and it had soared during the first six months of 2008 to around £90,000.

Mr Smith commented: 'The defendant's debts were increasing at a rate which was clearly unsustainable. The payment of money to foster his relationship with this lady in Cuba and the holidays he had spent there and continued to plan for could not continue to be funded by credit cards and overdrafts. Nor could a lifestyle which involved inviting Heidy Garcia Rios to England and driving a Ferrari.

'The evidence establishes that he was in receipt of correspondence from banks and financial institutions imposing pressure upon him during this time and the prosecution submit that he must have been becoming desperate for money. The letters from financial institutions and banks were coming in every day during May and June 2008, when the defendant was making preparations for his visit to Washington to sell the First Folio as the letters recovered by the police from his home demonstrate.'

Mr Smith said it was then Scott that decided to hatch his plan to sell the First Folio, using Heidy and Denny for his cover story and trying to remove anything which could identify it as the Durham copy.

'He was not sufficiently aware of the subtleties which surrounded the cataloguing and census of the book by experts such as Dr Anthony West.'

These subtleties included the addition of the handwritten words 'Troilus and Cressida' on the contents page, cuts and cut-outs in 26 pages of the Tragedies recorded before the theft, the gilded edges of the Folio which matched the Durham copy and fragments of goatskin left after the removal of the binding, which also matched the stolen Folio. There were other creases and tears, matching sewing supports on the binding and the fact no replacement leaves were found in the Durham Folio as none were found in the one Scott took to the Folger.

Mr Smith concluded: 'The prosecution say that the defendant is a dishonest con man. He carefully planned the sale of this book and destroyed the obvious signs which could lead to proof that it was the Durham First Folio. He has told many lies, to the experts at the Folger library, to other people and to the police.'

I met Scott after the day's hearing in Eldon Gardens in the centre of Newcastle. A regular gathering place for Goths, winos, junkies and people with nothing better to do, it was even more popular than usual because of the continuing heat wave that had the city perspiring.

'I think it went OK,' was his summary of the day's proceedings. 'Obviously it was very one-sided as the prosecution is first in to bat. But my time will come. He presented no evidence as to theft other than I was in possession of the stolen book. Lies do not constitute theft. The jury has to be sure beyond reasonable doubt that I actually took it.

'Toby said he thought we were all right with the Judge Richard

Lowden. He's a "red robe" judge who made his name as a prosecutor and they tend to have a natural bias towards the prosecution but Toby said he thought not in this case. We shall of course see.'

He took a drink from his bottle of Lucozade as a minor disturbance over whose turn it was to drink from a cider bottle took place in front of us. Scott tutted scornfully: 'They give drunks a bad name.'

He turned to me again: 'I am of course drinking lemonade during the trial.'

'Funny looking lemonade,' I said.

'During the day I am drinking lemonade. After the day's proceedings is a different matter.'

He was wearing a fawn-coloured pinstripe suit. Up close it was quite sober looking. He could have been a typical office worker or businessman – if you ignored the snakeskin shoes and the bling. I pointed this out to him.

'It's been a bit strange this week. It's like having a job for the first time in my life. Nine-to-five. Get up early, shave, breakfast. Regular hours. I keep thinking of Reggie Perrin and making excuses for being late. Sorry CJ, Puma on the line at Chester-le-Street, that sort of thing.'

I asked if his mother had been following proceedings.

'Oh, no. She doesn't watch the news or read the papers. She thinks it's just a dispute about ownership of the book. I was relieved she wasn't on the jury or my fate would have been sealed. She would find me guilty for my own good.'

The next day the main exhibit was produced – the First Folio. It was carried into court amidst great security in a padlocked black plastic strongbox. As it was removed and placed on a cushion next to the witness box, the packed court strained to catch a glimpse of it. As Scott said, "it didn't look like much".

Compared to what it did look like in 1998 before its theft, with its binding and leaves in place, it certainly didn't look much. Before, even in its plainness, it had a certain majesty. Any old or ancient object which has been preserved in pristine condition reflects well on its owners. Now it looked like a book that had been left with a bored teenager with destructive tendencies. Something knocked about and carelessly dealt with, which, of course, created a certain impression about the person who last had it in his hands. Particularly so when the prosecution stated it had been mutilated for criminal ends.

The former Durham University librarian and Keeper of Rare Books, Ian Doyle, who gave evidence about the importance of the First Folio and later Richard Kuhta, flown in from Washington DC, cut earnest, academic figures with whom you could trust your life savings. Dressed soberly, they spoke reverentially of the book on the cushion next to them. In Kuhta's case there was more than a hint of dismay at the ravages inflicted upon it.

A not-so-sober-suited Scott, occasionally adjusting his designer shades, sat impassively in the dock a few feet away from it as the jurors' eyes flicked from the First Folio to him and back again.

As much importance as what is said in a court case is how the defendants appear and conduct themselves. Scott, to labour the point, had done himself no favours. The penny, eventually, dropped a couple of days later.

I had met up with him again at Zizzi's restaurant for a post-hearing meal and chat and, even for Scott, he was wearing the loudest shirt, so loud I was tempted to borrow his Tiffany shades to protect my eyes from its glare. It was an electric-blue Versace shirt with ostentatious gold trim. He was wearing it beneath a leather jacket, the image completed by black jeans and dark winkle-picker boots.

'I wanted to look like Romeo but ended up feeling more like Falstaff,' said Scott, as a waiter arrived at our table, gave him a slightly stunned once-over and took our order.

'It's a Versace shirt at the height of his creative powers just before he was shot in Miami. It's the same vintage as Liz Hurley's safety pin dress. That was one of his more conservative ones. I have about half a dozen of them in all, which I bought from the Versace shop in New Bond Street. They're worth hundreds and hundreds of pounds. A bit of an investment.'

However, if it was unwise of him to wear such a shirt at all during the case, his timing of wearing it that specific day was particularly bad. After much legal argument the Judge had agreed to allow evidence from the defence about Jacques and his alleged connection with the stolen First Folio. However, to allow that, the prosecution had successfully argued for Scott's previous to be outlined to the jury. Today, his previous had been presented in court.

'I must say I came to regret my choice of apparel,' admitted Scott. 'Someone once said that all men wearing Versace looked like cocaine dealers and the women looked like high-class hookers. Perhaps a more conservative approach was what was needed. But I am what I am and what's done is done.'

Typically, the hint of self-doubt disappeared quickly. 'It's all very theatrical, the courtroom. The judge, the barristers all have their black gowns and wigs. I have my costume. The intent is to intimidate and I won't be intimidated.'

Then it reappeared just as quickly. 'My moods swing. You know when people say "I'm worried to death"? I didn't actually know what that was like but for some reason last weekend I was worried to death. I wasn't thinking of taking my own life but it was an awful time. My sleeping is fitful at the best of times but my mind was racing. I spent the night pacing up and down. Everything is out of my control; my fate is in other people's hands and for what? A book. For love. I keep asking myself again has it all been worth it?'

We talk once more about the letter to Heidy saying he had died. 'It arrived yesterday from Sunderland. It cost £25 to translate into the Spanish language. I haven't decided yet. I think if I'm convicted, I'll send it.'

His phone rang. 'Hello, Mother. I'm with the journalist, having a bite to eat. Everything went great in court today. Yes, fine. Soon be over. I'll be on my usual train. Yes, see you then.'

He hung up, for a moment contemplating his half-eaten dish, then turned to me again. 'I've written two other letters and given them to my solicitor to send if it goes wrong. One is to my cousin, Adrienne; the other is to my mother. To my mother, I say I'm sorry.

I didn't steal the First Folio but there is circumstantial evidence that I handled it knowing it was stolen.'

I referred back to the previous conversation about Heidy and Denny, how he said it was all about the money for them.

'I didn't mean they wanted money in such a mercenary way – *in vino veritas*, perhaps. Perhaps people might think I'm mercenary too. But I'm not a monster. I'm kind, I'm a considerate man. It wasn't just about sex. I would have gone round with Heidy as a friend. I wasn't just interested in shagging. For me it was important to be seen out and about Havana dressed to the nines with a beautiful young Cuban girlfriend.'

'Shagging' wasn't a usual Scott word. In the past he had been coy about giving any details about his sex life with Heidy. Out of respect to her, I assumed, or out of respect to what he saw as the character of their relationship. He was painfully aware of how it seemed to the outside world, but company – the more attractive the better – was perhaps more important. It allowed him to play the part of 'the ageing Lothario', his favourite description of himself in newspaper reports.

'Lothario not being a character from Shakespeare's plays but *Don Quixote* by Cervantes,' said Scott.

As to who was the seducer and the seduced in Scott's world, there was one point on the forming of the 'triumvirate' that was still not nailed down conclusively. Did Heidy introduce Scott to Denny, as he first said, or did Denny introduce Scott to Heidy, which he had occasionally alluded to in the past but backtracked about when pushed? The answer could be of significance.

'There's a possibility we're talking now about a lonely male traveller who had come to Cuba. Not a sex tourist – they go to Thailand. But you have a guy, he's all alone, that sort of thing …' Scott's voice trailed off.

I asked again who did the introductions to whom.

'Do you know the test they do for colour blindness?' he asked.

'No.' I sighed heavily.

'They have those colour cards within which is contained the

shape of a number and if you haven't got it you see 69.' He sniggers briefly at the mention of 69.

'If you can't see it, or see 96 or something, then you are colour blind. It's about what you see and how it can be interpreted differently.'

He lost me there.

Scott added: 'It's a chicken and egg situation, sort of thing.'

I resisted the temptation to bang my head on the table. Among Scott's haul during his shoplifting spree from 1993 onwards as detailed to the court were books, whiskey, brandy, a crystal vase and a smoke alarm. An eclectic mix. There were two more shoplifting charges while on bail since his arrest for the Shakespeare First Folio case – books again and two figurines worth £150 from the John Lewis store in Eldon Square.

Scott consoled himself with the fact that while the list was lengthy, the items taken were of a mundane nature and nothing like the First Folio. 'Like an inveterate bike thief being accused of pinching a Rolls-Royce,' he said.

It was just as well that Scott – no doubt at the strenuous insistence of Hedworth – was sticking to the decision not to take the stand. For what happened next gave an insight into the damage he could inflict on his own chances when left to his own devices. Perhaps he had become bored or frustrated listening to the prosecution and defence crossing swords in front of him while he watched impotently from the dock.

He had spoken to me about disagreements with his counsel and had offered his opinion as to how the case was proceeding, but it seemed to Scott that Hedworth had adopted the stance of legendary football manager Brian Clough. 'If anyone disagrees with me,' Clough had said, 'we have a discussion and after fifteen minutes decide I'm right.'

As time went on, Scott's unquestioning belief in, and championing of, the adroit courtroom skills of Hedworth were waning. He had positively gone off Hedworth's junior counsel, Caroline Goodwin, mainly it seemed for always backing up Hedworth. On the Friday at the end of the third week we had gone to Vujon's, an upmarket Indian restaurant off Newcastle's Quayside. Next week was going to be the final week of the trial and Scott was in philosophical mood.

'Come what may, whatever the outcome, I've given them a fight and I'll continue to give them a fight. I've not been remanded in custody but I've had it hanging over for me for so long. I'm sure the police would have liked to have sorted it out quicker but what sticks in my craw is the seizing of the property which belongs to my mother and late father, basically what they worked all their lives for.'

The sound of a text arriving on my mobile disturbed his reverie. It was from a colleague at work. It said 'U know Raymond Scott walked in 2 cop shop with new rare book last nite?'

I didn't. I could have screamed or punched Scott in the face or both. I took a deep breath and asked about it as politely as I could through gritted teeth.

'You didn't know about it?' he asked, all innocence.

Work commitments meant I hadn't been able to physically go to the trial, instead following it from stories in the paper and Scott's interpretation of events. I had soon become aware of the wild discrepancy in content of these two sources. While the newspaper reports appeared damning, Scott seemed in the main upbeat with only the occasional brief period of doubt. Now I kind of guessed why. He was censoring out the bad stuff and only repeating the good which explained why his synopsis of a day's hearing usually took just a few minutes.

What happened and why? I asked.

'I went in to Peterlee police station and surrendered two paintings from Fenwicks. There was a security camera on the wall of the store. The footage showed me walk by the paintings with a bag but not actually take them. I said to Toby it was like walking into a room and finding a bottle of cream upturned then seeing a cat at the other side of the room and putting two-and-two together. Toby said "no, it's like seeing the cat tip over the cream". I said I didn't think so. He said "I do".'

'They're valued at about a thousand pounds. It was on a Saturday and what motivated me to do it were the Picasso prints taken from my mother's house by the police. Pencil drawings, done mainly in 1946 of his mistress Francoise Gilot. 'Francoise au Noeud dans les Cheveux' – 'Francoise with a Bow in her Hair'. Beautiful, serene. I thought it right I get something to hang on the wall in their place. It was an opportunist theft.

'I knew today they were going to show the video footage of the theft to the jury. I thought it would be damaging to me if they thought I'd sold them so I decided to hand them in. I decided to hand in a Latin ecclesiastical dictionary I'd bought in Cuba as well. It was published in 1627 – four years after the First Folio – and was bound in Vellum.

'I thought it was time, like Tal would do, to make a sacrifice, just to confuse the jury basically.'

Mikhail Tal was a chess grandmaster who became the youngest world champion in 1960, before Gary Kasparov assumed the mantle 25 years later. Tal was a famously attacking player, similar to Bobby Fischer.

'I'm concerned that the jury, because of my travel itinerary, will think I've never been to Cuba. Toby wasn't best pleased.'

Oh, why's that? I asked, imagining the irony dripping from my tongue. Obviously, my delivery wasn't up to scratch as it didn't seem to register.

'He said the prosecution will say it shows I steal things, hide them away and then produce them at a later date when it suits me. It matches their theory that I stole the First Folio and kept it hidden for 10 years. I don't think so, but what's done is done,' said Scott, not for the first time.

'Toby and Caroline Goodwin – I'm actually really starting to dislike her in fact – they profess to know how juries think. I don't think that's true. I think they afford the jury too much intelligence and sophistication. But, you know, life goes on.'

Was it stolen?

'Not as far as I'm aware.'

How can you not be aware whether it was stolen or not?

'I got it in Cuba in 2008.'

It was his final answer. Like the jury and no doubt his learned counsel, I was well and truly 'Tal-ed' too. And, of course, it showed he had a place unknown to police where he kept stuff. A special room in Durham Constabulary HQ had been set aside for all the items they had taken from his house and they pretty much filled it, Argos catalogue and all. There was no way they would have missed the two paintings, not to mention the Latin dictionary which, as well as in age, was similar in size to the First Folio.

Part of his defence was that if he had stolen the First Folio, where were the other items from Durham University which had been taken at the same time? They had never surfaced since, and they weren't found at his house. The implication now was, like Jacques, Scott had a secure place known just to him. What else could he be keeping there?

Jacques had been found guilty of the theft of 13 books from the Lindley Library in London. Before adjourning the case for sentencing, Recorder Michael Holland QC rather pompously told Jacques: 'You are a Cambridge graduate and should know better.'

Jacques, his criminal past and his alleged connection to the theft of the First Folio, were going to be examined by Hedworth the following week in defence of Scott – the grammar school boy who seemed to rejoice in not knowing any better.

Which is why I shouldn't have been surprised when I met him the following day, he confessed to the Durham University theft.

Chapter Twenty-Two

The Unusual Suspect

We'd met up again at the Fallen Angel hotel in Durham. Scott stepped out of the Pecanto wearing another of his Versace shirts, nuclear yellow being the best way to describe its colour and effect on my eyeballs. I waved at his mum as she drove off and he handed me another set of gifts – two Che Guevara readers on politics and revolution and two Cuban cigars.

We walked into the hotel, 18 months since we had first set foot in the place together on that freezing January night when we ended up in the New York suite. Today, as it had done for weeks, the un-British-like sun continued to beat down and we headed to the garden in the back. Less than a mile away was Durham University library where the First Folio was again *in situ*. Closer to us was Durham police station. More ominously, just 200 metres away was Durham prison, Scott's destination after the trial if things didn't go his way.

He began by talking about Bruce Reynolds, the mastermind of the great train robbery. Over the months I'd learned to let him go on with his anecdotes, as more often than not there was a point to them.

'He wrote an autobiography about his life in crime. I haven't read many, but that is one of the best. He's a very intelligent man. He mentioned the jobs he'd been on, serious armed robberies, like the hold up of an armoured car in Chelsea and also the London airport job – nicknamed the 'bowler-hat job' because two of the thieves were dressed as city gents. The proceeds were £62,000, which was a hell of a lot of money in those days, but they were disappointed as the man who marked their card – the inside man – said there would be something like £300,000. After paying each of the robbers a £6,000 cut, they used £5,000 to buy Leatherslade farm, the hideout for the Great Train Robbery.

'The interesting thing was he was never charged with the robbery on the van in Chelsea, but in his autobiography he mentions it in detail. It was a long time ago, but this country doesn't have a statute of limitations and you just wonder what the legal situation is. Here he is admitting to something for which he hasn't been charged. Maybe it was true, maybe it wasn't. I think it was.'

The relevance of his paean to Bruce Reynolds was yet to become clear. We went on yet another walkabout in Durham, this time it had the aura of a farewell tour. We strolled along the cobbled streets, stopping off at various newsagents for Scott to flick through copies of the papers to see how much coverage his court case was getting. There was no two-for-one meal voucher this time – Scott seemed too distracted to eat just yet – so we went into a couple of bars to buy a drink for me, while he sipped from his Lucozade bottle.

We looped back round to Old Elvet and the County Hotel where Scott finally decided he was hungry and we ordered something to eat after much deliberation. There wasn't any lobster thermidor on the menu, or filet mignon or langoustines, so he went for cheeseburger and chips, which we shared. We sat out in the garden at the back as kids from a wedding party went about dirtying their posh clothes and lobbing toilet roll at each other as their parents drank and let them get on with it. The party had obviously been going on for a while, as the garden resembled the goalmouth of a football match, circa 1970.

After a moment contemplating the debris, Scott said: 'Turn the tape recorder off.' An hour later, I turned it back on as I drove away from Durham and hurriedly recounted everything he had told me. I remembered quite clearly the first thing he said, 'You know I did it, don't you?'

I had replied, I didn't. I thought such a theft was beyond him. Too much planning and preparation had gone into it and there must have been a fair degree of patience, first with the checking out of the library and then having the tools and wherewithal to force entry into the cabinets and take the books and documents. Scott struck me as someone who on a whim stole soft targets from shops. Even at this, judging by the amount of past convictions he had, he wasn't very good. He was a petty thief and would have had to be in front of a draconian judge to face jail time for these petty thefts.

The Durham First Folio theft was in a different league altogether. It was high risk, relying on timing and the perpetrator being discreet, as well as unobtrusive, faculties that did not come naturally to Scott. And if he got caught, a custodial sentence was inevitable.

I told him my theory had him getting to know Jacques after bumping into him by chance in Cuba. Although seemingly fanciful, I had reasons for the assumption. When we first met, Scott had said he was probably in St Moritz or Pontresina at the time of the Durham University theft. Months later he texted me about having found a picture of himself at a party in Havana around the time of the theft in 1998. When I texted him back saying I thought he had said that he was in one of those two Swiss ski resorts, he expressed surprise and said I must be mistaken. However, while I knew of St Moritz I'd never heard of Pontresina before he mentioned it. I could hardly have mistakenly identified somewhere I didn't know existed. Later, he described how he went to Cuba three times a year from around this time, one of the periods coinciding with Jacques' flight there.

My theory was that he had either bought the First Folio from Jacques or that Jacques had given it to him for safe keeping. Many months previously, Scott had come up with the rather theatrical scenario of receiving a letter containing a note with just a mobile phone number which he rang and spoke, he assumed, to Jacques. During the conversation he was given certain information about First Folio thefts in the past. Yet, judging by reports, Jacques was a classic case of someone who 'kept himself to himself' and volunteered nothing to people he didn't know. To have acted as Scott said, appeared as much out of character for Jacques as Scott actually stealing the First Folio from Durham University.

Scott seemed genuinely surprised that I thought him incapable of the theft. He said that in 1998, he had indeed been 'scoping' out

Durham library and had seen five cabinets – two wooden and three metal ones. 'The three metal ones were an absolute no-no,' he said. With him he had a screwdriver and a plastic bag and when no one was around he broke into one of the wooden cabinets that contained three books and two manuscripts which he put into the plastic bag and then made his way out.

During Scott's case, the court was told of security arrangements in the library, which included a 'manned desk'. Scott said that as he walked out, the desk wasn't manned and he got outside unchallenged and made his way off. The First Folio had been in the second wooden cabinet and Scott said he saw it but decided it was too big to get away with. He then kicked himself because he hadn't been stopped and it had all been so easy. Then Scott asked: 'Do you remember that copse I mentioned a few months ago?'

I nodded and he said that he emptied the contents of the plastic bag and hid them there before going back to the library, forcing the other cabinet, and taking the First Folio. Again, he was not stopped, the desk remained unmanned, and he made his way back to the copse to collect the other books and documents, and then went home.

He said he kept them all, but in 2007, when he reached the age of fifty, he decided to do something about them. By then he had met Heidy and Denny, and had enjoyed a night to remember in Havana on his fifty-first birthday. In 2006, he had read with great interest about the Dr Williams' copy of the First Folio which had sold for around £3 million at auction. The Durham copy was in a similarly pristine condition and it was only then, according to Scott, that he realized quite how much it might be worth. Now, with visions of his dream life of wealth and a beautiful young woman on his arm, he decided to sell the Folio. He came up with the idea of a Cuban provenance for the book and set about removing the pages and binding which could identify it as the Durham First Folio.

I reminded him that in court, expert Daniel De Simone said that the person who did this had shown a degree of expertise in removing the leaves and binding. Scott said: 'Not really. All I needed was a hacksaw and a pair of pliers.'

I said I thought that he then took it to Washington DC. Scott admitted a large part of him knew it was 'madness' going there and didn't think the Folger would take it. He hoped they might buy it privately, assuming they had the money.

'I paused outside the front door for a while then said to myself "let's do it, let's go for it", like a First World War army officer exhorting his troops to go over the top.'

He said that when he was in his twenties, he decided to become a thief as it was the only way to achieve the means to get out of his 'socio-economic status'. Scott described how he had stolen numerous modern books over the years and would take them to London and sell them to second-hand bookstores, making around £500 a time.

He claimed that he got to know several members of the Newcastle criminal fraternity, one man in particular who he had given alibi evidence for when the man had come to trial. Scott's testimony had been ignored. With the man, Scott claimed he planned a jewellery 'heist' in London in the 1980s. 'I said we needed to do one big job and then retire on the proceeds,' he recalled.

He said it wasn't Graffs, the well-known Mayfair diamond store in the news recently after it was robbed, but somewhere near it. Scott described how he had bought a car in Manchester to use for the getaway and parked it in a London lock-up. On the day of the planned raid he had gone to collect it, but couldn't get to the vehicle as someone had changed the locks on the lock-up.

As for Jacques, Scott said that he was not involved. Scott just took advantage of the fact of the 'massive coincidence', uncovered by his defence team, of Jacques having fled to Havana. As far as he was aware, Jacques had never met Denny.

When I asked what happened to the rest of the books and documents stolen from Durham University, he said they were being kept safe somewhere and hinted that other people might have them.

That was basically it, Scott had claimed. Was it the truth, the whole truth and nothing but the truth – or anything but the truth?

There was much more detail compared to the earlier 'fairy story' he had told me at our first meeting. Then, there was his interest in how Bruce Reynolds had seemingly confessed to a crime he hadn't been charged with and wondering how he got away with it. If Scott was found guilty of the charges, he said Hedworth already had plans to appeal on the grounds that Judge Lowden had allowed his previous convictions to be heard by the jury, which had had an adverse effect on the fairness of the court proceedings. It would look odd, to say the least, if he appealed against a conviction for a crime he was now admitting to carrying out.

And if he was cleared of the charges, how would the authorities react to his 'confession'? As I was pondering the latest Scott conundrum, a text duly arrived from him.

> ALL LIES AND JEST STILL A MAN HEARS WHAT HE WANTS TO HEAR AND DISREGARDS THE REST
> (SIMON AND GARFUNKEL'S THE BOXER ONE OF THEIR GREAT LYRICAL TRIUMPHS).

My initial reaction was 'you bastard', but on reflection it was predictable for the reasons outlined. It was a high-risk strategy and he needed deniability.

Or was he indeed just making it up? The film *The Usual Suspects* had been on TV recently and my mind strayed to its main character Roger 'Verbal' Kint, played by Kevin Spacey. Kint, a seemingly pathetic petty conman suffering from cerebral palsy, is interrogated by a police officer about what happened on a boat in which five people are massacred after a drug deal goes wrong, and he is only one of two survivors. He comes up with an elaborate explanation and speaks of a criminal mastermind, Keyser Soze, as being behind it.

After Verbal is released, the detective suddenly realizes that Verbal had used objects in his cluttered office to provide names and details to make up his elaborate tale, and Verbal is in fact Keyser Soze.

In his story, Scott said he used the 'massive coincidence' of Jacques, the notorious 'tome raider' who went on the run to Cuba, as the basis of his elaborate tale. His friend, Denny, who he said had been entrusted with the First Folio by Jacques before giving it to him, is beyond British law and cannot confirm or deny this. He spoke of his criminal past and a 'heist' gone wrong on a jewellery store close to Graffs when only that week a jewellery heist on Graffs was in the news.

Scott seemed incapable of stealing a modern book without being caught, yet talked of trips to London with what must be large batches of stolen books, if, as he says, he was earning £500 a time.

However, unlike Verbal, who is doing his utmost to evade being unmasked as Keyser Soze, Scott seems hellbent on implicating himself before the usual last moment back-tracking.

In the final scene of *The Usual Suspects*, Verbal is seen limping away on a crooked leg which slowly rights itself while it dawns on the officer that he has been hoodwinked. The last line of the movie has Verbal describing the near mythical Soze as someone who appears 'and like that, he's gone'.

Verbal – or rather Soze – is then seen getting into the back of a limo and being driven off as the detective tries in vain to catch him. While Scott was given to arriving to court in a limo, the chances of him getting away in one were slim.

On the Monday morning of the final week of the trial, the press benches were packed. During the trial's course, their numbers had waned, but this day it was going to be revealed, once and for all, whether Scott was going to take the stand, and they had arrived for the possible spectacle.

However, their hopes were soon dashed when Hedworth stood up to tell the court that Scott would not be giving evidence as whatever he said would be 'rubbished' by the prosecution because of his dishonest past. He added that allowing Scott to be cross-examined would be like 'throwing a Christian to the lions' and prosecutors would 'turn him inside out' with ease.

The press bench quickly emptied for, much to Scott's chagrin, a more dramatic story was unfolding just a few miles from Newcastle Crown Court. On the Thursday when Scott had walked into Peterlee police station to hand over the Latin dictionary and two paintings, a certain Raoul Moat had been released from nearby Durham jail. Moat was a man with a grudge against the police which was exacerbated by his former girlfriend who told him she had started going out with a policeman. This was untrue. Her hope that this would put off reprisals by Moat was in vain. He had quickly armed himself and begun to run amok.

A few hours before I'd met Scott on the Saturday, Moat shot his ex, Samantha Stobbart, and her new boyfriend Chris Brown, seriously injuring her and killing him. In the early hours of Sunday morning, he'd turned his gun on police officer David Rathband, leaving him permanently blind, before going on the run.

The hunt for Moat provided a dramatic backdrop to the finale of Scott's trial. As armed police spent the week running him to ground, with the world's media not far behind, events at Newcastle Crown Court unfolded more or less out of the spotlight.

As a result, the introduction of Jacques into Scott's case went unreported. Scott later described how an officer who had investigated his original crimes in the 1990s identified similarities between Jacques' *modus operandi* and the Durham University theft.

'Lerner and Callan went down to Wandsworth prison where Jacques is on remand for the theft of old, rare books and interviewed him. However, it wasn't tape recorded, as it was just a general interview of which Lerner made rough notes.

They asked Jacques are you aware of this case? He said "yes I've read about it". They asked him did you steal the Durham First Folio? And he said "no". He said, "I know what the First Folio Shakespeare is and as far as marketing it it's a white elephant. It's not worth stealing." But then again, as Toby will say in his closing speech, he stole two copies of Newton's *Principia Mathematica* which are equally white elephants.

'Asked, "did you take any books to Cuba with you?" he said "no". They then asked "are you prepared to assist us further?" "Well," said

Jacques, "I'm prepared to make a written statement and tell you about Cuba if you can get these current charges against me dropped." DC Lerner said there could be no chance of a deal like that, at which time Jacques said "well I can't help you" and then indicated to the screw he wanted to go back to his cell in Wandsworth.'

According to Scott, the previous interview in 2002 with Jacques was mentioned, while DC Lerner also admitted that paperwork from the original inquiry into the First Folio theft had been destroyed. While he said that happened before his time with the force, Lerner had spoken to one of the officers, now retired, who investigated the original theft and said as far as he recalled they had no leads. In other words, the only person interviewed about it other than Scott was Jacques, albeit not under caution.

Scott commented: 'It was a brilliant point but it ended on a not so brilliant point. Toby made a submission that there was no case to answer on the first count of theft and made a good argument. Smith then got up and made what seemed not such a good argument and the judge went out to consider them. Toby said to me it would be advantageous for our case for the theft charge to be dropped as it would seem like the prosecution are backing off. The Judge returned and said the jury are going to have to consider the theft charge. I'm not bothered about that. I don't think it's a disaster.'

In his summing up, described by Scott as a master class, Hedworth sought to make sense of his client to the jury and shift the blame for everything to Denny and Heidy. Scott was the innocent dupe, the thought of which he had previously appeared to find so distasteful. But this was crunch time and no place for being precious.

'Raymond Rickett Scott, shopper and shoplifter, serial credit card user, of cards sometimes not even obtained in his own name, a Walter Mitty fantasist, international traveller and playboy with an extensive line in sharp clothes from the apparently bygone age, a Ferrari driver and fine-cigar smoker, no doubt last seen in a cinema near you starring in *Boogie Nights*; a fifty-three-year-old, still living at home with his elderly mother, complaining in text messages about having to ask for permission for another night or two away; international playboy with a single bed in Washington, Tyne and Wear; pockets empty, bank accounts stripped by a beautiful young woman in Havana who seems to have got through one-hundred-and-eleven times the national average wage in six months.

'You may have done a bit of a double take when you saw Mr Scott. So much of what he is and what he does is outwith our normal expectations.'

He concluded: 'Yes, he's a shoplifter. But does that mean he's guilty of any other type of theft? Yes, he's feckless and a spendthrift. He is, you may think, of questionable taste. Yes, he's had his head turned – he fell into a honey trap. But is he just the sort of bizarre, naïve, out-of-the-mainstream type character who could be taken in by someone much more worldly and cynical in Cuba? Is this naïve mummy's boy simply out of his depth? He's someone who genuinely believes a twenty-one-year-old dancer is his fiancée. Ladies and gentlemen, there's no fool like an old fool. May it be that he's been had over? No doubt loving every minute of it. But if that may be the case, your verdict in respect of these charges would be not guilty.'

Judge Lowden's summing up followed and the jury was sent out. They weren't able to reach a verdict that day so they were sent home for the evening to return the next morning. I met up with Scott and we went to La Tasca, a Spanish tapas restaurant on the Quayside. The sun had relented and it was cold and blustery but we sat outside anyway looking out at the Gateshead Millennium Bridge. He was subdued. 'It's like "The Last Supper". Or the condemned man's final meal. You can report Scott ate heartily.'

He talked of his plans for the future, whether immediate or after a period at Her Majesty's pleasure, he did not specify. 'I'll get away to the South of France. I'll take the Ferrari and a caravan. I won't need much to live on. I can be frugal.'

'A caravan on the back of a Ferrari? That'll impress the women,' I said.

He smiled. 'I'll of course leave the caravan on a site and drive into town in the Ferrari. I'll enjoy the company far, far away from cold, cold England. I'll tell my stories on a night and then return to the caravan, alone. I couldn't have people see where I'm staying – bad for the image. That's not the only reason. I'll just enjoy the company and the warmth of the sun on my back.'

A waiter came out to clear the table. As ever with Scott, he started up a conversation with him. It turned out he was from Barcelona whose club team had seven players in the Spanish national side, which at the weekend was to play in (and win) the World Cup Final.

Scott fulsomely praised the skills of the Spanish team and denigrated the inept performances of an unimaginative England side. It seemed another reason in his mind to leave these shores, to escape to a country where football was a thing of beauty, not a slog. France, it has to be said, had been worse than England, but that was an unmentioned detail.

Scott's mood visibly picked up during the chat, a welcome distraction. As the waiter was about to return to the restaurant with our dishes, Scott said: '*Visca el Barca il visca Catalunya.*'

The waiter seemed impressed. '*Bravo senor, bravo.*'

Scott explained: 'That was Catalan. Different from Castilian, the state language of Spain. The language of Franco and oppression.'

And then we left the restaurant, Scott returning home to sleep in his own bed for perhaps the last night in a long while. How long was not only going to come as a terrible shock to him but, as seemed par for the course in his case, was going to cause not a little controversy.

Chapter Twenty-Three

A Shakespeare Tragedy in a Sentence

By the Friday the jury in Newcastle's courtroom 10 returned to pass judgement on Scott. They found him not guilty of theft, but guilty of handling stolen goods and removing stolen property from England. He also pleaded guilty to a charge of theft of two paintings from Fenwicks in Newcastle in October 2008 – the paintings he handed in at Peterlee police station along with the Latin dictionary. He was remanded in custody to Durham Jail after the Judge asked for psychiatric reports before passing sentence, which he warned would be 'substantial'.

When I heard about the verdict I fired off a quick text offering my commiserations in the hope he might have a chance to reply before he was taken into custody; but none came back. So I settled down to write an article for the newspapers I work for about my time with him.

I remembered once how he said with a hint of bitterness during the trial that if found guilty, 'They'll say showman Scott arrived at court in a chauffeur-driven limousine and left with his tail between his legs in a police van.'

And to my shame, that's more or less how I started the article. As I was writing the article, the Moat story had reached its own endgame with him eyeballing police marksmen across a narrow strip of grass while holding his own gun to his throat, threatening to kill himself if they came any closer. It was going to be a long night.

I met colleagues in a pub after finishing my Scott piece and watched with them the Rothbury stand-off on the large flat-screen TV above our heads. To the right you could see the armed officers behind bullet proof shields, a couple of them pointing Tazer guns to the left at Moat, tantalizingly out of view. Seconds, minutes or hours from death, it was his own choice as he was to make good his promise he wasn't going to give himself up alive. Although nothing happened, the scene held a curious fascination. If you had watched long enough, you would eventually get to see – or rather hear – a man die, live on TV. *Big Brother*, eat your heart out.

Looking at the screen and Moat's situation, made me think of Scott's state of mind now, and I genuinely feared for him. How would he cope with the prospect of doing time? He was fifty-three now and what was there left for him? No book, no riches, no woman of his dreams, no life in the South of France – at least not in the foreseeable future – and not even the compensation of being in the spotlight, which had now been brought abruptly to an end.

Early Saturday morning, after a six-hour standoff, Raoul Moat shot and killed himself. For a brief period he was elevated to cult status and a Facebook appreciation site called 'RIP Raoul Moat – You Legend', gained much notoriety. His funeral was attended by scores of mourners, some of whom had never met him but travelled hundreds of miles to the North East to pay their respects. The antihero worship led to a heated national debate and a wide-ranging search for answers or, more accurately, scapegoats, until things settled down.

There was less sympathy for Scott, the general line being he had got what he deserved. Everyone seemed really angry that, by implication, he had 'vandalized' the First Folio even though it was supposition that he had. Of course, he had confessed to having done so to me – then quickly retracted his comments. So who really knew?

Still, my fears for him were allayed four days after he was found guilty when a brown envelope dropped through my letterbox, my address written in Scott's unmistakable hand. 'From prisoner number A1347AV, Mr R. R. Scott, E1-10 Wing.'

> He did not wear his scarlet coat for blood and wine are red and were on his hands when they found him with

A Shakespeare Tragedy in a Sentence

the dead. The poor dead woman whom he loved and murdered in his bed. To all let this be heard. All men kill the things they love some with a bitter word the brave man with a sword, the coward with a kiss'
The Ballad of Reading Gaol – Oscar Wilde.

Yeah well not guilty of theft, but guilty of receiving/handling. Was that an honourable draw? No it was a 1-0 defeat for my side. I'd like to know the jury's reasoning i.e. how did they unanimously come to the sure and certain decision that I knew the book was stolen? We'll never know.

Toby, hating to be on the losing side is angered by the judge who wanted to have the last word in The First Folio Case. He is to appeal on grounds of the judge wrongly allowing the jury to hear of my previous as the price for letting in Jack and the unfairness of the summation. We live in hope.

Anyway for the time being convicted and remanded in custody for psychiatric reports. Not quite sure the exact date for sentence at Newcastle Crown Court in front of Lowden but I think I heard August 11, obviously not the next day as he'll be on the grouse moor. Professor Turkington is to carry out psychiatric report. Certainly handling is preferable to guilty of the actual theft thus implying I was responsible for the vandalism and took the other outstanding books.

I'm in the reception wing E-wing that housed Ronnie Kray (though not Reggie – they were reunited in Parkhurst) some of the Great Train Robbers (including the Raffles style Bruce Reynolds, an early role model, Charlie Richardson, mad Frankie Fraser and other notable alumni. I'm the latest celebrity.

The history of the wing has a darker past as when it was closed by the Mountbatten Report in the early 70s for men it became the maximum security prison for women (dubbed she wing) and was home to Myra Hindley. Also there was the IRA's Judith Ward and The Price Sisters, not sure if Rose West was here.

Anyway, when I came on the wing compared to my experiences in the late 80s I thought I'd come to Claridges. So clean and bright. Cells although the same size now boast a hand basin with hot and cold water, a flushing toilet with screen and a portable colour TV (no remote, 5 channels and DVD channel). A kind of air con (no pun intended) and a large south facing window with quite attractive white bars. Three pool tables outside for association and numerous wall telephones to make calls from. You have to supply a list of numbers to call and once approved you can call the numbers at your own expense. Your mobile is on my list.

This OL (ordinary letter) is a free one every week which they put a 2nd class stamp on. I've obviously phoned my mother who sounds v. surprisingly cheerful. Her visits will take up all my allocation so unless you can see me as a press visit we won't meet. Letter will be our conduit.

I'll only be on E-wing for one week but all cells in Durham have these en suite facilities and TVs. When sending me a letter you must include my number and name and yours, as anonymous mail will not be given out!

I exercise for one hour every day walking around a garden. Weekends are the most boring. Monday I start my induction course. Getting librium to help me with alcohol withdrawal. You can have £25.50 a week sent in to spend on luxuries at the canteen. You can have a hot shower every day. Three square meals a day. The local open prison is Kirklevington beside Yarm I think. No walls no cells – a key to your own room.

A Shakespeare Tragedy in a Sentence

According to the alcohol de-tox team I'll feel great in about 14 days. When I visit the canteen I will buy stamps (firsts) and stationery (so be warned – but I won't need to write so small).

I'm reminded of Tom Courtney in *Billy Liar* who gets caught nicking pointlessly loads of calendars from his boss's undertaker business (played by Leonard Rossiter) and fantasizes about being sent to prison and writing a best seller about penal reform – the Governor says, "Well done you've used your time well!" Mmmm.

I have a cell mate (only two per cell on custody unit in these enlightened times) a canny lad, bit simple whose first mistake was to choose the wrong parents to be born to.

Actually apart from one or two they are a sad bunch. They are inadequate, woefully insipid personalities. They invariably visited their fathers in Durham as children as theirs now visit them. I feel most sorry for the old men who sit on the benches during exercise and then shuffle back to the wing (D wing exercise with us too). The screws call them by their first names. One of these old lags was actually born in Durham, his mother a prostitute serving a sentence in the women's wing. They look like they've escaped from Hogarth's London. I think they like it here, it's their home. There but for fortune go you and I. Well you anyway.

You can, even convicted, wear your own clothes but I'm not yet. I want to fit in. Don't want them to say "Who does he think he is?" RS.

We had never directly speculated what jail sentence he would receive if found guilty. In our first chat he had pointed out the maximum term for handling was longer than that for theft. But that was 14 years and I could not believe it would be anywhere near that. A pointer, I thought, was given on July 20th when Jacques was sentenced to three-and-a-half years for his latest crime. If Scott was given a similar term, he could be out in under two years – less if his appeal against conviction was successful.

A few days later a documentary on Scott's case called *Stealing Shakespeare* was broadcast on BBC. He did not come across well. Detailing in depth the police investigation, it was interspersed with interviews the production crew had done with him in the weeks before I met him, mainly in the library room at the Fallen Angel hotel. He was sporting his trademark jewellery and a peculiar designer T-shirt, the cut and style of which was perhaps more suited to a man half his age. Inevitably he was drinking champagne and puffing on a Cuban cigar – he had all but given up smoking long before the end of his trial.

Scott spoke in sound bites throughout: 'I'd rather have one item of quality rather than 100 items that were indifferent' and 'It's possible to live a champagne lifestyle on a lager budget if you're careful' were but two.

DI Callan commented: 'He's an eccentric character. He's a man who thinks he's James Bond.' More Austin Powers I thought after one clip of him on Seaton Carew beach near Hartlepool passing comment on the local beauties there, comparing them unfavourably with the heavenly Heidy. I groaned when the programme detailed how Scott had the name of a luxury Monte Carlo hotel and a Liechtenstein bank as his addresses in his passport, not his home address, Wigeon Close, as he had told me.

I had written a newspaper article in his defence just the previous week, with him strolling into the Folger giving his correct name and full home address and asked, 'was that the act of a man guilty of carrying a stolen item?' As it turned out, he had been tracked down to Wigeon Close through the monitoring of his mobile phone calls.

The intended answer to my original question was somewhat different now. I'd written to Scott alerting him to the programme to make sure he tuned in. Sure enough, he had. When he wrote back, it seemed my article in which I'd alluded to his 'fairy story confession' had caused a bit of a stir with the Crown Prosecution Service.

A Shakespeare Tragedy in a Sentence

Scott wrote to me:

> I got a letter off the solicitors dated 21 July which seems to indicate that I will be sentenced on Monday 2 August. It included two things, firstly the psychiatric report by Professor Turkington who I saw for one hour on Thursday 15th July and secondly it went on, "I have also enclosed a copy of a newspaper article published by the Sunday Sun on the 11th July 2010, which was sent to me (Judith Curry) by the Crown Prosecution Service, no doubt along with a copy to the judge". They obviously take a dim view of it. I do not. I wrote them a letter by return explaining how I had said many, many things to you over the 18 months, mostly under the influence of alcohol, including a categorical denial of the theft which I considered to be par excellence an inside job. I pointed out that in your short article there are two outright mistakes, factual errors, viz the Louis Vuitton case and the fact that I left the Folger my address at 3 Wigeon Close.

Thanks for that, I thought. The 'battered' Louis Vuitton case was a detail Scott had insisted on me including and I didn't need reminding about the Wigeon Close howler. The letter continued:

> I have included the conclusions of Prof Turkington's report, he holds a chair at Newcastle University (no I won't say that must cause his arm to ache after a while).
> 'It starts at point or paragraph 29 but the preceding ones are his reports of what I said to him about the case which you know better than him and run to a bulky 8 pages. When you dropped the hint in your article about "the reports should make interesting reading" I picked it up.

Great, I thought. God knows what was in the first part of the report he hasn't sent me and I'm left to wonder how much of the second part he actually has sent is based on anything other than what he wants people to think he is like, rather than what he is actually like.

He reiterated Hedworth's plan to appeal on the grounds he outlined before – the inclusion of his past record as well as what was perceived as the unfair summing up of Judge Lowden. It was to be submitted to the Court of Criminal Appeal after sentence. If the application was denied, Hedworth could still go to the CCA to plead the case, but this wouldn't be covered by legal aid and could potentially cost a lot of money. Scott wrote:

> BUT GAWD BLESS HIS SILK ROBE he will do it free PRO BONO (for the (common) good). "I hate being on the losing side," said Toby to me down in the cells.

He added:

> I will appear in the dock at Newcastle Crown Court in my prison uniform – a blue and white striped short sleeve shirt with a pair of blue denims (non-designer) and a pair of black plimsolls. Why? Why not! And because I AM NOW A CONVICT i.e. A CONVICTED PRISONER OF THE STATE (as once was GHANDI, MANDELA, KENYATTA, CASTRO, LENIN, STALIN, HITLER, SOLZHENITSYN IN THE GULAG, MENACHEM BEGIN, PERON inter alios (amongst others). Why change into my designer finery for a few hours. Come what may I am going to keep a prison uniform. Primo Levi kept his Auschwitz uniform and looked at it every day. Have you read IF THIS IS A MAN, an account of his descent into the cradle of evil?

There's nothing like a sense of perspective and, even though it couldn't possibly be the case, I imagined Scott pacing up and down his cell dictating his thoughts for his cellmate to write down. He had been transferred to C-wing and concluded his note by asking for a name check of his fellow inmates who appeared to be treating him very well.

> I must say that I am a celeb and have NOT come across any resentment or jealousy. On the contrary I have been welcomed with open arms by the names, the faces, the chaps who matter.

He also insisted there be a launch party for our book at Howard Marks' Tequila Bar in Leeds. Marks, at one time one of the world's biggest dealers in hashish, became quite a celebrity himself thanks to his autobiography *Mr Nice*. Scott said his mum, 'Lady Bountiful', would hand over a £1,000 cheque towards it.

> Open at least one bottle of champagne and toast your absent friend.
> I've taken my literacy and numeracy tests and passed with straight As, flying colours, top of the class (the competition was not too exacting). Inevitably I've been pencilled in for a job as a library orderly (assuming I pass the security vetting). Once a week I play chess with Martin the mortgage fraudster and other white collar crims (birds of a feather) in the library.

Scott was in great form and any fears for him I had before had disappeared. He seemed in his element, surrounded by people he viewed as kindred spirits.

The nature of crime and the way he conducted himself during all his court hearings probably amused the hardened criminals, so he had nothing to fear from them. In his quieter moments he could take himself away to the library and read. 'They have the Complete Works of you know who, often taken out judging by its date stamps,' he wrote. Or try his 'Queen sacrifice' on Martin the mortgage fraudster.

A Shakespeare Tragedy in a Sentence

His psychiatric report – anyway, the section he sent to me – contained no surprises. The gist of it summed up Scott's personality.

> This gentleman has strong schizoid and obsessive-compulsive traits within his personality. He is basically introverted with low self-esteem and has a very deep rooted belief in his own lack of achievement. His compensatory fantasy life relates to him being a fabulous success in life and is centred around the trappings of wealth. His obsessive-compulsive traits include a tendency to perfectionism and a desire to have life highly organized. He said that socially without alcohol he was very anxious and described himself as a wet blanket. He described himself as a romantic, a dreamer and as a spiritual man but also one with communist leanings. He said that he could not cope with any kind of responsibility towards relationship or work.

The worst thing for Scott was the absence of mitigating circumstances to minimize his sentence. The report said he fully knew what he was doing and there was a high risk he'd do something similar in the future. Drink played a role and while inside he could attend a CARAT programme – Counselling, Assessment, Referral, Advice and Throughcare – to curb his thirst and lessen the chances of him offending again. In other words, a spell inside would do him good. Just like his mum thought, as Scott had previously said to me.

He had a change of heart about turning up at court in his prison outfit, instead plumping for a beige linen suit. The jewellery had gone but the designer shades were in place. Perhaps as his last public performance in a while he thought it only appropriate to turn up in some of his finery.

When Scott appeared in the dock again, Judge Lowden labelled him a 'fantasist' involved in 'highly sophisticated criminal matters'.

A Shakespeare Tragedy in a Sentence

'You wanted to fund an extremely ludicrous playboy lifestyle in order to impress a woman you met in Cuba. It [the First Folio] was worth in its condition some million pounds. It would be regarded a priceless but to you it was definitely a very big price and you went to great lengths for that price. Your motivation was of course for financial gain. The book had to be kept for many years, it had to be defaced to hide its true identity.'

Scott shook his head but Judge Lowden told him: 'You either did it or you embraced the obvious fact that someone had already done it.'

However, the judge seemed convinced that the damage done to the book, which he described as 'cultural vandalism', was actually done by Scott who was attempting to strike a balance between doing enough to hide its identity but, in doing so, not lose too much of its value. It was, as Judge Lowden said, Scott's attempt to 'take on the world's experts at their own expertise'.

He added: 'You were confident that that balance was achieved. You were however overconfident because the experts were more confident than you.'

It was then Scott found out exactly how substantial the sentence Judge Lowden had in mind for him. He was jailed for a total of eight years – six years for handling stolen goods and two years for removing it from England, the sentences to run consecutively.

Elsewhere in Newcastle Crown Court that day, Michael Ridley, an amateur boxer and bodybuilder, was jailed for five years for the manslaughter of off-duty soldier Chris Chacksfield – who had served in Iraq and Afghanistan – and injuring Chacksfield's wife, Adele, in an unprovoked attack. A few weeks earlier the notorious 'tome raider' Jacques had been jailed for less that half of Scott's sentence, his latest court appearance in a life of crime which had seen him plunder well over 100 antique and valuable books. Scott's sentence was just shy of those two combined. It was an incredible shock, not just to Scott and his defence team, but to people with no previous concern as to how the case was to end, some of whom had been previously scornful of Scott.

A Shakespeare Tragedy in a Sentence

The handling of a stolen Shakespeare First Folio which, granted, had been 'vandalized' by a person or persons not properly identified, was seen, judging by the sentences meted out, as a more serious crime than beating an off-duty soldier to death.

Another coincidence was that three weeks earlier when Scott had been warned of receiving a 'substantial sentence', two officers from Durham Constabulary, former colleagues of the men who had investigated Scott, had been given suspended sentences after appearing at Newcastle Crown Court for selling-on guns which had been handed in.

I really feared for Scott's state of mind and, from a personal standpoint, I was furious. It's only a bloody book, I thought; he didn't beat anyone to death. I sat down to write a column for the paper about it both as a means of giving vent to my feelings and to show I was thinking of him, for what these were worth.

Before the article was published I got a letter from prisoner Number A1347AV, Name R. R. Scott, Wing C – 4 – 9 and in brackets (it adds up to 13, notice).

> Hi Mike, well old mate, I've had better days. Keep calm, carry on and appeal. In every life some rain must fall, this is my first shower in almost 54 years, my sternest test to date and also that of my mother who will be 83 next January. This day some have been killed in road traffic accidents, some have been told they only have months to live and some have received "a substantial custodial sentence". On the other hand some have had good fortune. C'est la vie, such is life, so it goes. Nonetheless I'm devastated, shocked and very depressed "in a word Barry, sick as a parrot – gutted". I know your thoughts are with me at this time Mike. I well remember fondly our many meetings of the past and recent past and as you knew I was carefree and quite content because I did not think I would be convicted but if so the sentence would be a few years, say two or three. I genuinely was not worried. Ignorance was bliss.

A Shakespeare Tragedy in a Sentence

I should have known "The First Folio Case" would go out with a big bang and not a whimper.

Continuing this after the hiatus of association where I've had nothing but sympathy from outraged lads, some of them doing or themselves expecting long double figure sentences. Most valuable of all I was taken aside by Jim, a real life freedom fighter, an Irishman who has done 30 years and is soon to be repatriated to The Republic, he gave me some invaluable advice about doing my time and more encouragement about an appeal and how for me a 5 or 6 year sentence can shrink to 2 or 2½ years in an open prison with home leave and a job out in the local prison community. Most of all it was just seeing someone caring, sheer human decency. A prison officer who revealed he was a Salvationist branded the 8 years as "unchristian". Ironically I shared cell 7 at Newcastle Crown Court with Mike Ridley, gaoled for five years for the manslaughter of the soldier in Newcastle. He also got two years for assaulting the widow BUT concurrent. I got 6 years for dishonestly handling and 2 years for removing it from England BUT consecutively 6 + 2 = 8. Toby and Caroline thought 5 years in total was just and are zealously taking up the appeal against conviction and sentences as a cause célèbre. On the blackboard outside cell 7 the guard had chalked "Ridley Scott" (director of *Blade Runner* etc and born like me in South Shields). The solicitor spoke to my mother on the phone and I've spoken to her twice since sentencing and she is standing up well. She knows I'm not going to do "anything silly" and I know she won't.

"Condemn me. It is of no importance. History will absolve me." Fidel Castro on getting 15 years for the failed assault on Moncada Barracks (a fiasco in 1953). Two years later Batista released him in an amnesty, Fidel went into exile in Mexico and 6 years later he was Commandante en Jeffe (President/Dictator). I'm not throwing my hand in either – mein kampf (my struggle) continues. Not against the prison system, they are not responsible for me being here, indeed I intend to be a model prisoner who will use all the facilities available to facilitate an early release. Sooner rather than later I will be a free man (on licence, if appeal against conviction fails) and fit with hopefully years still ahead of me. I'm tired now after a hard day and I'm sure to get a good night's sleep. I wonder if the judge and the jurors can sleep tonight with a clear conscience. VENCEREMOS! (We shall overcome – Che).'

He seemed to have taken it quite well, summoning up the spirits of Castro and Che Guevara – a good sign he was in reasonable humour – mapping out future battles to distract him from his present predicament. Tilting at windmills again.

A couple of days later my piece duly appeared in the paper:

> Perhaps it is appropriate that society has got its pound of flesh from Raymond Scott.
>
> Last Monday, Scott was sentenced to eight years in jail for handling a First Folio, the first collection of William Shakespeare's plays published in 1623, stolen from Durham University in 1998.
>
> In Shakespeare's *Merchant of Venice*, Shylock demands his pound of flesh from Antonio after he defaults on a loan. It is his revenge on Antonio who had previously insulted him.
>
> Scott insulted the powers-that-be by not looking suitably chastened when facing court, turning up in ostentations clothes and arriving in a stretch limo, smoking cigars and drinking champagne.
>
> To borrow a line from another English literary giant – Charles Dickens – 'the law is a ass', as has been proven by Scott's sentence.

A Shakespeare Tragedy in a Sentence

Before I go on, I better hold my hands up here. I've got to know Scott well over the last 18 months as I'm writing a book about the case and he has become a friend in that time. But the following are facts and I leave it up to you to decide whether I'm biased.

On the very same day at Newcastle Crown Court when Scott's trial ended last month and he was warned of a substantial sentence, two officers from Durham Constabulary – Maurice Allen and Damian Cobain – were also up before a judge. They had been entrusted with disposing of firearms surrendered by members of the public and admitted to selling them on. Both got a suspended jail sentence.

Part of their mitigation was that they only sold the weapons to gun-licence holders. Derrick Bird was a gun-licence holder. Remember him? (Bird shot and killed 12 people and injured 11 others in Cumbria in June 2010) To my knowledge no-one has ever killed anybody with a First Folio.

Then, by another trick of the British judicial system, on the very same day at the very same court when Scott was sentenced to eight years in jail, another case concluded.

Michael Ridley pleaded guilty to killing a soldier – Staff Sgt Chris Chacksfield – and injuring Chris's wife Adele in an unprovoked attack outside a nightclub in Newcastle.

Ridley, who is 22, was sentenced to five years in jail. Yes, five years, a little over half of Scott's sentence. As Ridley pleaded guilty to manslaughter, he could be out in less than three.

From the outset of Scott's case it seemed clear he was not just being tried for the theft and handling of an old book – he was actually cleared of the theft charge – but as a direct assault on a cultural icon for which we were all supposed to be outraged. The First Folio had been badly damaged in an attempt to disguise its provenance. When sentencing him, Judge Richard Lowden said Scott was guilty of "cultural vandalism" but it was never proven that he did the damage.

Let's hope that Lowden is presiding if a gun sold by the two Durham police officers is used to commit, say, a robbery or a murder. For, going by his logic, then the two officers who sold the guns in the first place should be brought to book. In that instance I wouldn't take issue with him, but it's not going to happen.

Let's face it, Scott's other, unspoken crime in the eyes of those who tried him was to court publicity. Arriving at court in a stretch limo, quaffing champagne while dressed head to toe in designer gear was seen no doubt as someone cocking a snook at society. He had no visible means of paying for his extravagant lifestyle and it was largely funded by credit scams from banks (he wasn't on trial for this either, by the way). In my more jaundiced moments I thought this was a pleasant change as it is usually us punters who get ripped off by banks.

Who were the victims of his crime? You or I? He was not found guilty of depriving society of this cultural icon – I repeat, again, he was not convicted of stealing it. He didn't beat anyone to death, he didn't sell anyone a gun. Someone who gave evidence at Scott's trial said that while the First Folio belonged to Durham University, the contents belong to the world. Really? How easy do you think this universal tome is to see in its ivory tower? Try going to Durham University for a look. Take a Thermos as you might have to wait a while. Meanwhile, Scott is in prison serving a more severe sentence than those meted out to many rapists, paedophiles and killers.

No doubt Judge Lowden thinks he has made an example and it is this. If you kill a soldier, if you're a cop

A Shakespeare Tragedy in a Sentence

and abuse your position of trust, that's a bit naughty. If you are found in possession of a book by Shakespeare, watch out. The full title of the First Folio is *Mr William Shakespeare's Comedies, Histories and Tragedies*. Now, thanks to what's happened to Raymond Scott, you can add 'travesty'. Travesty of justice.

The article was a bit over-the-top in places but it generated as much positive as negative reaction in letters to the paper over the next week. Scott always divided opinion. He appreciated the thought although a simple 'thanks for the support' message would not do for him.

> Do you recall amongst my long texts, the many of them, there was one where I said if it all went horribly wrong I expected you to be my Emile Zola railing against the injustice of it all as he did in The Dreyfus Case. You know Zola wrote the open letter "J'accuse" to the French Establishment published in the liberal press as Captain Dreyfus sat on his rock on Devil's Island. Right now looking out of the bars "at that little tent of blue which prisoners call sky" (Oscar in Reading Gaol) a view of the Atlantic Ocean or the Caribbean Sea from a subtropical island is most appealing. I'll have to get Papillon out of the library. Papillon (real name Henri Charrière, I think) was of course innocent of murder, as Dreyfuss was of treason. That makes three of us. I was awoken this morning at 7.45am precisely by Mr Bell with a crisp copy of the Sunday Sun. "There's a great article in here about your injustice!" "Ah," I thought, Emile Zola lives!"

Hopefully he didn't also get a copy of *The Daily Mail*. As Scott looked out at the 'little tent of blue which prisoners call sky', dreaming of the Caribbean, it appeared that Heidy had been doing a bit of blue-sky thinking of her own to provide for her future. A reporter had actually been to Cuba, evidently tracking down a friend of hers, and fellow dancer, Marissa Barrios.

She was quoted as saying: 'Heidy didn't fret for long when her fiancée was gone. She told me Raymond, or Raymondo as she called him, was fun while it lasted but she had no intentions of waiting for him to come back to Havana.

'As soon as he stopped sending her money she could not pay for her mobile phone, and that was it. He was out of her life. For a sensual woman like Heidy to be without a man, that will not happen. Raymondo was her passport to a new life. I don't think she loved him, but when he proposed she was not going to say no. Heidy wanted to go to America, but she would have settled for Britain. She is not a stupid girl and when you have someone who is prepared to spend money then she will do all she can to keep hold of him. Did she love him? Of course not. He was a means to an end.'

At the same time as the story was published, I got another letter from Scott, giving the article about Heidy a poignancy that it didn't deserve.

> Heidy will have received the letter in Spanish from my cousin around the end of July with the very bad news contained therein. It reminds me of the Don McLean weepie 'American Pie' about Buddy Holly. My cousin posted it in a DHL envelope to Heidy's house. Shit happens. Perhaps 'Another Suitcase, Another Hall' sung by Siobhan McCarthy in the original London production of Evita would be more appropriate for Heidy: "I don't expect my love affairs to last for long, never fool myself that my dreams will come true …"
>
> Maybe it's for the best, all things considered after all, at the end of the day. Ever heard of pollyannaism? If not look it up – or think Monty Python in The Life of Brian when Eric Idle sang 'Always look on the bright side of Life' whilst being crucified. Que sera, sera.

A Shakespeare Tragedy in a Sentence

Retiring to bed perchance to dream, ay there's the rub. To sleep to sleep.

P.S. I Forgot to mention I think there is a con man on my wing called David William Shakespeare. True! Honest!! Raymond.

Chapter Twenty-Four

Keep Calm and Carry On Appealing

By the time I got to visit Scott in jail, he had been moved first from Durham to HMP Acklington and then to its near neighbour in Northumberland, HMP Castington.

It was a bit of a leap of faith booking-in a visit, as it was in the middle of the coldest December in the UK since records began. Northumberland had endured the worst in England of it, nearly a foot of snow falling on one night alone and temperatures at times plunging to minus 20.

Castington is in a remote part of the county, in the village of Acklington. You could not book a visit fewer than six days in advance and as the BBC weather forecasts I relied on only came in five-day cycles, I had to take pot luck and signed up for one Saturday, hoping the snow would hold off. As the Saturday approached, the forecast was for a blizzard.

However, when I set off, the weather was cold and sunny, and while the temperature gauge in my car dropped to below zero, the snow looked like holding off for a while.

The prison, which was also home to a young offenders institute, is built on the site of the former RAF Acklington. It had a bit of a lively past, being named the most violent detention centre in 2001 by the Prison Reform Trust, although four years later it had improved sufficiently to be declared a 'safe, respectful and purposeful' environment by Her Majesty's Chief Inspector of Prisons.

Over the weeks, Raymond and I had kept in touch via a series of letters. In them, as with our meetings before he was jailed, his moods swung widely, although it now seemed that they swung within a narrower arc.

Rather than dwelling on melancholia, he sought humour mixed

with perversity by looking for incidents and circumstances he thought that would amuse both of us.

His change of surroundings appeared to help. While, to me at least, he had been a little star-struck at first by the more hardened criminals at Durham, there seemed little to keep him occupied apart from awaiting his sentence.

At Acklington, then at Castington, there seemed more to do. From Acklington, he revealed he was taking a course in, of all things, bookkeeping. He wrote:

> I kid you not – the double entry type with red and black ink. No wonder they call prison "a university of crime".
>
> After I have completed the Bookkeeping course (to Asil Nadir standards) I may enroll in the Metalwork Faculty to study the modular option 'Advanced Welding and Thermic Lance Techniques'. Then there are the courses in The Printing Shop. My future possibilities are limitless. One con has an OLL degree in sociology obtained at Parkhurst in the 90s whilst serving 15 years for armed robbery. On release he went back to stealing but crucially he now knows precisely why he does it.

Even at such a distance from home, his mum Hannah had still been regularly visiting him.

> Lady Bountiful visited me on Wednesday despite me trying to stop it on humanitarian grounds – arguing to the Governor that 90 minutes of lambasting and "I told you so's" amounted to "cruel and unusual punishment". He is obviously a sadist. No not really, she is taking it very stoically and points out that the drinking of the previous decades could not continue. She is of course correct. Que sera sera. OK point taken but I don't need years of incarceration to drive it home. The excessive drinking of the past few years, especially those awful two years on

bail, were beyond enjoying alcohol and all to do with decline and fall.

Even in jail he found echoes of his court case.

> In the TV documentary about the case DI Mick Callan, the man leading it, described me as thinking I was some sort of James Bond. At Castington my cell number is E1 – 007. They seem to be adding concrete to my imagined fantasy.'

A couple of weeks before my visit I had received a letter in which Scott revealed some bad news. His initial appeal against his conviction and the length of his sentence had been refused by Mr Justice Davis in the Court of Appeal. If he was to pursue his appeal further, he would now be without legal aid.

Regarding the conviction and the claim the introduction of his 'previous' had prejudiced the case, the gamble of introducing Jacques had seemed to do for that. Mr Justice Davis wrote: 'By virtue of the defendant's attack on Jacques, the gateway was undoubtedly there ... to empower the Judge to permit evidence of the defendant's own bad character to be adduced.'

In relation to the length of sentence, there was a hint of sympathy in which he described the eight years as 'perhaps a stern sentence'. However, he continued: 'But it was a grave offence, involving a national treasure of great financial and cultural value.'

Scott described himself as 'not daunted, discouraged, dismayed or even depressed', and again used for encouragement the experiences of his role model Fidel Castro when things went against him. In this instance he wrote of the shambolic voyage and landing of the Granma, a boat designed to accommodate 12 people which carried Castro and 82 revolutionaries, including Che Guevara, from Mexico to Cuba in 1956 to overthrow Batista.

While most of them were captured or killed, a small group, which became the core of the revolution, escaped and the Granma expedition is seen as the start of the armed struggle which eventually overthrew Batista three years later.

Scott himself appeared to be prepared for the long haul, although he would have to rely on the largesse of his barrister, Toby Hedworth, and the hope that he would fulfil a promise Scott said he had made to represent him for free.

'Remember,' he wrote, 'the British Army lost all the major battles of World War I – Mons, Ypres, the Somme, Passchendaele but they (we) won the war. Mmmm. Someday we'll look back on this and it'll all seem funny (Bruce Springsteen, 'Rosalita', *The Wild, The Innocent and the E Street Shuffle*).'

After parking up, I trudged towards the visitors centre with a gaggle of quietly muttering fellow visitors to get my number and wait to be escorted across to the prison complex itself. Inside, the centre was packed, it was standing room only with a few frayed magazines to read or the Omnibus edition of Coronation Street to watch on the small TV bolted high on the wall until my number was called. It had the feel of a doctor's surgery or an A&E hospital department with the injuries of those gathered not altogether obvious.

There was a mixture of over-made-up loved ones, bored kids, the ever-patient elderly parents and friends and confederates who had the air of not having to wait too long before they were to find themselves on the other side of the security doors.

After a half-hour wait my number was called and I walked the short distance to the jail itself. Having been fingerprinted, I was buzzed through into the search area where I walked with some trepidation. My visitor order had spoken of a Body Orifice Security Scanner, basically a moulded chair upon which you sit for staff to detect weapons, mobile phones and the like hidden up your backside. While I had nothing to hide, it certainly gave me pause for thought. Fortunately I didn't have to take my chances on the chair and I was more conventionally frisked and walked into the visiting area where Scott was waiting.

The last time I had seen him was about four months ago in the Spanish restaurant on Newcastle's Quayside in his court finery.

Today he was dressed in prison regulation grey sweatshirt, blue jeans and his designer Fendi glasses, the only nod to his dapper past. He looked well. It had taken a while for Scott to get used to being off the booze. Famed for his champagne swilling and smoking of Cuban cigars, both these luxuries were of course not available to him and he admitted it was doing him good.

'I'm looking at my time as extensive re-hab. I was given a course of Librium at first to get over my drinking and I've never felt so fit. I was on Prozac, too, but not any more. There are people who spend thousands to go to places like the Priory for the treatment I have received inside which I, of course, get for nothing.'

In the corner was a WRVS snack shop. No lobster on the menu there and I bought him a hot chocolate and a mint chocolate Aero. 'It makes a change me not doing the buying,' he said a bit pointedly.

We talked about his time inside, how he had signed up for a Motor Mechanics course to pass the time. He'd been amused by a story in the papers about how he'd got a job in the prison library.

'Not true. I don't know where the story came from. A prison source, it said. Not a particularly good one. I'm not bothered. It's an amusing thought.'

Around us a steady stream of visitors arrived. At the head of the room a group of prison guards presided over the goings-on perched on an elevated platform, like teachers invigilating an exam or priests watching their dubious flock. The low buzz of conversation was disturbed by a commotion in the room as a row broke out between a guy and his partner, which was quickly calmed.

He revealed with a chuckle that he was in trouble again over a book. However this one was published four years ago and you can buy it for 97p on Amazon – *Villains Paradise* by Donald Serrell Thomas, which he borrowed from the Castington prison library. He had received a warning letter that it is overdue for return. He handed me the warning letter as proof.

It read: '1st Notice: These library books are now OVERDUE please return on the next library visit.' There was a 2nd and 3rd Notice telling him what would happen if it wasn't returned. At the bottom Scott had written a 4th Notice of his own. 'You will be subjected to an unfair trial and sentenced to 8 years in prison.' After which he added: 'He bangs his forehead with his right palm. "Why oh why didn't I borrow The Complete Works of You Know Who and keep it beyond its return date?" Things to do, perhaps.'

He seemed at ease with his surroundings, which he had mentioned in a letter I received before my visit. It read:

> It's a lot better than when I last spent time on remand all those years ago. Castington, or The Country Club cum Health farm as I've dubbed it, is very civilized and light years distant from Durham with its shadow of the treadmill and mangle. Durham Gaol – somehow the archaic word seems so apposite to the place – is such an oppressively claustrophobic monolith where it is impossible to escape from the fact that you are in a Victorian House of Correction. Its depressing effect is palpable. I reckon the nick actually dumps in the region of a kilo of melancholia on its inmates and staff in any 24-hour period in accordance with Einstein's equation $M = mc2$ where M = Melancholia – or the blackness – m = mass and c = speed of light in vacuo. No wonder they say Durham nick made more people honest than the Bible ever did.'

I said the paper I worked for was interested in a story of his time behind bars. 'Shakespeare in the slammer,' he volunteered.

As the visiting time was being wound up by the guards, I wished him well and we shook hands. He said: 'My motto is Keep Calm and Carry On appealing.' With an eye to Christmas he added: 'If you get me a present don't get me a five-year diary.'

A couple of days after my visit another letter arrived from Scott with another Visiting Order included.

> It was really great to see you on Saturday (and I mean that most sincerely folks!). Did you know that the idea

for Truman Capote's Breakfast at Tiffany's came when he met by accident a lovely high-class pricey call girl in New York City who was paid to visit a mafia Don on remand awaiting trial in Sing Sing upstate New York? Yes it's true. Of course, little Truman wasn't using her professional services himself; as he put it near the end of his colourful life, "I've devoted my life to wine, women and song … well two out of three isn't bad." Anyway, here's another VO for you to use any time, any place, any where, it's the right one it's the bright one it's Martini.

I look forward to seeing you. Do you know any high-class call girls? Do try and find one whose name is not an amalgam of her dog and her mother's maiden please! Irrepressibly yours, Raymond.

The Shakespeare-in-the-slammer story caused a bit of a stir after it had appeared in the paper. When I tried to book another visit by phone I was put on hold for a while. I was then politely told I had been in breach of my visitor order and was effectively banned from seeing Raymond. While I could continue to write to him, all correspondence would be strictly monitored.

At around this time, the Shakespeare First Folio went on public display again at Durham University's Wolfson Gallery amid much fanfare. It seemed appropriate to pay a visit and so, on a wet Sunday afternoon, I travelled to Durham University's Palace Green to take a look. According to the lady selling tickets, 'The Treasures of Durham University' exhibition of which it was the centrepiece had proved very popular, particularly during the recent half-term holidays. I suspect a hell of a lot more people have heard of the First Folio today as compared to 1998, when it was last on show.

However, that Sunday attendance was sparse. There was just me, my two young sons who I had coerced into visiting on the promise of a Burger King afterwards, two elderly couples and a student sitting at a desk by the entrance frantically scribbling in a jotter.

It was all very peaceful beneath the imposing oak beams and the sterile calm of the air-conditioned room. Everything was set out neatly. Around the outside were a series of glass cases containing books and documents dating from as far back as the 9th Century and at the centre was the First Folio itself, fairly dramatically flanked by two white pillars, in a glass case all of its own.

Work by the conservation unit to restore it to its former glory had not yet begun and it was still in the same condition, in what seemed like a lifetime ago, when Scott had strolled into the Folger Shakespeare Library in Washington DC and wafted it flamboyantly under the nose of its head librarian, Richard Kuhta. It rested reverentially on a white pillow, presumably the same one as when it was taken to Newcastle Crown Court for the trial. As Scott had said, it really did not look much.

Opened at the dedication page to the most noble William, Earle [sic] of Pembroke and Philip, Earle of Montgomery, it seemed naked with the front cover removed. The frayed bindings of the spine gave it a sad, down-at-heel look, while in 1998, when it was stolen, it was complete and in possession of all its glory.

On the pillars at the sides, notes to exhibition visitors described, with a hint of anger and a touch of apology, how the book 'was brutally damaged in an attempt to disguise its identity' and how it was 'displayed in the condition it was returned in'. The inference was clear, I thought – it's all Scott's fault, the dastardly knave.

On the back of the pillars were pictures of the evidence that snared Scott – the handwritten *Troilus and Cressida* title prominent, pictures of Scott, Heidy and Denny and the latter two's letters describing the First Folio's fake Cuban provenance – as well as thanks to all those who helped in its return, from the Durham officers who headed the case, Mick Callan and Tim Lerner, to the experts at the Folger who identified it as stolen and those from the Shakespeare Birthplace Trust who confirmed this.

There was even a picture of Callan and Lerner, looking slightly sheepish, alongside university staff in a celebratory picture, all somber-suited and furrowed gravitas. Then, with a laugh, I saw a picture of Scott on the opposite pillar. The contrast could not have been greater. It was taken outside North Durham magistrates Court, Consett, in his 'Macbeth' period, Scott dressed in tweeds, a pheasant feather sticking out of his top pocket, brandishing a bottle of Drambuie and a cigar. Alongside him stood his glamorous assistant, Claire, and they were both leaning on his 'Boss Hogg' limo.

Apart from the First Folio there was an impressive collection of First Editions, including Jane Austen's *Pride and Prejudice* (1813), Charles Dickens's *Oliver Twist* (1838), the *Diary of Samuel Pepys* (1825), Samuel Johnson's *A Dictionary of the English Language* (1755).

Even the atheist Scott couldn't have failed to be impressed by its copy of 'The Byble in English' (1541). Commissioned by Thomas Cromwell and Thomas Cranmer, both leading reformers under Henry VIII. Cromwell was executed the year before it was published, his downfall precipitated by his recommendation to Henry that he should marry the less-than-pretty Anne of Cleves.

As a result, in 16th Century terms, Cromwell's contribution to the book was airbrushed from history – his coat of arms having been removed from the printer's woodblock, leaving a blank circle on its front page.

Scott would have liked the exhibition, I thought, and for some reason I suddenly became aware that there were no security guards present. No one was searching bags, and literary treasures worth millions were in plain view with nothing but a glass case to protect them from an opportunist thief idling his time away on a wet Durham afternoon.

Perhaps the glass was reinforced and, if attacked, metal barriers would come crashing down at the door to prevent escape, alarms would sound and the Palace Green police, on red alert for the duration of the exhibition, would come running.

Or maybe, as the First Folio is the most documented and exhaustively researched book in the history of English literature, they think that nobody would be stupid enough to try and steal an unsellable book a second time.

After all, there can only be one Raymond Scott.

Epilogue:
Exit Raymond, Stage Left

On the afternoon of March 15th 2012, I was working for my newspaper, deep into a phone interview with a former Newcastle United footballer turned TV commentator, Ray 'Rocky' Hudson.

Only true Newcastle aficionados could ever recall his playing days in the North East which amounted to about 40 games in the mid- to late-1970s before he headed to the US to join Fort Lauderdale Strikers in Florida as part of the football revolution which brought the likes of Pele, George Best and Franz Beckenbauer to the North American Soccer League.

Hudson had made a name for himself as a football broadcaster, with his explosive outbursts, extended metaphors, heart-on-the-sleeve rants and near-the-knuckle comments on the matches he covered. He was as amusing during the interview as on screen and I was enjoying the chat when a note was put on the desk in front of me.

It read: 'Raymond Scott found dead in prison.'

I squinted at it disbelievingly and read it a second time as Hudson continued on, oblivious to my growing unease at the other end of line. I paused briefly as the news sunk in. Hudson, a nice man and obviously used to being quizzed by occasionally hesitant interviewers, just came out with another anecdote to fill in what could have been an awkward silence. I had to turn the note over to be able to finish the interview, which I then brought to a fairly abrupt halt.

The Press Association news feed on my computer had a brief one-paragraph flash repeating what was said on the note. I trawled other news websites, some of which were talking of it being suicide.

I sat for a while staring at the screen trying to take it in. An awful thought hit me: Back home, a letter written to me by Raymond

Epilogue: Exit Raymond, Stage Left

lay unopened. I had received it perhaps three or four weeks before and had set it aside, but had never got round to reading it.

It was one of numerous letters I had received from Raymond over the 18 months of his incarceration that he had written to fill in the hours before lock-up. I would reply less frequently as each letter I sent seemed to spur his pen, and his subsequent reply to it would be much more bulky, one running to about 10 sides of A4 paper.

They were full of anecdotes from prison, news of the snail-like progress of his appeal against conviction, the occasional bouts of anguish at his lot, but always by the end he had talked himself round to a state of sardonic acceptance at his contribution to the mess he was in.

They were always well written and funny, but at times repetitive and this was why I had put aside his last letter for so long. One of my New Year' resolutions had been to ring up the Governor at the prison and try to persuade him to allow me to visit Raymond again and to write him more letters. I had done neither.

Over my time with Raymond I had got to know him, as he would say, 'more than anyone else has'. But he was a difficult person to get to really know, as he protected himself with a wall of artifice which, if breached, would be shored up with some fresh whimsy. So I was surprised at the depth of my reaction to his death.

I was completely thrown off-kilter by the particularly upsetting news in one report later that day which said he had killed himself by cutting his own throat – an awful, painfully slow way to take your own life. The prison authorities wouldn't comment other than to say there had been an act of self-harm and that he had been found alone and unconscious in his prison cell at 8.30 in the morning.

The image this conjured up was just too much and I left work early. I thought of Raymond alone in his cell and of his mother, Hannah, and the pain she must be going through.

I bought a bottle of wine before arriving home and opened his last letter to me, selfishly hoping there was no hint in it of what was to come.

Epilogue: Exit Raymond, Stage Left

Reckless gamblers Mike the unrealistically optimistic, the wild chancers the dreamers (yes the Walter Mittys) they all end up outside in the rain skint.

This is my 'De Produndis' was that not the letter Dear Old Oscar wrote to Bosie or about Bosie when he was at his low or lowest ebb? I'm sick, writing this I am ill physically and mentally and hoping opening up my veins will help me feel a little less wretched. Since the last letter I've deteriorated physically and mentally lost lots of weight and no appetite not eating not difficult as food is inferior to what it used to be hardly sleeping looking haggard I now look fully my soon to be 55 years. My mother has noticed my lack of vitality on the phone. She's coming up on Wednesday. I'll try put a brave face on it. So what's happened? In common parlance it has "just hit me". The sheer gargantuan catastrophe that this is to me and my mother, nothing in the past even comes close at all. When I think of the life I used to have compared to now I want to cry but can't find the tears. It's a calamity. How was I so optimistic before in the sentence? Fools paradise and all the carnival whilst on bail – I must have been mentally ill mad raving bonkers fuelled by all the booze. 19 months I've done out of 4 years i.e. half of the 8. The first 18 months no problem then my mother's birthday 12th January that's when it started. Everyone has been trying to help me - the lads, officers, teachers and healthcare – I'm due to see a CPN seen the doctor and seeing him again on Monday. Especially the chaplains have been counselling me. Great blokes offering me advice and contemplation in the lovely tranquil chapel. An oasis for a troubled mind. What happened after the 12th? Well the mirror started to crack. My mind, my personality my world was what I saw when I looked in the mirror. The mirror was made of lego bricks with mirrored silver surfaces . . . Then the bricks took a shock, something shook them and they started to crumble a few at a time, bits of my face not there in the reflection until they all lay in a heap on the floor. You go to look in the mirror and there's nothing there, well not quite, just beyond the mirror used to be is a sepia tinted distorted mirror so you barely recognise your face. The chaplains seem metaphysically to understand this most of all.

SUNDAY AFTERNOON. Spent whole morning at the chapel talking to Eric an ordained minister and a smashing bloke. Judith from McKeags (Scott's solicitors) coming up on Tuesday as I sent out an urgent call for her. I want some sympathy and reassurance. Time is different in prison. 19 months outside goes very quickly but 19 months in pain of suffering is a very different thing. Imagine walking around with a drawing pin in your shoe for 19 months, it's a very long time. How did I get here? You struggle to find something good coming out of it all some hidden concealed thing but can't. An odd conman I met knew the surgeon Vickers who killed his wife in Gosforth with an experimental anti-cancer drug (I'm sure you recall the case and his notorious scarlet mistress who was acquitted) and did the full 17 years of his life sentence and walked out of the age an old but sprite man. The indomitable human spirit – instinct for self survival. Not all possess it. In prison you might as well be dead, I feel, the only thing that keeps you going is the ever approaching release. You might remember Captain Blackadder in the trenches of The Somme who said, "when I joined the British Army I never imagined anything as bloody awful as this." I echo his sentiments about prison. If the appeal fails (I'm naturally less optimistic) I'll transfer from here to any one of many more open CAT C Gaols. My mother won't be able to visit but I'll be able to call her every day and save up visits to

Epilogue: Exit Raymond, Stage Left

have in Durham. She'll understand it is much more important for me to feel comfortable in a new prison. Ah, if only we could turn back the clock. What a disaster in reality. Something wrong with my thought processes, I think, sometimes. This is, for me, a severe punishment but just got to do it. CAT D open prison is the window the light at the end of the tunnel but it's not (contrary to popular opinion) easy to get there and there's a waiting list. Although eligible after ¼ of your sentence the majority wait months longer to get there and if you infringe the many, many rules you get CAT D status taken off you for 6 months. It's tough. I dream of walking in Monaco and Havana but will it ever happen? Mike me old mate be very, very careful and circumspect out there you don't want to come here or any other prison. If only the various gates and doors here would throw themselves open and you could walk out free. What I and the other lads would give for that. Not going to happen. You wonder how The Great Train Robbers did their circa 12 years from 1963-1975 in old Victorian nicks with slopping out, no TVs and other privations, sewing mail bags etc for 40 hours a week just to buy an oz of burn. But they did it. Lifers usually did a 12 too. Tomorrow morning I'll be at the office for business administration with a cappuccino from the Bistro at 10.30 but it's not where I want to be. No. Adjust. Go to the gym. Forgot Monday morning I'll be seeing the Doctor. Just do it one day at a time.

FRIDAY 10th FEBRUARY. Just had the absolute worst week of my life. Total breakdown pacing round the cell all night shaking. I thought I was in a bad way last Saturday night when I started this letter. The scales have fallen from my eyes it's a waking nightmare. Not eating.

Epilogue: Exit Raymond, Stage Left

Not sleeping. Mother came up on Wednesday – difficult visit she left worried naturally. How did I get into all this? Rescue me somebody please give me a second chance. Can't cope. On suicide watch "the orange book". Dear me what a disaster, when I think what I had now look at me living like an animal in a cage. Seems like a million miles away those days on bail you and me on the book. The drunken buffoon attending court. YUK. The ludicrous enterprise with the Folio surely THAT person was mentally ill deluded not real in cloud cuckoo land. The first 18 months in here optimistic with the fresh evidence 'una cerveza camarero por favor'. I would be out. Solicitors up on Thursday and here's a thing I've abandoned my appeal on Toby's advice against conviction but he still wants to appeal against the length of the sentence. I signed the abandonment notice of course it's all obvious now. My mind is done in. I look in the mirror but see a stranger's reflection. What a waste all this. I'll not bounce back from this. How could I have been so deluded and that is it DELUSIONS I now think in fact I'm sure I'm mentally ill schizophrenic I think certainly not normal. Why could I not see the obvious? Where's it all going to end? God alone knows. What a disaster. I genuinely thought when convicted that after a few months I'd be released on appeal and marry Heidy in Havana, no honestly I did yes I know fucking ridiculous. There's something wrong with my thought processes MUST BE, no other explanation. Ah Mike I'm at my wits end honest. Such a mega debacle no way back. No can't see it. Thought last night it's be nice to die peacefully in my sleep no more pain a panacea. Come back and have better luck next time in the cycle of reincarnation. Me in my cell picture Hitler May 1945, all around destroyed. Such a failure. Oh Dear oh dear can't get my head round it. This will finish me. I'm a stupid bastard got to be. Day in

Epilogue: Exit Raymond, Stage Left

day out the same old shit. It's killing me. I'll have to get a transfer to a better nick even if she can't visit me. How have I held up until now? I'm genuinely worried about my ability to deceive myself. What really is real? Well Mike this is the letter from HELL.
RS.

For a moment I was consumed by awful self pity. If only I'd read it earlier. If only I had done what I'd set out to do at New Year. If only.

To add a bitter coincidence, David Rathband, the policeman blinded by Raoul Moat, had also committed suicide shortly before Scott. In one of Scott's most ill-judged comments – which was saying something – he had accused Moat of stealing his thunder when he had gone on his infamous gun rampage, murdering his ex-girlfriend's boyfriend and seriously injuring her before his attack on PC Rathband, then killing himself, during Scott's trial.

PC Rathband and Scott, two men who for very different reasons couldn't deal with the hand fate had dealt them, had chosen to end their personal misery. One as the result of being in the wrong place at the wrong time through no fault of his own. The other who had no one else to blame but himself.

PC Rathband was remembered as a hero. Scott not so, recalled as the Shakespeare fantasist, the criminal as clown, the serial show-off who thumbed his nose at the authorities with his court demeanour, the ageing lothario who fought the law and the law spectacularly won.

His death and the reasons for it showed he was human after all, and displayed a side of him the public did not know as he had, until his final letter, refused to show it. Too late now.

Perhaps if he had, he wouldn't have got the eight-year sentence which, in the end, was his undoing. Society likes its criminals contrite and humbled. Pride and a sense of mischief prevented him from playing the game by its rules.

The question I've been frequently asked since his passing is 'did he do it?' Did he steal the First Folio, the charge he was cleared of?

Epilogue: Exit Raymond, Stage Left

The truth is he didn't give a definitive 'yes' to at last set the record straight. As revealed earlier, he hinted at his guilt during our first meeting before qualifying his response by labelling it a 'fairy story'. Shortly before his trial ended he went into much greater detail about how he might have done it, breaking into the display cabinets not once but twice, the second time going back for the First Folio as he had been surprised at how easy the first theft had been. But again he stepped back from a full confession with his subsequent 'All lies and jest' text.

On reflection, he knew so much about the First Folio and its provenance, his knowledge representing years of study and understanding which would have done an academic justice. Surely more than he could have learned at the Biblioteca Nacional in Havana, as he had claimed.

Yet, if he knew so much about it, he would have also known that the chances of him getting away with selling it and pocketing the resultant riches to live the good life with Heidy were practically non-existent.

But he was backed into a corner, the credit card companies he had fleeced for nearly £90,000 to fund his extravagant lifestyle were, at last, wise to him and in hot pursuit. 'Lady Bountiful's' purse was not bottomless. It was a gamble beyond recklessness, but perhaps he thought 'what have I got to lose?' and decided to take the chance for a final hurrah and to live, as he said, one day as a lion, not as a lamb.

So, for what it's worth, I am as certain as I can be that he did steal the Shakespeare First Folio from Durham University in 1998. That he chanced upon it, as he related in his 'fairy story', and had stolen it as he had described to me shortly before the conclusion of his trial. And I can well imagine him at night in his room, as his mother watched *Coronation Street* or some other soap opera downstairs, reading the most celebrated book of plays by perhaps the greatest playwright who ever lived, pacing the floor as he declaimed his favourite passages to the four walls.

It was poignant that even as he approached death, he thought of

Epilogue: Exit Raymond, Stage Left

Heidy. He loved her, in his own way. For him it wasn't just sex – he had been coy to the point of recalcitrance when it came to discussing the intimate side of their relationship. A gentleman perhaps, of sorts.

I always hoped for Scott that there would be a happy ending, if not the one he had originally planned. I liked his idea of driving around the South of France after his release, towing a caravan behind his Ferrari. Parking-up, he would walk into the nearest town where he would prop up the bar and regale locals with one of his stories. He was a great, though unreliable, storyteller.

And a friend.

First published in Great Britain by:

Ashgrove Publishing

an imprint of:

Hollydata Publishers Ltd
27 John Street
London WC1N 2BX

© Mike Kelly, 2013

The right of Mike Kelly to be identified as the author
of this work has been asserted by him in accordance with
the Copyright Designs and Patents Act 1988.

No part of this publication may be reproduced, stored
in a retrieval system or transmitted, in any form or
by any means, electronic, mechanical, photo-
copying, recording or otherwise, without
the prior permission of the publisher.

ISBN 978 185398 178 4

First Edition

Photographs courtsey of ncjMedia

Book design by Brad Thompson

Printed and bound in England